Augsburg Commentary on the New Testament
II CORINTHIANS
Frederick W. Danker

Augsburg Publishing House

Minneapolis, Minnesota

AUGSBURG COMMENTARY ON THE NEW TESTAMENT
2 Corinthians

Copyright © 1989 Augsburg Publishing House

Scripture quotations, unless translated by the author directly from the Hebrew or Greek, are from the Revised Standard Version of the Bible, copyright 1946, 1952, and 1971 by the Division of Christian Education of the National Council of Churches.

Quotations from Greek and Latin authors are translated by the author.

Library of Congress Cataloging-in-Publication Data

Danker, Frederick W.
    2 Corinthians / Frederick W. Danker.
       p.   cm. — (Augsburg commentary on the New Testament)
    Bibliography: p.
    Includes index.
    ISBN 0-8066-8868-8
    1. Bible. N.T. Corinthians, 2nd—Commentaries.   I. Title.
II. Title: Two Corinthians.   III. Title: Second Corinthians.
IV. series.
BS2675.3.D36   1989
227'.307—dc19   89-51
                                                  CIP

Manufactured in the U.S.A.   APH 10-9026

1 2 3 4 5 6 7 8 9 0 1 2 3 4 5 6 7 8 9

To John Tietjen, Endangered Benefactor

CONTENTS

Foreword 7

Abbreviations 9

Acknowledgments 11

Introduction 13

Outline 27

Commentary 29

Selected Bibliography 215

Index of Ancient Authors and Writings 219

Glossary 221

About the Author 223

FOREWORD

The AUGSBURG COMMENTARY ON THE NEW TESTA-
MENT is written for laypeople, students, and pastors. Laypeople
will use it as a resource for Bible study at home and at church.
Students and instructors will read it to probe the basic message
of the books of the New Testament. And pastors will find it to
be a valuable aid for sermon and lesson preparation.

The plan for each commentary is designed to enhance its usefulness. The Introduction presents a topical overview of the biblical book to be discussed and provides information on the historical circumstances in which that book was written. It also
contains a summary of the biblical writer's thought. In the body
of the commentary, the interpreter sets forth in brief compass
the meaning of the biblical text. The procedure is to explain the
text section by section. Because the readers of the commentary
will have their Bibles at hand, the biblical text itself has not been
printed out. In general, the editors recommend the use of the
Revised Standard Version of the Bible.

The authors of this commentary series are professors at sem-
inaries and universities and are themselves ordained. They have
been selected both because of their expertise and because they
worship in the same congregations as the people for whom they

are writing. In elucidating the text of Scripture, therefore, they attest to their belief that central to the faith and life of the church of God is the Word of God.

The Editorial Committee
Roy A. Harrisville
Luther Northwestern Theological Seminary
St. Paul, Minnesota

Jack Dean Kingsbury
Union Theological Seminary
Richmond, Virginia

Gerhard A. Krodel
Lutheran Theological Seminary
Gettysburg, Pennsylvania

ABBREVIATIONS

Most of the names of modern scholars are readily identifiable through the bibliography. The following abbreviations and short titles will simplify other identifications.

APOT	See bibliography, Charles.
BAGD	See bibliography, Bauer.
Benefactor	See bibliography, Danker.
Betz	See bibliography, Betz, *2 Corinthians 8 and 9*.
CIG	See bibliography, *Corpus Inscriptionum Graecarum*.
Gk:	Designates the word that follows as the Greek term being translated or commented on.
IG	See bibliography, *Inscriptiones Graecae*.
IGR	See bibliography, *Inscriptiones Graecae ad res*. . . .
LXX	Septuagint, Greek version of the OT.
MeyerK	H. A. W. Meyer, Kritisch-exegetischer Kommentar über des Neue Testament.
MT	Masoretic text of the Hebrew Bible.
NT	New Testament.
OGI	See bibliography, Dittenberger, *Orientis*. . . .
OT	Old Testament.
Priene	See bibliography, Gärtringen, *Inschriften*. . . .
RSV	Revised Standard Version of the Bible.
Sammelbuch	See bibliography, *Sammelbuch*. . . .
SIG[3]	See bibliography, Dittenberger, *Sylloge*. . . .

ACKNOWLEDGMENTS

A research grant from Lutheran Brotherhood gave considerable encouragement to the completion of this commentary. I am grateful to Clayton Publishing House, St. Louis, Missouri, for permission to quote at length from *Benefactor: Epigraphic Study of a Graeco-Roman and New Testament Semantic Field* (1982). To Dawn Hass, scholar of the Lutheran School of Theology, Chicago, I express public appreciation for her expert technical assistance in the preparation of the manuscript.

INTRODUCTION

Few pieces of correspondence by St. Paul have attracted so much controversial comment as has 2 Corinthians. Among the principal factors accounting for this phenomenon are: (1) unavoidable ignorance of the precise circumstances that elicited some of Paul's discussions; (2) the probability that 2 Corinthians in its present form is composed of two or more pieces of correspondence; and (3) failure to take sufficient account of the cultural environment within which the letter took its shape.

1. Corinth and St. Paul's Mission Activity

Apart from Paul's autobiographical references and historical notes, the principal source for information about Paul's Corinthian connection is the book of Acts (18:1-17). From these two sets of data it is possible to make a rough outline of Paul's activities at Corinth and his correspondence with the Christians in that city.

In keeping with Hellenic custom, Corinthians took pride in the antiquity of their city and recited its origins in mythological terms. Being the chief city of the Achaian League, it was viewed as a threat by Rome, which undertook its total destruction in 146 B.C.E. under the generalship of the Roman consul Lucius Mummius. So thoroughly did he raze the city that few remains of its

13

ancient walls have been recovered. Refounded by Julius Caesar in 44 B.C.E. as a Roman colony, it began to assume some of its former prestige.

In the earlier centuries of its existence Corinth came under criticism for alleged licentiousness, but it is questionable whether it majored in immorality to a greater degree than does any major United States metropolis, especially a port city. Allegations of temple prostitution belong in the category of gossip rather than serious historical recital, for such activity was contrary to Greek custom. Moreover, the literary references that denigrate the reputation of Corinth refer to a time long before Paul's stay in the city. In any event, the types of moral problems that harassed the people of God at Corinth are present to varying degrees, and in some respects perhaps to an even greater degree, in any contemporary Christian congregation. In addition to sexual morality, other socially destructive practices and thought processes, such as protection of traditional turf at the expense of others, snobbery and class consciousness, bureaucratic power plays, and use of religion as a screen for entrenched self-interest may be even more finely honed in contemporary ecclesiastical circles. Indeed, one of the more compelling reasons for the popularity of commentaries on the Corinthian correspondence among other than biblical specialists is the practical contribution they make to related problems that bedevil Christian congregations today. The Corinthian correspondence therefore is a fertile source for contemporary proclamation and exhortation.

Luke's reference in Acts 18:12 to a Roman official named Lucius Junius Gallio Annaeus, a brother of the philosopher Seneca, finds support in an inscription (A. Plassart, "L'inscription de Delphes mentionnant le proconsul Gallion" [*Revue Étude Grecques* 80:372-78]). The fragmentary nature of the inscription is belied in translations that fail to indicate the many missing letters, but it clearly identifies Gallio as a proconsul in Corinth, with term of office either in 51–52 or in 52–53. Combined with the account in Acts, these data provide New Testament students with a fixed point for determining the approximate time when Paul first came to Corinth, and they make it possible to construct a plausible temporal framework for Paul's career and his correspondence.

According to Luke, Paul made his initial visit to Corinth on the missionary journey described in Acts 15:36—18:22. Paul arrived in Corinth after a brief stay in Athens and "shortly after" Aquila and his wife Priscilla came to the city because of an edict by Claudius ordering the expulsion of Jews from Rome (Acts 18:2). If the date 49 for this expulsion is correct, Paul's arrival in the city corresponds approximately with Gallio's period of office. Luke states that Paul remained in Corinth 18 months (Acts 18:11), perhaps from 50 to 51.

Being a center of commerce, Corinth was filled with a variety of tradespeople and visitors from many parts of the Mediterranean world. Many of the permanent and temporary residents were members of clubs and associations, not a few of which were probably organized on the basis of trade affiliation. No such club or association would meet without engaging in some kind of religious activity. The minutes of such a group located in Athens were unearthed in the winter of 1892–1893. They describe the reorganization meeting, held in the second century of our era, of a group called the Iobakchoi, which met in the name of Dionysus. Of special interest, because of some scholars' malicious gossip concerning alleged immoral conduct in connection with Dionysiac rites, are the regulations concerning appropriate decorum in the meetings and the responsibilities of "bouncers." For details, see *Benefactor,* pp. 156-166.

According to Acts 18:3, Priscilla and Aquila shared Paul's trade of tentmaking. Since religious rites were intimately connected with Greco-Roman clubs, these three Christians would not have associated themselves with such organizations. Instead, they formed their own "club" and soon gathered adherents for the celebration of the gospel of Jesus Christ. Like the members of clubs, the Christians in Corinth would have formed a number of groups. It is inappropriate therefore to refer to them as a single congregation. Meeting perhaps in numbers of 10 to 15 at a time in homes scattered throughout the city, it was natural for each of the assemblies to develop its own polity, and the liturgical practices would vary. It is also readily understandable how factionalism and petty partisan politics could mushroom. To help all the Christians of Corinth develop some sense of corporate identity across their limited meeting room boundaries was a constant challenge for the apostle.

Partisan Politics

After Paul's departure from Corinth, partisan politics became a serious issue. In addition, a number of moral and theological problems surfaced. Because of his conscientious concern for new converts (2 Cor. 11:28), Paul appears to have carried on an extensive correspondence. From 1 Cor. 7:1, it is clear that 1 Corinthians was in part formulated to answer questions expressed in letters sent by the Corinthians. In 1 Cor. 5:9 Paul expressly alludes to an earlier letter that he wrote in answer to a query.

As can be deduced from 1 Cor. 3:1-17, partisan politics was a prime source of impediment for success of the gospel mission at Corinth. To assist the Corinthians in dealing with this and other problems, Paul wrote 1 Corinthians. Unfortunately, storms continued to raise high waves in the congregational life at Corinth, and Paul felt that his personal presence was needed. He therefore made a special visit, only to find the congregations in turmoil and even encountering open hostility from certain leaders and self-styled ecclesiastical and theological authorities, who had succeeded in intimidating many of the members. Unable to resolve matters, Paul appears to have left in disgust. This visit, his second, is therefore termed, in Paul's own words, his "sorrowful visit" (2 Cor. 2:1). In all probability he returned by ship to Ephesus, from which he wrote a strong pastoral letter, which he labeled his "sorrowful letter" (2 Cor. 2:4). The writing of this letter drained him emotionally (cf. 7:8), and Paul could scarcely endure the interval between its dispatch and some news about the response of the Corinthians. In the meantime a "door" of evangelistic opportunity opened up in Macedonia (2:12), and Paul headed for that area, where he also expected to meet Titus and hear about developments at Corinth. Finally Paul was able to join his colleague, who reported that Paul's sorrowful or severe letter had appeared for the most part to have restored corporate sanity at Corinth (7:8-15). In gratitude to God (2 Cor. 1:1-7) Paul wrote 2 Corinthians, in which he assured his addressees that he would soon be making a third effort to see them (13:1).

Introduction

From 2 Corinthians it appears that two major related problems had surfaced at Corinth. The first involved an open attack by a specific individual on Paul's apostolic role at Corinth. Paul's discussion of it in 2 Cor. 2:5-11 suggests that the problem was resolved. The second had to do with interference, evidently from outsiders, who claimed to have impressive credentials, including letters of recommendation (3:1), perhaps from Jerusalem itself. Since Paul was not authorized by human authorities, but through a direct commission from Jesus Christ (see Gal. 1:15-17), he was at a tactical disadvantage in the face of narrowly construed bureaucratic claims. Critical of Paul's personal characteristics and administrative pastoral style, the interlopers endeavored to bring the congregations within the orbit of their own control (cf. 1 Cor. 4:19-21; 11:19-20).

Additional grist for the opposition's mill was furnished by Paul's alteration of his travel plans. At 1 Cor. 16:5 he had announced his intention to visit the Corinthians on the way from Ephesus through Macedonia. After the writing of 1 Corinthians he changed the plan, intending to make a double visit by coming first to Corinth, then to Macedonia, with immediate return to Corinth (2 Cor. 1:15-16). Evidently the emergency that occasioned the sorrowful visit was responsible for this change in plan, but Paul's opponents used the circumstance to cast doubt on his integrity (1:17-22). Much of the debate about the circumstances under which 2 Corinthians was written therefore revolves around the issue of Paul's problems with his detractors. In short, the visit of Titus with the sorrowful letter in hand had helped resolve some problems, but pockets of resistance remained, with some of Paul's detractors pointing to his strongly worded letter and saying that Paul was tough in his letters but weak in presence and therefore incapable of handling affairs at Corinth (cf. 2 Cor. 10:10). Since 2 Cor. 10–13 appears to contradict the rosier picture of restored congregational harmony expressed in chaps. 1–9, it is probable that chaps. 10–13 were written after additional reports about Corinth had reached the apostle. This view is to be preferred to the conclusion that these chapters are a fragment of the sorrowful letter, for the contents are scarcely such as to suggest the kind of concern expressed by Paul in 7:5-13. On the other hand, it was only natural that in his eagerness to celebrate the least sign of repentance by the Corinthian congregations he should have spoken as glowingly as he did, especially in 7:5-16. At the same time, 3:1; 5:11-13; 6:11-13; and 7:2 suggest that all was not yet well. Hence 12:19-21 is written in a vein that contrasts strongly with 7:8-11. As will be indicated below, there are rhetorical traditions that help account for some of the data, but the probability is strong that 2 Corinthians was not written in its present form at one sitting, but consists of at least two letters. Yet in the course of making such judgments, it must be noted that a similar disjunction in thought and emotion begins at Phil. 3:1, and the relevance of Romans 9–11 to the rest of Paul's argument of Romans has been questioned, along with the coherence of Romans 16. In other words, caution must be observed, lest one's own contemporary conceptions of literary unity control verdicts about ancient productions. At the same time, the fact must be faced that numerous documents in antiquity are composites generated by later editorial effort, and it is this phenomenon that has invited suspicion especially about the status of 6:14—7:1 and chaps. 8–9 as original parts of 2 Corinthians.

2. One or More Letters?

In the case of 6:14—7:1, there appears to be a disruption of Paul's appeal, a disruption that is punctuated by some diction not otherwise found in Paul's letters. But closer scrutiny reveals that the passage is in effect a digression, a rhetorical device that was frequently used by ancient orators to amplify a point that was being made. In this instance, the central thought of the digression is fidelity, a theme intimately associated with Paul's appeal for inclusion in the Corinthians' affections. As for the terms to which exception is taken, most of them are synonyms relating to the very problem whose exploration dominates 2 Corinthians. Greco-Roman orators used hapax legomena, words that occur only once in a specific document or body of literature, for striking rhetorical effect. And Paul, by heaping them up as he does, reinforces his point. It is also significant that 7:1 appears to anticipate the concern expressed in 12:21.

The gathering of moneys for Jerusalem's poor is the burden of chaps. 8–9. According to 1 Cor. 16:1-4, the collection was being made under Paul's instructions as a collegial effort with the assemblies in Galatia (cf. Acts 24:17; Rom. 15:25-33). The criticism that chap. 8 appears to begin abruptly and therefore indicates that it and the succeeding chapter are not an integral part of chaps. 1–7 is a demonstration not of historical circumstances but of personal literary taste. On such a basis it could be assumed that 1 Corinthians 12, which begins just as abruptly, was not a part of the letter in which it is incorporated.

Hans Dieter Betz, who has put biblical students in debt for his comprehensive analysis of chaps. 8–9 on the basis of ancient rhetorical techniques and administrative terminology, follows the lead of Hans Windisch and argues that these two chapters are fragments of two business letters that were independent of the rest of 2 Corinthians. The first, chap. 8, was addressed to the Corinthian Christians. The second was dispatched to Christians in the broader area of Achaia. There is no question concerning the accuracy of Betz's judgment on Paul's use of business terminology in chaps. 8–9. His conclusions receive support from a study made of related diction and formulation in Romans (see Frederick W. Danker, "A Form-Critical Study of Linguistic Adaptation in Romans" [see bibliography]). But the hypothesis of an independent origin of the two chapters requires further scrutiny. As the commentary will endeavor to demonstrate, chap. 8 deals with details respecting the project, whereas chap. 9 concentrates on motivation for completion of the project. This is not to state that the case against the possibility of 2 Corinthians consisting of fragments is closed—for such scholars as Günther Bornkamm and Dieter Georgi argue persuasively for as many as five fragments—but that the canonical document in its present form conveys an overall argumentative consistency that may ultimately be traceable to post-Paul editors who were responsible for circulating what remained of Paul's correspondence to Corinth. On the other hand, there are rhetorical considerations that have been overlooked in the history of interpretation of 2 Corinthians and these suggest that some cautions are in order against a too-ready adoption of partitionist hypotheses without some compelling modifications.

3. Cultural Context

In *Benefactor: Epigraphic Study of a Graeco-Roman Semantic Field* (1982), I called attention to the Mediterranean reciprocity system as primary background for understanding certain passages of a theological and moral-ethical character in the New Testament, with numerous references to the Corinthian correspondence. In this commentary I extend the exploration in an effort to resolve some aspects of the literary problems that have remained in contention for lack of consideration of a broader data base.

Since Corinth was part of the very heart of the Hellenic world, it is important to consider a primary feature of Hellenic culture, namely, the important role that consideration of excellence of the highest order played in Greco-Roman society. Goodness was a civic virtue from Homeric times, and exceptionally good beings and persons were those who made signal contributions to the welfare of humanity and their immediate society. At the very apex were deities, whose recognition was dependent on their ability to preserve the fortunes of their devotees. Hence they were frequently called "saviors" and recognized as bestowers of all the blessings and bounties that delight the heart and make life enjoyable. Heads of state and mighty warriors were traditional candidates for recognition. Homer gives Hector recognition for daring to stand alone against the fearless Achilles. Both of these warriors are outstanding examples of arete, a loanword from the Greek *aretē*, meaning "superior merit." Distinguished athletes also received recognition, and the odes of the Greek poet Pindar are filled with praise of arete exhibited at the Olympic, Pythian, Nemean, and Isthmian games. With the passage of time, philosophers shifted emphasis from physical prowess to acceptance of moral and ethical challenge. Upright people, Plato pointed out, are prime candidates for recognition as benefactors of humanity.

Thousands of inscriptions attest the importance that was attached to recognition of heads of state and other public officials.

A number of these are recorded in *Benefactor* and are referred to from time to time in the commentary. Of special interest, because of its nearness to the time when Paul wrote to Corinth, is the decree published in honor of Nero's visit to Hellas (*Benefactor*, pp. 284-85).

Shortly after he had won more than 1800 trophies or crowns in all the competitions that Hellas could stage in the year 67, Nero ordered an assembly to be held at Corinth on November 28 of the same year, at which he made the following declaration (the bracketed material indicates erasures or unreadable portions of the inscription).

> There is nothing that one could not expect from my generosity; yet it is an unexpected boon that I grant to you, the people of Greece, and one that you could never have found it within you to request. As of this moment, all of you Greeks in Achaia and in what till now has been known in the Peloponnesos, are in receipt of liberty and exemption from tribute, something that none of you experienced even in your finest days, for you were either slaves to others or to one another. If only I had been able to grant this gift while Hellas was in its prime, how many more could then have benefited from my grace! As it is, I can only blame the passage of time that has exhausted before me such magnitude of grace. And now it is goodwill, not pity, that prompts me to be your benefactor; and I take the opportunity to requite your Gods, of whose concern for me on land and sea I have made trial, and they have granted me the opportunity to practice benefactions on unparalleled scale. Other commanders have liberated cities, [but Nero] an entire province.

Thereupon the following decree was read:

> Epaminondas, son of Epaminondas, the chief priest of the Augusti for life and also of Nero Claudius Caesar Augustus, made the motion. The preliminary decree had been proposed by him to the Senate and the People. WHEREAS Nero—Lord of all the Cosmos, Supreme Imperator, designated Tribune for the 13th time, Father of his country, New Sun that brightens Hellas, who has chosen to be the benefactor of Hellas, and with piety requites our Gods, who are always at his side and look out for his safety—is unique in the annals of time and as Supreme Imperator has proved himself the friend of Hellas, [Nero] Zeus Liberator, and has granted to us our liberty

that from of old was so characteristic of us and germane to our land, but then was snatched from us; (and whereas this liberation) is his gift to us, and he has restored (to Hellas) its ancient autonomy and freedom, and has added to his great and unexpected gift release from taxation, something that none of the Caesars ever granted before; IN VIEW OF ALL THIS, it is DECREED by the magistrates, the council, and the people forthwith to consecrate the altar hard by Zeus SAVIOR and to inscribe it: TO ZEUS LIBERATOR [NERO] FOREVER, and to consecrate the sacred images of [Nero] Zeus Liberator and Goddess Augusta [Messalina], in the temple of Apollo of Ptos in joint dedication with our Ancestral Gods, so that, with all things perfected in such fashion, all the world may know that our city renders all honor and piety toward the [house] of our Lord Augustus [Nero].

This decree is cited in full in order to illustrate a number of features that require consideration for fuller understanding of 2 Corinthians: (1) Nero's emphasis on his imperial grace (Gk: *charis*) renews one's perspective on Paul's references to divine grace or beneficence. Throughout 2 Corinthians Paul expresses his wonder over the surpassing nature of God's extraordinary beneficence exhibited in Jesus Christ. (2) Nero emphasizes liberation. Indeed, if Nero could say that he liberated an entire province, one can note that about a decade earlier Paul had proclaimed God's liberation in Christ for the entire world (2 Cor. 5:19). Hence Paul expresses concern that the Corinthians are willing to return to bondage (11:20). (3) Nero has gone to some risk in coming to Hellas. Similarly Paul recites the hazards he experiences in proclaiming Christ's good news (6:4-10; 11:23-33). (4) In both sections of the inscription the deities of Hellas are credited with bringing Nero safely to port. Throughout 2 Corinthians Paul credits God for his successes and his survival in trials and tribulations. (5) Nero is recognized in his act of beneficence as an imitator of Zeus. Likewise Paul projects himself as God's instrument of beneficence for the Corinthians. (6) The Hellenes acknowledge that recognition of beneficence is a sacred obligation and they give due praise to Nero. Paul chides the Corinthians for siding with nonbenefactors, while giving him the cold shoulder. (7) Nero is recognized for his piety. Paul insists that the Corinthians ought to recognize him for his total dedication to the cause of God's gospel. (8) The honorands wish all the world to know that the city renders all honor and piety to Nero. Paul takes satisfaction in knowing that all the world recognizes the Corinthians as his "letter" (3:2). (9) Bureaucratic diction and formulation are characteristic of this inscription. Paul similarly makes use of numerous bureaucratic expressions, including the elaborate form of address in 1:1.

Greco-Roman cultural tradition and economics were intertwined. In place of an income tax, wealthy individuals were expected to render public service by filling administrative posts, which often involved defraying costs of public works or entertainments. An inscription from 145 C.E., in honor of a benefactor named Vedius Antoninus, illustrates some of the advantages and drawbacks in the system (*Benefactor*, pp. 69-70):

> Titus Aelius Hadrianus [Antoninus] Augustus Imperator Caesar, son of God Hadrian, grandson of God Traianus Parthicus, great-grandson of God Nerva, Pontifex Maximus, Tribune for the eighth time, Imperator for the second, Consul for the fourth, Father of his country, to the officials of Ephesus, the Council, [and the People]: Greeting.
>
> I learned about the generosity that Vedius Antoninus shows toward you, but not so much from your letters as from his; for when he wished to secure assistance from me for the adornment of the structures he had promised you, he informed me of the many large buildings he is adding to the city but that you are rather unappreciative of his efforts. I on my part [agreed] with every request that he made and was appreciative of the fact that he does not follow the [customary] pattern of those who discharge their civic responsibility with a view to gaining instant recognition by spending their resources on shows and doles and [prizes for the games]; instead he prefers to show his generosity through ways in which he [can anticipate] an even grander future for the city. His Excellency Proconsul [Claudius Ju]lianus is transmitting this letter. [Farewell.]

This inscription reveals the importance attached to recognition by communities for benefits conferred within their midst. Indeed, the biblical principle expressed by Paul in 2 Cor. 9:7, "God has affection for a cheerful donor," would have been well understood in the Greco-Roman world, where the principle "It is better to give than to receive" prevailed in many circles. And, as Aristotle (*Nicomachean Ethics* 1120b) put it, "liberality is not judged in terms of the amount given but on the basis of the spirit with which it is given." Since Paul understands himself as an envoy of Jesus Christ, the Great Benefactor, in the service of God, the Supreme Benefactor, he emphasizes his insistence on defraying his own expenses at Corinth. Thus he reinforces his role as representative benefactor to the Corinthians, a point that is made with devastating satire in chaps. 10–12. It is a mistake, therefore, to conclude, as some commentators have done, that the Corinthians are the patrons and Paul the client. Rather, Paul is like Greco-Roman envoys of whom it could be said that they defrayed expenses out of their own purse so as not to burden the populace.

Beyond a doubt, the cultural model of distinctive excellence as displayed especially in highly ethical performance, generosity, and ability to survive perils maintains a high profile in 2 Corinthians. But second in importance is the demonstration that Paul gives of his rhetorical competence. In his commentary on chaps. 8–9, Betz offers the most informative demonstration to date of rhetorical criticism applied to discussion of a biblical passage. Whether Paul was conscious of all the refinements that Betz notes in his analysis of the structure of the two chapters cannot be decided here. What is now needed is a comparative study of Paul's rhetorical techniques at the hand of recognized masters of the rhetorical art. I have tried to meet some of this need by exploring themes, topics, and rhetorical techniques that are common to 2 Corinthians and Demosthenes' speech *On the Crown*. My reasons for doing this are threefold. First, Paul engages in a good deal of self-praise, satire, and sarcasm, all of which dominate Demosthenes' speech. Second, the speech by Demosthenes in defense of his right to be awarded a crown for public service parallels one of the major cultural themes in 2 Corinthians. Third, the speech by Demosthenes was recognized in Paul's time as a rhetorical model. Hence I make frequent reference to Plutarch's essay *On Inoffensive Self-Praise*.

The data relating to the identity and tenets of Paul's opponents at Corinth are so very meager, and frequently so tinged with irony and satire, especially in the "Fool's Speech" (2 Cor. 11:1—

12:13), that it is impossible to formulate any satisfactory conclusions beyond a few general assessments. On the whole, Paul's opponents appear to assert that they have a stronger claim than Paul has on apostleship for proclamation of the gospel. In 2 Cor. 10:12-18 Paul makes a counter-claim concerning jurisdiction. Since Paul does not refute his opposition for adherence to Mosaic legislation at the expense of the gospel, they are probably not to be classed as Judaizers. And allegations of Gnostic association find no solid footing in 2 Corinthians. In view of the plurality of house churches at Corinth, it is probable that the opponents were not a unified group, but in competition even among themselves for the allegiance of Christians in Corinth. Their intrusive presence thus led to the partisan politics against which Paul inveighs in 12:20. Since, as indicated above, Paul's self-defense is contained in numerous rhetorical ploys, it is impossible to conclude with certainty that the opponents actually laid a claim to visions and revelations. Paul's statements in 12:1-5 are perfectly understandable on the assumption that he was under attack for laying claim to special revelation for his apostolate. In self-defense he declares that it is not his habit to recite all of his extraordinary experiences.

Because of the fact that Paul goes to extraordinary lengths in 2 Corinthians to communicate on the Hellenic wave-lengths of his addressees, I have made extensive reference to classical authors in addition to the data from public Greco-Roman documents. Except when otherwise indicated, all translations, including departures from the RSV, are my own. Parallels are not to be viewed as sources for Paul's thought, but they can illuminate the points at which people who were formerly outside Jewish-Christian traditions could find a foothold for grasping some of the things that were being independently expressed. Paul knew how to be "all things to all people" in the best sense of the phrase, and no document of his displays this characteristic better than does 2 Corinthians.

OUTLINE

I. Introduction (1:1-11)
   A. Greeting (1:1-2)
   B. Thematic Proposition—Triumph over Obstacles (1:3-11)
II. Struggle for a Meeting of Minds (1:12—7:16)
   A. Facing the Problem (1:12—2:13)
      1. Affirmation of Concern (1:12-14)
      2. Explanation for a Non-visit (1:15—2:4)
      3. Resolution of a Disciplinary Problem (2:5-13)
   B. Self-affirmation (2:14—5:10)
      1. Credentials (2:14—4:6)
      2. Credentials Confirmed (4:7—5:10)
   C. Appeal for Reconciliation (5:11—7:16)
      1. God's Reconciling Effort as Motivation for Paul (5:11-21)
      2. Price for Paul's Proclamation of Reconciliation (6:1-10)
      3. Transition (6:11-13)
      4. Personal Appeal (6:14—7:1)
      5. Paul's Anxiety about the Sorrowful Letter and His Joy over the Return of Titus (7:2-16)
III. The Collection: A Statement of Unity in the Gospel (8:1—9:15)
   A. Description of the Project (8:1-24)

27

   B. Motivation for Completion (9:1-15)

IV. A Declaration of Loving Concern (10:1—13:13)

   A. Paul's Claim on the Congregation (10:1-18)

      1. Disciplinary Power (10:1-6)

      2. Jurisdiction (10:7-18)

   B. "Fool's Speech" (11:1—12:13)

      1. Prologue (11:1-4)

      2. Declaration of Love and Protest against Rivals (11:5-15)

      3. Credentials and Crises (11:16-33)

      4. Ecstatic Experiences and a Thorn in the Flesh (12:1-10)

      5. Transition (12:11-13)

   C. Final Protestation of Affection (12:14—13:10)

      1. Paul No Free-loader (12:14-18)

      2. Fears about the State of the Community's Health (12:19-21)

      3. Paul's Wish for a Pleasant Visit (13:1-10)

   D. Closing Words (13:11-14)

      1. Plea for Mutual Affection (13:11-13)

      2. Benediction (13:14)

COMMENTARY

■ Introduction (1:1-11)

Greeting (1:1-2)

1—The portion of the greeting in this verse in the main follows Greco-Roman convention for personal correspondence. First the source of the document is cited, followed by the identity of the addressees. Unusual is Paul's citation of his credentials. He writes in the manner of an imperial bureaucrat. He is the official delegate or envoy of **Christ Jesus.** This means that he does not owe his credentials to any human assembly (see the comments on 3:1). On the contrary, **God** is the ultimate arbiter of all that he does, for God has put him under the jurisdiction of Christ Jesus, and he carries out part of his responsibility by writing to God's people in **Corinth** and identifying them with all other Christians in **Achaia.**

The two chief corporate political entities in Greek political life were the *boulē* (council) and the *ekklēsia* (public assembly). In keeping with his initial bureaucratic imagery, Paul calls the Christians in Corinth an assembly (**church**), but with the qualification **of God** he distinguishes them from the public assembly as normally understood. The letter is for the publics specified. Matters discussed in it call for public action, and the authoritative tone that one encounters throughout the epistle is in complete harmony with the magisterial beat sounded in its first verse. This

29

verse sketches the drama that is about to be played out in the rest of the epistle. Paul will have hard words to say about those who discount Paul's credentials and exploit the Corinthians with appeal to their own authority. The Corinthians belong to his care, and he will fight for their security in Christ as a bear fights for its cubs.

Much of Paul's success lay in his political acumen, with a flair for recognition of the potential of others for service. If politics is the art of mobilizing power and resources, material and human—with whatever bureaucratic structures are necessary—to satisfy the optimum requirements for justice and to ensure the safety of the powerless, St. Paul qualifies as one of its masters. There are those who shy away from the use of the terms *politics* and *bureaucracy* in connection with ecclesiastical matters. But if politics is presumed to be so intrinsically tainted that the institutional church is embarrassed by the term, there is no reason to expect "politicians" to think better of themselves. There is no escape from reality—politics and bureaucracy are facts of life, and it is primarily a question of whether there will be good or bad politics and good or bad bureaucrats. It is also true that groups of people ultimately determine which kind will prevail. In this letter to Corinth, Paul exposes practitioners of bad politics and invites his addressees to insist on good politics. He himself claims to be a politician dedicated to the interests of God and Jesus Christ, and therefore of the Corinthians' interests. It is not surprising therefore that many of Paul's statements in this letter relate to matters of morale, authority, teamwork, and obedience.

Paul displays his understanding of basic principles of good management. As part of his many administrative responsibilities, he keeps close touch with affairs in Corinth by maintaining a network of communication through use of capable people, such as Timothy and Titus. Never narrowing his vision to a single area or issue, he maintains a challenging perspective as he endeavors to relate one constituency to others: he calls the Corinthians to join the Macedonians in the welfare program for Jerusalem's poor and he solicits their support for his mission objectives in the West. In the face of obstacles he maintains extraordinary maneuverability. Although he tends to wear his heart on his sleeve, he alternates spontaneity with carefully orchestrated diction that dramatizes selections from his own and the Corinthians' social and cultural reality. He intends thereby to arouse emotions of loyalty and commitment and to persuade them to rechannel their thinking and behavior in specific directions that are compatible with their avowed claim to be the people of God. Completely sold on God's program, he radiates an infectious confidence in the ultimate success of the divine venture.

The term **brother** was frequently used in the Greco-Roman world in reference to a member of an association. Paul appears to have introduced **Timothy** to Christ (1 Cor. 4:17) and in keeping with his participatory management technique the apostle used him for a variety of missions (1 Cor. 16:10; Rom. 16:21; Phil. 1:1; 2:19; Col. 1:1; 1 Thess. 1:1; 3:2, 6; 2 Thess. 1:1; Philemon 1; 1 Tim. 1:2, 18; 6:20; Acts 16:1; 17:14, 15; 18:5; 19:22; 20:4; Heb. 13:23).

Timothy was indeed known to the Corinthians (see 1:19), but since Paul's letter is to circulate throughout Achaia, it was necessary to identify this particular Timothy as Paul's colleague. According to 1 Cor. 4:17, Timothy had been sent to Corinth, but details concerning this mission are shrouded.

In 27 B.C. the Peloponnese and part of mainland Greece, together with a number of islands, became the province of *Achaia*, which is mentioned in 1 Cor. 16:15; Acts 18:12, 27; 19:21; Rom. 15:26; 1 Thess. 1:7-8). According to 1 Cor. 16:15, the household of Stephanas were the first converts in Achaia. Arguments based on silence in the sources are always hazardous, and the paucity of references to congregations in Achaia cannot therefore be used to limit the presence of converts in Achaia to only a few localities.

Paul's use of the word **church** in the singular attests his sense of the unity of God's people. Every Greek city-state had its popular *ekklēsia* or assembly, in which the people's voice was heard. Although its powers were severely curtailed under Roman control, the use of this term in reference to Christians would call attention to their communal responsibilities.

2—Greco-Roman heads of state communicated their own goodwill. Paul concludes his greeting with a Jewish type of benediction, but focuses on two terms that dominate secular political statement: beneficence (**grace**) and **peace.** Imperial administrators displayed their grace in public works, gifts of food, and especially in spectacles. Relief from internal and external turmoil incurred especially fulsome expressions of gratitude from their subjects. Paul's addressees are the recipients of unparalleled benefits, which are bestowed by the Supreme Parent (**Father**) and by **Jesus Christ,** who is called **Lord,** a declaration of imperial status. God functions through Jesus as viceroy. The sum and substance of their benefaction is **peace.** The term signifies God in outreach to humanity, and especially to the believers, who are invited to explore fresh possibilities of individual and corporate well-being through cultivation of the many and varied divine gifts.

Triumph Over Obstacles (1:3-11)

3-7—The theme of divine beneficence comes to elaborate expression in vv. 3-11. Much of this letter is devoted to clarification of Paul's credentials as an apostle and to resolution of problems encountered in his dealings with the Corinthians. Therefore Paul immediately brings up the subject of his troubles in other parts of the world and rings changes on the theme of consolation. Basic to his line of argument in vv. 3-7 is awareness of his auditors' involvement in various forms of reciprocity, a fundamental ingredient of all human interaction. His main point: the more trouble, the more opportunity to thank God for all the consolation that God offers. Subpoints: (1) The apostle's own experience of consolation is in direct proportion to the sufferings that he undergoes as a consequence of identification with the Anointed One and his program. (2) His experience of divine consolation makes him an expert in consoling others. (3) The more consolation the addressees experience, the easier it will be for them to imitate Paul in endurance of suffering. (4) Their partnership in suffering on behalf of the Anointed One warrants partnership in consolation.

3—The adjective **blessed** reflects Semitic usage and is used almost exclusively of **God,** who is so praised out of appreciation for benefits conferred. In Greco-Roman circles the cognate verb *eulogeō* appears in reference to praise of people or of such deities as Pan (*CIG* 4705b) or Isis (4705c). By defining God as the **Father of our Lord Jesus Christ** (so also Eph. 1:3; 1 Pet. 1:3), Paul declares that Jesus is the optimum benefit conferred by God. At the same time, since Jesus suffered the extremity of crucifixion, the apostle implies that God is especially tuned in to the sufferings that Christians undergo because of their affiliation with Jesus Christ.

To say that God is **the Father of mercies and God of all comfort** means that mercy and comfort become especially meaningful in association with God. Psalm 40:11-12 (LXX 39:12-13) is a reliable commentary on the thought. The term **mercies** refers to God's compassionate concern. **Comfort** in this context refers to the assurance that God is not against the sufferers but for them.

Consolation was a recurring topic in Greco-Roman books of essays, and much of it owes a large debt to Krantor, the most esteemed consoler in the Greco-Roman world. To be even moderately successful, the consoler must establish affinity with the sufferer. Prometheus expresses a common complaint when he says to the chorus (Aeschylus, *Prometheus* 263-265):

> How light for those who feel no pain to give
> advice to those whose life is weal and woe.

With related strains in Sophocles' *Trachiniai* (729-730), Deianira chides the chorus:

> Such things no partner in grief would say,
> but one who knows at home no bane.

And Shakespeare (*Much Ado about Nothing*, act V, scene 1) echoed the sentiment:

>   Men
> Can counsel and speak comfort to that grief
> which they themselves not feel.

Quite evidently, consolers will be assured of some success if they can show that they themselves have attended the school of suffering, for awareness of democracy in suffering can aid in suppressing indignant protest against one's fate. As Greek poets were wont to remind their publics, even God's favorites cannot escape troubles. Simonides (Diehl, fragment 7) writes:

> Not even those of olden time, offspring of
> the immortal Gods, reached hoary days and
> ended life sans trouble, grief, and pain.

Since, as the extant tragedies of ancient Greece attest, the problem of human suffering was a dominant theme, it is evident that Paul would readily attract the attention of his addressees through his opening thematic gambit, and by calling attention to his own involvement in disasters he would find an opening into the hearts of his beloved Corinthians.

4—Paul's repeated use of the Greek word *pas,* rendered **all** and **any,** highlights the plentitude of divine resources for assisting Christians in their troubles. Greco-Roman honorary documents make frequent use of the term in recognition of generous benefits conferred by civic-minded persons. Being the recipient of a large amount of God's consolatory benefits, Paul in turn becomes the benefactor of others through the prodigality of his consolation.

5—Paul sets up a balance sheet. The expression **share abundantly** renders the term *perisseuō,* part of a family of words that is commonly used in commercial contexts to express profit or surplus. In effect, Paul images two columns. In the one column, headed "Sufferings for Christ," he enters the sufferings that he has experienced on behalf of Christ (cf. v. 6). The addition line shows a surplus. That is, they are almost unbearable. But the other column reads "Consolation" and also shows a surplus. For the same Christ who is ultimately responsible for Paul's sufferings provides generous consolation. And because Paul has more consolation than he needs for himself, he can be a source of consolation to others.

Some interpreters think that Paul is alluding to·the sufferings that are to attend God's people in the time of the Messiah. It is not improbable that Paul might have been thinking along such lines but, in view of his remarks in 4:10-12, it is more probable that he has in mind the sufferings that befell him because of his proclamation concerning Jesus Christ.

6—So, concludes Paul, the troubles we experience are **for your comfort and salvation.** With these words Paul poses himself as an endangered benefactor, who experiences perils on behalf of his clients. (For details on this theme see the comments on 6:4-10; 11:24-29.) In turn, the comfort that Paul receives through association with Christ spells consolation for the Corinthians. The sufferings that the Corinthians experience are the same as the apostle's in the sense that they derive from the same association that he has, namely, with Christ. Therefore, since they are linked with the same source of suffering, they will also share in the same abundance of consolation that the apostle described in v. 5. Through this line of reasoning Paul goes far beyond the democratization of suffering described in Greek tragedy. Paul's experiences merely provide the opportunity dramatically to communicate the surpassing consolation that God offers in Christ Jesus. Thus at every step in his opening remarks Paul keeps faith with his motto: "I am determined to know nothing among you, but Jesus Christ and him crucified" (1 Cor. 2:2).

7-8—The translation **unshaken** renders a common commercial term (*bebaios*), in the sense of "guarantee."

Not much is to be gained by guesswork about the locale for what was almost a terminal hazard for Paul. It has been suggested that he may have fallen deathly sick, but in view of the experiences he describes in 11:23-27, it is more probable that he refers to external hazards. In support of this view is the word **unbearably,** which translates an expression (*hyper dynamin*) that is frequently used in reference to officials who render services beyond the call of duty. Of Phaus, an official in Cyrene, it was said that he exposed himself to much danger in behalf of Cyrene, and that he carried out his obligations to the deity Apollo "with fervent piety" and to people with "extraordinary generosity beyond his resources" (*OGI* 767.15-19).

As though anticipating his later boast that he did not make himself a burden to anyone (11:9), Paul emphasizes that he himself was put under a heavy burden. Such willingness to endure personal discomfort is cut from the same cloth as the accolade accorded to the philanthropist Opramoas, of Lycia, who himself paid for the statues that were voted in his honor, because he did not wish to "have the province burdened" (*Benefactor*, no. 19.9.30.57-58). So also merchants residing in Puteoli have expenses for imperial celebrations charged to their account, "so that," as they state, "we might not burden the city" (*OGI* 595.15).

The troubles to which Paul refers took place in the province of Asia. Unfortunately, the record we have of his career is so fragmentary that all attempts to define them are pure guesswork. But they were of such intensity that Paul despaired of life itself.

9—On the other hand, Paul exploits possibility in such apparent personal disaster: "We have gotten in ourselves the death sentence." The diction is carefully chosen. Paul is not referring to condemnation by secular authority. He notes that his experiences have taught him to face at the depths of his being the harsh reality of mortality. "Where the fire has been, the fire can no longer come," said an Indian in answer to someone who asked him why he had set the brush ablaze near his teepee in the face of a roaring forest fire. Once having faced death to a depth beyond mere attack on his body, Paul is prepared for anything. At first sight, Paul appears to express thoughts expressed by Epictetus (2.1.14-17):

> Our courage ought to be directed at death, and our discretion aimed at the fear of it. But as it stands we are careless, remiss, and indifferent about forming a judgment concerning death. Socrates did well in labeling it and related matters "hobgoblins." It is well known that masks fill children with fear and terror because they lack experience. In the same way and for the same reason we are affected by circumstances. . . . What is death? A hobgoblin. Turn it over, examine it and discover what it is. See! It doesn't bite. This trifling little body must be separated from its wee spirit. So it was before, and it is now only a matter of time for the separation again to take place. Why, then, do you take it so hard, if the time is now? And if not now, certainly you must face the fact later.

But a deep chasm separates Paul from the Stoic philosopher.

Whereas Epictetus teaches self-reliance and dependence on resources developed within oneself, Paul has learned the opposite—not to rely on himself, but **on God who raises the dead.** The present tense of the verb "raises" emphasizes the ongoing resurrecting activity of God. In any event, God, who rescued Paul from a situation that led him to despair of life itself and to ponder things anew, will continue the beneficent activity.

10-11—The Corinthians can through their prayers be of assistance to the apostle, for God will heed their requests and grant further deliverances, with the result that there will be an outpouring of thanksgiving for the benefaction (**blessing**) bestowed on Paul. Through emphasis on the **many** who will express such gratitude, Paul evokes the understanding that a benefactor's performance ought not to be buried in forgetfulness. Paul's addressees would readily recall what is commonplace in Greco-Roman decrees: "That all may know that we know how to render due thanks to our benefactors." The **many** prayers that are voiced in Paul's behalf will result in an equal number or more of thanksgivings for the deliverances that follow upon the prayers. Thus God's prestige will be magnificently magnified—and for Paul that is the goal of all living and dying. In sum, four major points emerge in Paul's presentation on the extraordinary beneficence of God: (1) In his brush with death Paul became less confident in his own resources and more intimately acquainted with God's resurrection power. (2) God's rescue in the past is a warrant for future rescue operations in Paul's behalf. (3) The Christians in Corinth are cooperating by petitioning God on Paul's behalf. (4) The many benefits that result from so much prayer will require a multitude of thanksgivings.

◼ Struggle for a Meeting of Minds (1:12—7:16)

Facing the Problem (1:12—2:13)

By emphasizing the beneficence of God and depicting the unity of the Corinthians in their concern for Paul, the apostle prepares his auditors for his succeeding presentation. Since much of that presentation deals with the matter of his credentials, he had to make it clear at the beginning that he requires no lessons in humility. God has taught him well through his tribulations. Any suggestion of arrogance derives from the demands of the situations that he encounters at Corinth and is not to be attributed to personal pique or self-aggrandizement.

Affirmation of Concern (1:12-14)

In these verses Paul writes in the vein of a public benefactor. A Lycian billionaire named Opramoas designed a mausoleum for himself in the second century and covered its walls with a record of his numerous benevolences. Among the documents are numerous letters of attestation informing the emperor of Opramoas's character and of his many contributions to the public welfare. Paul does not require such letters. His own **conscience** and the perceptiveness of his addressees are all the witness he needs.

Numerous ancient monuments record of their honorees that during their tour of duty they behaved in a manner worthy of their city. Paul cites the character of God as his model for performance wherever he goes as the emissary of the gospel. God has no hidden agenda in his dealings with people, and neither does Paul. Paul approaches others without guile (textual variant **holiness**), in all candor and **sincerity.** He does not take advantage of others with intellectual tricks. The beneficence (**grace**) of God dominates his thinking and expression. He does not write one thing and mean another. He is straightforward in all his expression. What they see is what they get. He anticipates such mutual understanding that they will be as proud of him as he will be of them when **Jesus** is openly revealed as **Lord** of all the universe.

From Paul's emphasis on his sincerity it now becomes clearer why he called such sustained attention to the theme of consolation in vv. 3-11. A Greco-Roman literary work known as *Consolation of Apollonius*, which was attributed to Plutarch, points out that flattery is the source of much apparent sympathy in grief (117f-118a; cf. Juvenal, *Satires* 3.101-102). Since calamity may lead sufferers to feel helpless and uncertain about the future, they will resent any exhortation that increases their sense of despair or suggests that the would-be consoler fails to understand their problems. Through his repeated reference to the divine role in his sufferings, Paul aimed to reinforce conviction concerning the genuineness of his concern for the Corinthians not only in their sufferings but in the problems that are subject to exploration in the rest of his letter.

Explanation for a Non-Visit (1:15—2:4)

15-22—In this passage Paul offers information about his travel plans as these relate to the Corinthians. Some time after the writing of the first letter to Corinth, Paul visited the Corinthian Christians. In the course of that visit he discussed his travel plans (see 1 Cor. 16:5-8). It was his intention to go from Ephesus to Macedonia and then on to Corinth, after which the Corinthians, he hoped, would join him in the planning of his further mission.

Unfortunately, conditions at Corinth were such that Paul had to pay an emergency visit. Instead of taking the overland route from Ephesus, he appears to have taken ship directly for Corinth. In the course of negotiations with the people at Corinth on this emergency visit, Paul had evidently laid out another set of travel plans. This time he intended to go to Macedonia and then return along the same route for another visit at Corinth (to confer on them a twofold benefit (**pleasure**), after which he planned to return to Judea. But Paul was so taken aback by the attitudes at Corinth that he scrapped his original plan and did not return to Corinth.

To protect himself against charges of waffling on promises, Paul writes as he does in vv. 17-22. As always, **God** is Paul's model. God does not talk out of both sides of the mouth, nor does Paul. His **yes** is yes and his **no** is no. In this respect he is in harmony with Jesus' exhortation concerning oaths (Matt. 5:37). Also, Paul never loses sight of the fact that God is the Supreme Politician and Benefactor. **The promises** (*epangeliai*) of earthly politicians frequently remain unfulfilled. Hence numerous Greco-Roman documents take special note of the fact that the honorands mentioned in them have carried out their promises. Paul declares that the Supreme Politician has a perfect record. In Jesus Christ

God's **yes** comes to dynamic expression, for in him all God's **promises,** especially those relating to the donation of the Spirit (cf. Gal. 3:14; 4:28-29) are constantly undergoing fulfillment.

In reciprocity, Christians pronounce **the Amen** (see, e.g., Rom. 11:33-36; Gal. 1:3-5; Phil. 4:19-20; 1 Tim. 1:12-17; 2 Tim. 4:17-18). (This expression is not the terminal word of a prayer. In keeping with ancient custom it is used to this day in response to a preacher's statements that evoke especially strong affirmation.) Through **the Amen** due recognition is given to God's beneficent display. Such recognition enhances God's prestige or reputation (**glory,** *doxa*) in the world. The liturgical act thus images Christian life as an ongoing doxology. At 7:1 Paul will again pick up the motif of divine promises, for God **guarantees** (establishes, *bebaioō,* cf. 1 Cor. 1:6-8)) to Paul and the Corinthian Christians receipt of everything that is theirs in connection with the Anointed One (**Christ**). And God does it by anointing them. For the term *anointing* RSV has **commissioned,** evidently limiting the term to Paul's receipt of apostleship. But such interpretation constricts the apostle's wordplay. Jesus is the Christ, and God makes *Christ*ians.

To image divine reliability, Paul uses legal and commercial terminology relating first to moneys or goods that are sealed (*sphragizō*) and thus secured for delivery, and then to the down payment (*arrabōn*) that guarantees full requital on a purchase price. Paul shows that God gives the Spirit as warrant (cf. 5:5, *arrabōn;* Eph. 1:13; 4:30, *sphragizō*) that fulfillment of all the promises in connection with Christ will ultimately follow.

Paul's line of thought is of a piece with his understanding that fullness of Christian living consists in complete control of Christian existence by the Holy Spirit. Such completeness of Spirit-life will become reality only "at the last trumpet" (1 Cor. 15:52), when the dead in Christ will rise and those who are yet alive will be changed. For "flesh and blood" as we know it "cannot inherit the kingdom of God, nor does the perishable inherit the imperishable" (15:50). Whether the apostle had baptism in mind when he drafted this portion of his letter cannot be determined with certainty. That he associates the Spirit with baptism is clear from 1 Cor. 12:13, but the custom of observing baptism in the second century with rites of "anointing" and "sealing" may be dependent on Paul's imagery without defining his intention in the use of it.

The verb **commissioned,** v. 21, renders the Greek word *chriō* (anoint), which appears only here in Paul's writings. In view of the reference to the extension of God's glory and to Paul's interest in demonstrating to Jerusalem the success of his outreach to the Gentile world (vv. 15-16), it is probable that Paul was thinking here of Isaiah's messenger, who, according to Isa. 61:1, has apostolic credentials through anointing of the Lord's Spirit. Since Paul was unfamiliar with the type of debate exhibited in modern discussion concerning the identity of Isaiah's suffering servant and the specific parts of Isaiah that are to be allotted to presentation of the Servant, it is also probable that he associated the possessor of the Spirit in Isaiah 61 with the Lord's Servant, who is specifically cited in the so-called Servant Songs of 42:1-4(9); 49:1-6(13); 50:4-9(11); 52:13—53:12. The vacillation between individual and corporate in Isaiah's depiction of this figure offered St. Paul the opportunity to set forth the Christian community as Servant Israel engaged in support of an ongoing outreach to the nations and at the same time to image his own credentials as the Servant of the Lord who is engaged in faithfully carrying out God's assignment to Israel (cf. 5:18—6:2).

23-24—Having shown that God is trustworthy, and that God has demonstrated it through Jesus Christ, the heart of Paul's proclamation, Paul now does the equivalent of crossing his heart and laying his hand on the Bible. In this phase of his presentation he is not in harmony with Jesus' urging to confine one's asseverations to yes and no, but it is highly questionable that he was acquainted with many of the Lord's sayings. In any case, the apostle's rare excursions into oaths (Rom. 1:9; Phil. 1:8; 1 Thess. 2:5, 10) contrast with the style of Demosthenes, who outswore all orators. Paul's point is to emphasize that his and God's interests and character coincide. Desiring to spare the Corinthians, he did not pay them the second visit that he had discussed with them. Lest someone misunderstand his meaning, Paul adds a disclaimer of unworthy motive in the initial clause of v. 24: "This statement of mine is, of course, not to be construed as suggesting a dictatorial stance. The fact is, we consider ourselves partners in your joy." (Other passages that include the "not that . . . but" form are 3:5; 2 Thess. 3:9; Phil. 4:17; cf. 3:12.) Paul had no interest in exercising apostolic clout over their faith. He would rather be their partner (*synergos*, cf. 6:1) in the experience of **joy.** The source of Paul's disciplined estimate of his authority is apparent from the model set forth in Phil. 2:5-11.

Reference to joy as the by-product of political stability was common in the Greco-Roman world. A decree of the Asian League, published about 65 years before the writing of 2 Corinthians, honored Caesar Augustus in these words:

> Providence that orders all our lives has in her display of concern and generosity in our behalf adorned our lives with the highest good: *Augustus,* whom she has filled with arete [exceptional merit] for the benefit of humanity, and has in her beneficence granted us and those who will come after us [a Savior] who has made war to cease and who shall put everything [in peaceful] order (*Benefactor,* p. 217).

Velleius Paterculus (2.89.2), an amateur historian and a contemporary of Augustus, echoed the sentiment:

> There is nothing that human beings could wish for from the gods, nothing that the gods can grant to human beings, nothing that the mind can conceive or good fortune bring to pass, that Augustus on his return to the city did not confer upon the Republic, the Roman people, and the world.

With the word **joy** used in association with his celebration of divine beneficence, Paul not only suggests the superiority of Christian over general Gentile experience but invites the Corinthians to explore the depths of one of the Spirit's primary gifts (cf. Gal. 5:22). Coupled with Paul's stress on joy is his caution that power plays do not promote corporate well-being. By faith, that is, in a commitment to God, whose trustworthiness is manifested in Jesus Christ, the Corinthians have and do find their stability. This evaluation is on the one hand a complimentary declaration that the Corinthians do not require a stern spiritual master, for they have firm moorings. At the same time it is a gentle reminder that loose footing may require firm intervention.

Excursus: The Corinthians and Corporate Israel

That Paul viewed the Corinthian congregations as part of corporate Israel is clear from the imagery he used in 1 Corinthians 10. Since corporate Israel had the assignment of functioning as the Lord's Servant, Paul viewed the Corinthians to be in partnership with Jesus Christ (cf. 1 Cor. 1:9; Phil. 1:5-7). Hence they were associated with Paul in the experience of suffering (2 Cor. 1:8-11). As a representative of Israel, in partnership with Jesus Christ (cf. 1 Cor. 9:23), and entrusted with the message of salvation (2 Cor. 5:19), Paul brought the gospel to the Corinthians and now mobilizes them also to fulfill the Servant's role. Besides this more general cooperative relationship, Paul has specific co-workers, through whom God gives shape and productivity to communities of believers (1 Cor. 3:9; cf. 2 Cor. 8:23; 1 Thess. 3:2; Phil. 2:25; 4:3; Phlom. 1, 24).

2:1-4—Chapter 1 concluded with the thought that Paul does not particularly enjoy using power plays. He now expands on this point in reference to some delicate matters that came up during his emergency visit. Since Paul's primary interest as God's instrument of benefaction is to fill others with joy, he determined not to visit them a second time on the previous trip. In view of the anarchical conditions prevailing in the congregations at Corinth, such a visit would have been too **painful.** Yet he had to accept his apostolic obligation. He therefore wrote a letter of strong admonition (vv. 4,9; 7:12), which took to task some members of the congregation who had evidently sided with someone whom Paul felt compelled to reprimand (cf. 7:8-12). The offender in this case does not appear to be identical with the one whose sexual offense is mentioned in 1 Cor. 5:1-5. It is more probable that Paul has here in mind someone whose challenge to Paul's apostolic authority threatened to destroy the unity of the congregations at Corinth. (On this lost "Letter of Tears" see the Introduction, pp. 16-18.)

The Corinthians are not to think that Paul enjoyed writing the sorrowful letter. On the contrary, his tears mixed with the ink. His ultimate purpose was not to inflict pain, but to communicate his abounding affection. But affection ought to be reciprocated, especially by the Corinthians (v. 3), who are deeply etched in the apostle's heart. Moreover, those who have been grieved by him and have thereby known his affection are in the best position to gladden the apostle's heart. By expressing his need for some receipt of affection, Paul discloses the intensity of his own love for the Corinthians and specifically for the offender whom he leaves unidentified. Had the apostle made the return trip as planned earlier, he would have been greeted with sorrow. As it is, he can now pay them a visit that will spell joy for all concerned. For Paul is confident that if the Corinthians know he is happy, they in turn will rejoice.

Paul's agitation shows through clearly. The heart of the gospel was at stake. The new age of God's reign in Jesus Christ ought to spell joy. It was of immense importance to restore stability to the Corinthians' congregational life. Paul therefore spends another paragraph on the theme of sorrow.

Resolution of a Disciplinary Problem (2:5-13)

Since precise details of the disturbance at Corinth are notoriously lacking, much of the speculation that finds refutation in commentaries belongs to the history of romance rather than sober exegesis. But, as indicated above, there is strong probability that someone had questioned Paul's administrative conduct.

5-11—Lest anyone think that Paul takes such questioning as a personal matter, he is quick to point out that sorrow has been inflicted on the entire community. His motive for involving all the Corinthians is translucent. By saying **in some measure** (v. 5) he heads off an overly stern attack from the corporate body, and at the same time suggests that their participation in the effects of the offender's action weakens a temptation to overreaction by the apostle. Paul's phrase *hina mē epibarō* (v. 5) is better rendered, "so that I might not bring weight to bear," with the verb used as in 1 Thess. 2:9; 2 Thess. 3:8, instead of RSV's **not to put it too severely.** Paul is well aware of Satan's designs (v. 11). Since the offending party remains in the community, it is necessary that the community reassure him of forgiveness and affection. The granting of such assurance is part of what constitutes obedience, and he wrote as he did, says the apostle, so that he might ascertain the genuineness (**test**) of their commitment (that is, whether they are **obedient**) to all aspects of his apostolic message. Paul does not present himself as an authority figure, but as an envoy who speaks for the Supreme Politician. God's expectations are to be taken seriously. Thus in 13:5 Paul advises his addressees to test themselves whether they have remained faithful. If the congregation forgives the man, Paul concurs. Thereby he demonstrates that he does not act high-handedly nor unilaterally, in a weighty manner, as though he alone has the right to pronounce forgiveness. Indeed, says Paul, if I do pronounce forgiveness in any circumstance, I do it under the eyes of Christ, with you always in mind.

Throughout these verses (5-11) Paul rings changes on the theme of beneficence and is in harmony with sentiments that were topical in Greco-Roman moral treatises. In an essay *Fraternal Love* (488a), Plutarch emphasizes the importance of forgiving (*charizomai*) rather than winning (*nikaō*). "Wise people," wrote Dionysius of Halicarnassus (5.4.3), "overcome hostilities with displays of friendship; fools and uncivilized people destroy their friends along with their enemies."

Paul is well aware of **Satan's** efforts to gain the upper hand, but the apostle is not easily taken in, and he accepts responsibility for protecting the Corinthians against his machinations. The apostle will have more to say about Satan in 6:15, where he appears under the name Beliar.

In Paul's writings, **Satan,** who is referred to with various terms, endeavors to mislead or entrap God's people (1 Cor. 11:3, the snake of Gen. 3:13; 7:5; 1 Cor. 7:5; 2 Cor. 4:4, the god of this age, who blinds the understanding of unbelievers; Rom. 16:20; 1 Thess. 3:5, the tempter; 1 Tim. 5:15) and serves as an undercover expert (2 Cor. 11:14; 2 Thess. 2:9), who inflicts misery on God's people (1 Cor. 5:5; 12:7; cf. 1 Tim. 1:20).

The reference to **the majority** in v. 6 refers to the action of the Christians as a body in contrast to decisions made by a handful of leaders. Paul wishes to emphasize the general obedience manifested at Corinth. The Corinthians would have been acquainted with such diction, which was firmly entrenched in Hellenic parlance from the time of Homer (*Iliad* 5.673) and used by Greek historians in reference to the people as oppposed to those in leadership positions (Herodotus 7.149; Thucydides 8.73.3; 89.2). References to analogous procedure in the Qumran community are of interest in demonstrating parallel parliamentary procedures (cf. Josephus, *War* 2.8.9), but cannot be presumed to establish the apostle's source for his choice of words. Paul writes Greek, not Hebrew, in this very Hellenic letter. Whether a minority was in disagreement cannot be determined from the meager data that Paul supplies. Everything would, of course, have been clear to the recipients.

12-13—The following sequence of events, much of it detailed in 1:15-24, appears to offer the best explanation for the temporal and geographical data in 2:12-13: After receiving information about discouraging developments at Corinth, Paul rushed to Corinth, but was unable to make any headway in resolution of the problems. Apparently on arrival he had laid out his travel plans, which included a trip to Macedonia, with return to Corinth, and from there to Jerusalem. But the apostle was so profoundly disturbed by what he encountered at Corinth that he appears to have taken the first boat back to Asia Minor without carrying out his promises of the return visit from Macedonia. Hence the charge that he spoke out of both sides of his mouth (1:18). In place of a longer stay and a return visit, Paul dispatched the "Letter in Tears" (v. 4), a letter so stern that he was tempted to question the advisability of sending it (7:8). After its dispatch, perhaps through Titus (cf. 7:5-6), he decided to combine a visit to his beloved Macedonians with an eventual visit to Corinth. On the way to Macedonia he disembarked at Alexandria Troas, a seaport city, about 200 kilometers northwest of Ephesus in direct flight, where he had planned on doing some evangelizing. At the same time he hoped to meet Titus with news from Corinth (2:13). Despite mission opportunities at Alexandria, Paul quickly went on to Macedonia, where he finally met up with Titus, who reported good news about the Corinthians' repentance (7:6-7). In response Paul wrote 2 Corinthians and sent Titus on ahead in the company of another respected "brother" and other associates

(8:17-23) to encourage the Corinthians to complete their collection for the poor in Jerusalem.

Paul's statement about his interest in the news from Corinth (v. 13) is one of his many protestations of love that find expression in this letter. That he could pass up a magnificent opportunity to engage in his favorite work of evangelization, must have made a profound impression on the Corinthians, who would be forced to admit that Paul did not make ego trips at the expense of personal relationships. Others could evangelize the region of the Troad. But he had to know how the Corinthians were faring. He wanted so much to hug them.

Self-Affirmation 2:14—5:10

Credentials (2:14—4:6)

14-17—Filled with recollection of the relief he felt when at last he met up with Titus in Macedonia (see 7:13-16), Paul ponders once more the beneficence of God. Gratitude for benefits is as natural to a Greek as the eating of olives, and for a Jew it is unthinkable that one would ignore God's generosity. Paul's formulation follows the pattern in 1 Cor. 15:57 (cf. 2 Cor. 8:16; 9:15; Rom. 6:17; 7:25). Like a Roman general who leads a long train of captives and exhibits the booty from vanquished places, God leads Paul and his associates in a victory procession (*thriambeuō*, as in Col. 2:15) throughout the world, with the Messiah as the dominating figure. God's victory over stubborn Paul (cf. 1 Cor. 15:8-9) was part of God's plan to overcome unbelief in the Greco-Roman world. God's victory is a victory of grace. Submission in faith to the Supreme Prince is the beginning of real life and a share in the victory over all enemies of the self. Overcome by God in Christ, Paul is happy to be led about in a triumphal procession. He may look defeated, but through his abject condition, as one rejected in the world, beaten and jailed, he is the instrument of salvation for many. Thus God becomes newly victorious more than triumphant. John Oxenham summed it all in a poem titled "Paul":

> Bond-slave to Christ, and in my bonds rejoicing,
> Earmarked to Him I counted less than nought;
> His man henceforward, eager to be voicing
> That wondrous Love which Saul the Roman sought.
>
> Sought him and found him, working bitter sorrow;
> Found him and claimed him, chose him for his own;
> Bound him in darkness, till the glorious morrow
> Unsealed his eyes to that he had not known.

Although the precise source of Paul's figure concerning the reference to **fragrance** is disputed, it is probable that Paul was thinking either of incense used along a triumphal route or of the aroma emanating from various spices that would be brought from conquered areas in the East. If the first of these is correct, Paul is imagining clouds of incense ascending in the course of a triumphal procession. If the second is to be preferred, Paul conceives of himself and his associates in ministry as the embodiment of such choice booty. Since the term **Christ** means "Anointed" and therefore suggests a sweet aroma, Paul's imagery is consistent. Auditors familiar with the Greek Bible might well have noted the imagery in Sirach 24:15 relating to wisdom ("aroma . . . odor . . . fragrance").

Fecund is the generating power of metaphor, and Paul himself undoubtedly made further associations, but the average auditor at Corinth would be left with the basic pattern suggested by the figure of a triumph, so characteristic of Greek acquaintance with Roman history. As captives in the divine procession, the apostles emit **the aroma of Christ.** Some like the aroma and others do not. To those who prefer **death** it is a fume that spells death. To those who prefer **life,** it is a perfume that spells life. In similar fashion Moses spoke to the assembly of Israel: "May my teaching drop as the rain, my speech distill as the dew, as the gentle rain upon the tender grass, and as the showers upon the herb" (Deut. 32:2), words that were earlier preceded by the following set of options: "See, I have set before you this day life and good, death and evil" (30:15). The problem is not with the fragrance, but with the resistance of the one who smells it.

But, asks the apostle, **Who is sufficient for these things?** That is, who is competent for all this? No mere human being is capable of determining the fate of anyone. The question implies that Paul takes his responsibility seriously. We are not, he says, like so many who seek status through unethical practices. The point is that unscrupulous merchants seek enrichment through unethical handling of otherwise fine wares, for example, selling wine diluted with water (cf Isa. 1:22 LXX). Plato's polemic against the Sophists (*Protagoras* 5, 313c-d), cited by Wettstein, set the pattern in the Greek world: "The Sophist is a merchant or peddler (*kapēlos*) of wares that are to nourish the soul. . . . These people conduct courses of study from city to city, and when they hold their sale they vend (*kapēleuō*) each one with words of high recommendation. And it's probable . . . that some of them don't even know whether the goods they peddle are good or bad for the soul." Lucian (*Hermotimos* 59), master exposer of charlatans, sarcastically observes: "I can't tell what philosophy has in common with wine, but this I do know, that philosophers hawk their wares like wine peddlers (*kapēloi*), and you can count on most of them diluting the merchandise and cheating you with short measure." Paul's emphasis on prior consideration of divine approval parallels the appeal of Epictetus (4.8.17) for moral integrity: "I knew that whatever I did well I did, not with a view to spectators but for my own sake. . . . I did everything with myself and God in mind." Paul insists on the quality of his wares. "We do not misrepresent them. Better yet, God guarantees their quality, for we make our proclamation in the sight of God. Christ controls us and our utterance."

Excursus: thriambeuō

The KJV renders the term *thriambeuō:* "causeth us to triumph," but the corrective addition in BAGD (s.v. 2) questions the validity of this interpretation. It has been argued by Rory B. Egan ("Lexical Evidence on Two Pauline Passages," *Novum Testamentum* 19 [1977]:34-62) that Paul's metaphorical use of the Roman triumphal procedure is unparalleled in literature prior to Paul (but note the usage by Paul's contemporary, Seneca, *On Benefits* 2.11.1); that it casts God in the role of an oppressor; and that a Roman triumph was not endless, but terminated in the execution of the prisoners, whereas Paul uses the term *pantote* (**always,** v. 14). Similar lines of criticism have resulted in censure of the Greek poet Pindar for mixed metaphors and the Roman poet Horace for exaggerated figures. But apart from the argument from silence, which is almost always specious, it is necessary to note that Paul was a genius and a poet, whose mind did not move at the pedestrian pace that is expected of those whose works have by historical accident become grammarians' hunting grounds or victims of "Shelfgeschichte." Moreover, not all triumphs terminated with execution of the prisoners. In the *Res Gestae* (tablet 1.4), Augustus reports that "during his triumphs, nine in all, kings or the children of kings were led before" his chariot. In this same account of his administration he repeatedly boasts of his clemency, a species of statecraft that was part of Rome's national ethos and commemorated by Livy (30.42) in his account of Carthaginian ambassadors who ascribed Rome's growing imperium to the sparing of her victims rather than to her victories over them.

3:1-3—Paul begins this section of his argument with a question that is designed to take the wind out of his opponents' sails. The very nature of their attack on his credentials requires affirmation of his authority, but at the same time lays him open to the charge of self-commendation. Therefore he heads into the eye of the storm and sets the stage for the numerous personal references that he will make throughout the rest of the letter.

Acts 18:27 notes that Apollos received letters of recommendation from Christians in Ephesus when he announced his intention to go to Achaia. And in Rom. 16:1 Paul adds a note of commendation for Phoebe. Apparently some of Paul's opponents had come to Corinth armed with such letters. Since one is left to guesswork in determining the possible sources, there is no point in further "darkening counsel with words without knowledge." The fact is that Paul, as he saw matters, needed no letters of recommendation when he came to Corinth, for he came on the scene in a new mission field with no other credentials than the persuasive power of the news concerning Jesus Christ. Nor does he need letters of recommendation from them when he goes elsewhere. All he has to say is, "Have you heard about the Christians at Corinth?" And people will respond, "You mean to say

that they are your converts? Why, everyone has heard of them!"
Similarly, Epictetus (2.3, cited by Wettstein) records the answer
of Diogenes to someone who requested him to write a letter of
recommendation:

> The man will take one look and know that you are a human being.
> As for determining whether you are good or bad, that will depend
> on his experience in distinguishing between good and bad people.
> And if he has no experience in the matter, it wouldn't help even if
> I wrote him a thousand times.

The basic figure of people likened to material objects as sig-
nifiers generated a variety of metaphors in antiquity. For example,
in the course of his funeral oration in memory of Athenians who
fell in the war with Sparta, Pericles pointed out that her heroes
were interred in the noblest of all tombs, the heart of humanity;
"for all the earth," he proclaimed, "becomes the sepulcher of
famous men" (Thucydides, 2.43). Distinguished merit wins the
respect of the ages. Spiritual accomplishment defies national
boundaries. In related vein Plutarch (*Moralia* 779b) observed that
the words of philosophers have the force of law when inscribed
in the souls of civic leaders and administrators. And Tacitus (*Annals* 4.38) reported that Tiberius Caesar desired no other monuments so much as being enshrined in the memory of Rome as
one who was worthy of his ancestors and constantly on the lookout
for her interests; such estimates of his person would be "the
temples in their minds and the most beautiful and enduring of
all monuments, for those that are erected in stone run the risk
of being turned into sepulchers when the judgment of posterity
turns into loathing."

In turn, Paul sees his beloved Corinthians as showpieces for
the gospel, living letters "known and read by people everywhere."
They are his letters of recommendation. Paul is the ministrant,
a *diakonos* or servant (here expressed by the participle of the
verb *diakoneō*) on their behalf, so that they can be an exceptionally expressive epistle. Whether Paul is likening himself to
the courier of a letter, as in the RSV with its rendering **delivered
by us,** or as the preparer of the letter, cannot be determined by

philological analysis. As indicated above on the metaphor of the triumph (2:14), Paul's rivers of imagery flood their banks. Paul's point is that the Corinthians are the product of his abiding concern from beginning to end. But in the last analysis they are **a letter from Christ.** Paul does not here image a specific writing process, whether by pen or by an engraving tool. When recorded on papyrus, letters were done in ink and then rolled up in the form of a scroll (cf. Rev. 6:14), after which senders put their signatures on the outside. Copies of ancient letters, especially those of official importance, were occasionally inscribed (*engraphō*, as in vv. 2-3) on stone (see, e.g., the correspondence in Opramoas's mausoleum, *Benefactor*, no. 19). Whether it is a pen or an engraving tool that is used, it is important to note that the same word, *engrapho*, can be used to describe either procedure. Much misunderstanding of Paul's metaphor in this passage would therefore be avoided by using the more neutral English term *record* in the rendering of the verb *engraphō* in vv. 2-3. In sum, when people look at the Corinthians, says Paul, they will read: "From Christ."

Despite Windisch's comment to the contrary, Paul's declaration that the Corinthians are a letter **known and read by all** people (v. 2) would patently suggest to the recipients that his imagery includes the inscriptional aspect, and the apostle's balanced phrasing in v. 3b further points in that direction. In the one scene, they are not recorded, as papyrus letters are, with the use of ink, but through the Spirit of the living God. In the second scene, with the props changed, the contrast is between solid stone and pliable hearts. Epistolary conventions thus offer Paul the opportunity to introduce a contrast between the product of the new age, namely, hearts that embody the goals and interests of the living God, and tablets of stone that register the decrees of God in the manner of an imperial magistrate. Paul is, of course, tipping his hand. Very shortly he will move into exposition and application of one of his favorite topics, the advantange of the presence of God's Spirit over mere dependence on Mosaic tradition. The inscriptional metaphor would, of course, remind some Corinthians of the tablets of stone on which God's finger had recorded the covenantal obligations (Exod. 31:18; Deut. 9:10). Some would recall Ezekiel's vision (11:19; cf. 18:11; 36:26) of a "heart of flesh" that would replace their "stony heart." And some would hear the echo of Jeremiah's (31:27-34) oracle about the law written in the hearts of Israel.

Excursus: Ancient Pens and Ink

Ancient ink was manufactured from carbon, probably from soot, and suspended in a gummy solution. Because of its hue it was called *melan* (black). Scribes would generally use a pen that was made from the reed known as *kalamos* (cf. 3 John 13), the hollow tubular stalk of grasses growing in marshy lands. Metal pens were not unknown, and the museum at Naples, which houses much of the treasure from Pompeii and Herculaneum, displays a bronze pen, which is nibbed much like the steel pen that still survives in the face of the ballpoint invasion. The high quality of ink used by some of the ancients is demonstrable from papyri and parchments.

4-11—"Who is competent [RSV: 'sufficient'] for these things?" asked the apostle in 2:16. Now he is prepared to give a carefully phrased positive answer. He argues that he considers himself competent to help the Corinthians be what he has just described—epistles, written with the medium of the Holy Spirit. As at 2:13, Paul uses the "not . . . but" formulation for his transition to his thought about the role of the Spirit. God has enabled him to be the minister of **a new covenant.** Paul's use of the term **covenant** compresses the line of thought that he used in Gal. 4:21-31, in which he showed that the promise to Abraham sponsors freedom and takes precedence over legislation that made its appearance later and made for bondage. The term **new covenant** echoes Jer. 31:31, and appears also in Paul's record of the eucharistic words in 1 Cor. 11:25 (cf. Luke 22:20). The word minister (*diakonos*, v. 6) echoes its cognate verb, which is rendered "administered" in v. 3. Since Paul's ministration is one of Spirit, not of letter, he can develop the eloquent kind of "letter" that characterizes the Corinthians.

The Spirit makes alive because it is the work of "the living

God" (v. 3), a term that appears frequently in the OT (e.g., Deut. 5:26; Josh. 3:10; 1 Sam. 17:26; 2 Kings 19:4; Isa. 37:4). For the NT see, e.g., Rom. 9:26 (citing Hos. 2:1 LXX); 1 Thess. 1:9; Acts 14:15; 1 Tim. 3:15; 4:10). The letter (RSV: **the written code**) kills, but the Spirit makes alive. To a Jew, who shares the sentiment of delight in God's "Law" that is frequently expressed in the Psalms, this would mean that God looks for integrity of creative commitment to God's interests and goals for humanity rather than for performance at the hand of specific rules and regulations. To a Gentile, Paul would be heard to say that people are truly free when they are not governed primarily by the sanctions of culture and custom, that which Greeks called *nomos*, but by the promptings of a spirit within that intuitively grasps the intentions of God and fulfills them through divine empowerment. For example, one of the participants in dialog in Plato's *Republic* (425d-e) points out that "there is no point in giving orders to people of exceptional merit, for they will readily recognize most of those items for which we ordinarily need legislation." From Paul's perspective all those who are motivated by God's Spirit are people of exceptional merit.

In Sophocles' *Antigone* (450-462), the heroic daughter of Oedipus informs despotic Creon, who has forbidden burial of her brother Polynices:

> It was not Zeus who published this edict,
> nor is it Justice, consort of the nether
> deities, who gave such laws to humankind.
> Nor would I value your commands so highly
> as to transgress, mere mortal that I am,
> the firm unwritten laws of heaven,
> which owe no birth to now or yesterday,
> and hide their origin in time's vast eld.
> No fear of any man's high prideful thought
> shall force me to their violation.
> That I must die, I knew, and needed
> no decree of yours to tell me so.
> Yet, if before my time, I count it gain.

In general, says Paul, dependence on specific directives impedes discovery of real personal identity and freedom. Tyrants rely on laws to keep people in line.

Paul's rhetorical skill in vv. 5-6 reveals itself in the *figura etymologica* or cognate expressions in vv. 5-6 ("our enablement" [*hikanotēs*], is from God, who "enabled" [*hikanoō*] us) and in the *epitasis* or emphasis that v. 6 gives to v. 5.

7-11—The apostle uses a common rabbinic line of argument, moving from the "lighter" to the "heavier," or the lesser to the greater, in the form: "if that . . . how much more this," with the conjunction **for** providing linkage in the chain. Making use of Exod. 34:27-35, he recites the story of Moses' encounter with God for 40 days and 40 nights on Mount Sinai. Moses neither drank nor ate during the entire period. During this period he wrote the law at divine direction. The account goes on:

> When Moses came down from Mt. Sinai, with the two tables of the testimony in his hand as he came down from the mountain, Moses did not know that the skin of his face shone because he had been talking with God. And when Aaron and all the people of Israel saw Moses, behold, the skin of his face shone, and they were afraid to come near him. But Moses called to them; and Aaron and all the leaders of the congregation returned to him, and Moses talked with them. And afterward all the people of Israel came near, and he gave them in commandment all that the Lord had spoken with him in Mount Sinai. And when Moses had finished speaking with them, he put a veil on his face; but whenever Moses went in before the Lord to speak with him, he took the veil off, until he came out; and when he came out, and told the people of Israel what he was commanded, the people of Israel saw the face of Moses, that the skin of Moses' face shone; and Moses would put the veil upon his face again, until he went in to speak with him.

Philo (*Life of Moses* 2.70) relates the tradition in the following form:

> Moses came down from the mount so much more beautiful in countenance than when he ascended that those who beheld him were astonished and dumbfounded and were unable to gaze for any length of time because of the brightness that matched the sun in brilliance.

To Corinthians who knew their Homer, Paul's account would have reminded them of the moment when Athena covered the shoulders of Achilles with her fringed aegis, whereupon a golden cloud, from which Athena kindled a brilliant flame, encircled his head (*Iliad* 18.203-206).

In the light of the account in Exodus, Paul argues: (1) The law (which was **carved** or engraved, *entypoō*, on the two tablets) carries with it penalties of death, yet it was a glorious moment when the law was given or came into being, so glorious that the congregation of Israel was not able to look steadily at Moses' face, which shone with extraordinary brilliance (*doxa;* Paul's experience on Damascus road was similar, Acts 22:11). If, then, the brilliance that flooded the countenance of Moses was so impressive, how much more glorious must the service of the Spirit be! (2). The law, which was transmitted so gloriously, serviced its violators with condemnation. How much more splendid and worthy of recognition is the service that is designed to effect acquittal and uprightness (*dikaiosynē*). Paul is the only NT writer to use the noun *katakrisis* (**condemnation,** here and at 7:3) and the cognate verb (Rom. 5:16, 18; 8:1). From the passages in Romans, where the same association of condemnation and uprightness is made, it is clear that Paul thinks of uprightness as the opposite of the condition that brings about the condemnation. The entire line of thought, then, follows the pattern in Gal. 3:19-22 and Romans 5–7, according to which the condition of humanity is such that legal structures are in effect conducive to death, for they evoke the sinful condition of humanity to break out in sinful actions. But our perversity is such that we try to determine our own acquittal. Hence it is that people caught in noncompliance customarily enter the plea that they were doing nothing wrong. In the aftermath of the "Watergate" and "Irangate" scandals, citizens of the United States have found this to be true at the highest levels of government. But the human tragedy is this, that the very resort to legal structures for self-justification leads to greater condemnation, for attempts to justify oneself preempt the judicial processes of God. The only way of escape is through the verdict of acquittal that God pronounces in connection with the gift of Jesus Christ and the new life of uprightness as the fruit of the Spirit's activity.

11—The apostle drives home his line of argument: when **splendor** is surpassed by splendor, that which is surpassed can be said to have lost its splendor. To put it another way, if something that fades has such short space of splendor, certainly that which endures, and in fact becomes more splendid as time goes on, can be said to possess far more splendor and certainly much greater claim on our attention.

12-18—The thought of permanence suggests the term **hope** (*elpis*). **Hope,** as ordinarily used by Paul, means expectation, not anticipation. Paul is confident that God will in good time make delivery of all the promises. In view of the expectation of abiding splendor and the consummation of the Spirit's activity, of which we now have an installment (1:22), the apostle exercises much freedom of expression (*parrēsia*) in his dealings with the congregation. That is, he deals openly with the members, as he will emphasize even more fervently, beginning at 4:1. So concerned is he that they not miss out on the glorious program that God has in store for them.

At this point Paul adopts a line of Jewish scribal argumentation, which does not adhere to the letter of the OT text (Exod. 34:34-35). According to the account in Exodus, the people of Israel were afraid to approach Moses when they saw his face aglow, but he encouraged them to remain and listen to his declaration, after which he put on a face covering and took it off when he returned to the mountain to speak with God. Paul argues that Moses put the covering on because he did not want the people to be disappointed with disappearance of the splendor. The implication is that the Israelites would not be content with a revelation that would give way to another in time. Their **minds were hardened,** that is, they wanted the law to remain and refused to face the fact that God had something further in mind. It is like that **to this day,** writes Paul. The veil is still in place when the old covenant is read in the synagogues, and the auditors cannot see that its glory is fading by virtue of the new developments that have taken place in connection with God's Anointed One, the Messiah (**Christ**). According to Paul, this hardness of heart can be removed only through conversion to **the Lord.**

Paul plays on words derived from the Septuagintal recital of the story in Exodus. "When Moses summoned [Aaron and the elders of Israel], Aaron and the leaders of the congregation 'turned' to Moses. . . . And when he had stopped speaking to them, he put a veil over his face. But when Moses went in to speak with the Lord, he removed the veil." Paul argues that under the new arrangement in Christ it is necessary to turn to the Lord, namely, Christ, and not to Moses, that is, the law. When such conversion takes place, the veil is lifted, and in place of the fading glory that once accompanied the revelation at Sinai there is now the abiding glory of the presence of the Spirit, as opposed to the letter of the law, cited at v. 6. From a rhetorical perspective, vv. 7-16 function as an insertion or *parembolē* that gives meaning to vv. 17-18, which serve as the conclusion to the statement in v. 6 concerning the life-giving function of the Spirit. We now know how the Spirit becomes reality. The Lord is the Spirit, that is, there can be no talk about the Lord apart from the Spirit. Colloquially put, as soon as one talks "Lord" one must think "Spirit." The rendering by the RSV suggests the equation of Lord and Spirit rather than the close relationship between the lordship of Jesus Christ and the activity of the Spirit. The presence of **the Spirit of the Lord** promotes **freedom,** that is liberation from the law, and Gal. 4:1-11 is the best commentary on Paul's meaning. To Paul such freedom also implied the privilege of speaking openly to the Corinthians (v. 12).

The Spirit may be said to be the Lord's alter ego. There is no need of a face covering, for there is no danger that the glory will fade. In ancient times Moses was the only one who displayed the glory of God on his countenance. Now Christians—**all of them**—are **beholding** or contemplating (*katoptrizomai*) that glory in the manner that one looks at one's image in a mirror. As a result of the Spirit's activity, what we see imaged is the Lord's character and personality that has so penetrated our own being that we in effect see God's own exceptional splendor. But not even yet is the ultimate reached. We have only the down payment of the Spirit (1:21). If such is the case, how can one conceive the quality of the splendor that still awaits us? Paul puts it this way: We **are being changed into his** (the Lord's) **likeness from one degree of glory to another.** This is Paul's rhapsody on the Christ-lives-in-me theme (cf. Gal. 2:20; Phil. 1:21).

Far from being a digression, as some have thought, vv. 12-18 are integral to Paul's argument. His focus is on the image of Christ. This passage shows how much is at stake. Because Paul knows the extraordinary possibilities of Spirit-filled Christian experience that await his beloved Corinthians, he cannot bear the thought of their being deprived by ego-tripping hucksters. Hence he appears to practice what some in Corinth interpreted as exercise of clout at a safe distance (cf. 10:10). But what they viewed as an effort inordinately to control the Corinthians is Paul's exercise of freedom in proclaiming the truth of the gospel. Therefore, as the transitional opening phrase of 4:1 indicates, he will not flatter the Corinthians, and he will not be intimidated to weaken his witness to the splendor of God's glory revealed in Christ.

By thus building up the superiority of the new age over the old, of the Spirit over the law, of Christ over Moses, Paul shows that his alleged demonstration of authoritarian control over the Corinthians is not a product of his own ego needs but derives from his overwhelming concern that the Corinthians do not lose out on the glorious privileges that are now theirs.

In Chapter 4, Paul continues his argument that the gospel proclaimed by him is superior to the proclamation made at Sinai, and that his concern for the welfare of the Corinthians accounts for his apparent arrogance.

4:1-6—Paul declares that he is in the service (**ministry**) of the Corinthians. Once more pointing to God as the Supreme Benefactor, Paul says that he has experienced such divine **mercy** (cf. 1 Cor. 7:25; 1 Tim. 1:13, 16) in permitting him to engage in such activity that he does not lose heart or enthusiasm in the discharge of his responsibilities. Similarly Julius Caesar boasted of his perseverance in time of peril on behalf of Rome (Livy, *Annals* 4.38).

Earlier Paul had said that he needed no letters of recommendation (3:1). Here he commends himself to the **conscience** (*syneidēsis*) of "every one." **Conscience** is recognition of a moral standard, an awareness of what is right or wrong in a given situation. Violation of the standard is attended by awareness of specific moral failure. Paul's generalization, "every one," is an appeal to universally recognized canons of moral conduct. The

Greek dramatist Menander (*Monostichoi* 654) expresses the ultimate criterion when he echoes a doctrine broadly held in the Greco-Roman world that "God is the moral standard (*syneidēsis*) for all mortals." The uniqueness of Christianity does not consist in its moral precepts, which are frequently stated as well or even more eloquently by non-Christians in the Greco-Roman world. Paul's life is open for review to every one. Humanity can serve as his jury. In a related vein Epictetus (3.22.13-18) advises those who desire to cultivate the best interests of their souls to live in such a way that their lives can readily be scrutinized. Morally questionable deeds and emotions require exterior protection, whereas self-respect is the only security needed by one who is committed to what is truly good. Such a person, says Epictetus, is free and lives "out in the open."

Windisch calls attention to the specific types of temptations associated with religious propaganda of the time, such as claims to special revelations (2 Pet. 1:15) and exploitation of believers. In view of Paul's hesitation to catalog his extraordinary performances (2 Cor. 12:12), it is probable that he disclaims the kinds of boasts made by emulators of a popular spiritual leader such as Empedocles, who is said to have made the following promise to one of his adherents:

> You shall learn of all drugs that can ward off ills and old age. . . .
> You shall restrain the unwearied winds that rush over the land and
> ravish the fields with their gusts. In turn, should it be your desire,
> you shall invoke requiting breezes, and after the tenebrous storm
> you shall give to earthlings a timely drought, and after the dryness
> of summer you shall bring forth tree-nourishing streams that will
> be found in the sky. And from the depths of Hades you shall restore
> strength to the dead.
>
> (Empedocles 111)

Especially significant is Paul's emphasis on the truth (*alētheia*). The RSV follows reputable exegetical judgment in its rendering, **by the open** (*phanerōsis*) **statement of the truth,** thereby suggesting that Paul uses the term **truth** as a synonym for the gospel he proclaims. Unfortunately, this rendering does not do justice to the fact that cognate terms relating to openness for the most part have personal attitudes or perfomance as their referents in

Paul's letters. This is especially true of 2 Corinthians. In fact, 2 Cor. 4:2 appears to echo 2:14-17, in which Paul expands on his use of the verb *phaneroō* (2:14) by referring to the purity of his conduct in proclaiming the word of God. Indeed, his record is of such a quality that the Corinthian believers are in their own persons an open (*phaneroō*) advertisement for Paul's type of ministry (3:3). In the immediate context of 4:2, Paul refers to Christ's life which is apparent (*phaneroō*) in his flesh (v. 11), and in 5:11 he certainly echoes 4:2 when he states that "what we are is open (*phaneroō*) to God, and I hope it is also known (*phaneroō*) to your conscience (*syneidēsis*)." What the Corinthians see is what they get. In 7:12 Paul notes that public advertisement (*phaneroō*) of his zeal in the Corinthians' behalf prompted the writing of one of his letters, and in 11:6 he uses the verb in reference to his general manifestation of sincerity. Furthermore, the formulation *ta krypta tēs aischynēs* ("the hidden things of shame") in 2 Cor. 4:2 follows the contours of the phrase *ta krypta tou skotous* in 1 Cor. 4:5, and both formulations refer to moral issues and are used in association with terms from the *phaner-* word family. In Rom. 1:18-19 the term "truth" (*alētheia*) is used in reference to moral conduct and in association with two terms from the *phaner-* word family. The balanced structure (cf. vv. 8-9, 16, 18, and passim) is typically Hellenic.

The Greek verb underlying the term **ways** in v. 2 is *peripateō*, whose central meaning is "walk." It is used occasionally in the OT to express commitment to God's expectations (cf. 2 Kings 20:3; Prov. 8:20), and Paul frequently applies it to moral behavior in either a positive or a negative sense. For other usage in 2 Corinthians, see 5:7; 10:2,3; 12:18. Paul's point is that he has refused to compromise his apostolic responsibility by clever and ethically questionable public relations maneuvers.

The Corinthians themselves can determine Paul's credentials, and they will be able to make a correct decision concerning him, for, as he affirms at the end of v. 2, he does not hesitate to have himself scrutinized by God.

3-4—At the beginning of v. 3 Paul picks up the theme of the veil, 3:14. How is one to account for the fact that the gospel is not welcomed by everyone, especially by Paul's own people? If the veil that fell over Israel is to be lifted in the time of the Messiah, how is it that so many reject Paul's proclamation? Is the revelation really so glorious, if so many cannot perceive it? Perhaps, allege his opponents, Paul has alienated many by his methods and lack of personal appeal (10:10). Others appear to have alleged that his approach to outsiders was either lacking in the kind of rhetorical sophistication to which auditors of Greco-Roman cultural background were accustomed (cf. 11:6) or was deficient in substantive appeal (cf. 1 Cor. 1). Both Jews and Hellenes displayed resistance to his message (1 Cor. 1:23). Or perhaps he has distorted the message to such an extent that its light does not beam forth.

Paul answers his implied critics by affirming that his message is hidden **to those who are perishing.** The perishing ones are not all members of humanity who have not heard the gospel, but those who, after exposure to it, have set themselves on a course of resistance (cf. 1 Cor. 1:18; 2 Cor. 2:15). In v. 4 Paul himself explains what he means. It is not the God and Father of Jesus Christ, but **the god of this world** who is responsible. He it is who **blinds the minds of unbelievers** (*apistoi*). The unbelievers are those who respond negatively to the proclamation of the gospel (cf. 2 Thess. 2:12). Satan prevents them from seeing the light of the gospel. For a similar association of Satan with unbelief, see 6:14, where Satan is called Beliar. According to a dominant strain of OT tradition, God at times removes internal blindness (Isa. 35:6) and at other times inflicts it (Isa. 44:18). In keeping with such views Paul interprets the sinful perversity of humanity as God's indictment on humanity's rejection of divine beneficence (Rom. 1:18-32; cf. 9:18). Similarly God consigns those who espouse unrighteousness in place of truth to be deceived by the "lawless one" (2 Thess. 2:8-12). Alongside such understanding of divine providence, there developed the view that Satan was responsible for unusual expression of folly. Hence 1 Chron. 21:1 qualifies 2 Sam. 24:1, by stating that Satan—not God—urged David to take a census of Israel. From this view of the matter it is but a short step to the conclusion that Satan is the principal cause of rebellion against God and is therefore termed the "god of this world." As Windisch notes, the Freer Logion of manuscript

W at the end of Mark has the disciples apologizing for their unbelief by alleging that "this lawless and unbelieving age is under the domination of Satan." The line of thought echoes *Test. Simeon* 2:7, in which Simeon declares: "The prince of deception sent a spirit of jealousy and blinded my mind to treating Joseph as a brother." The classic Hellenic statement of human capacity for inviting self-destruction is made by King Oedipus in a sarcastic response to the blind seer Teiresias: "It is you who are blind in ears, and mind, and eyes" (Sophocles, *Oedipus Tyrannus* 371). His words are of course an instance of supreme irony, for it is Oedipus himself who will later put out his own eyes because he has been blind to the truth about himself.

The gospel's glorious center is the Messiah. One who looks at the sun too long will suffer blindness. Since God's glory is of such a nature that no one can gaze on it and live, it is necessary to see the God of promise as it were by reflection. Jesus, the Messiah, serves that function. He is the likeness of God, even as Christians are the likeness of the Messiah (3:18).

5-6—Lest anyone misconstrue Paul's defense in v. 2 as self-congratulation, he is quick to point out that he is not proclaiming himself but Jesus Christ. And he proclaims him as "Master" (*kyrios*, rendered **Lord** by RSV). The correlative term is "slave," which is unfortunately rendered **servant** by the RSV, with Paul's bold metaphor noted in the margin. In the Greco-Roman world it was understood that no slave could render service to two masters. Paul owes allegiance to Master Jesus (cf. Rom. 1:1; Phil. 1:1; Gal. 1:10), but Jesus has put Paul at the disposal of the Corinthians. Hence the expression, "your slaves," a declaration that echoes Paul's express disclaimer of any intent to make lackeys out of the Corinthians (1:24). Some may say that Paul should place less emphasis on Jesus, especially since he was crucified and is a source of disgrace for the community. But, argues Paul, **it is God** who said that light should **shine out of darkness** (cf. Gen. 1:3). Well, concludes Paul, the light has beamed, and it has beamed in our own hearts, so that the glory of God may become all the more known, and in connection with the person (**face**) of Jesus Christ. In other words, the apostle's apostolic function is on a level of importance with the creation of light, for creation of that light was but one phase in God's total commitment to illumination for humanity's benefit. For this connection of ideas Paul had precedent in Isaiah's linking of creation's light with the saving effort that God would undertake on behalf of Israel (Isa. 45:7). A challenging feature of the second major part of the book of Isaiah is the figure of the Servant of the Lord, whose identity ranges from Israel as a corporate body to one individual who at times is the prophet's alter ego and at other times a unique figure, but the corporate image dominates. In Isa. 49:1-6 the corporate and individual identity overlap in a statement of responsibility for bringing God's salvation light to the world. Israel is to function as God's slave (*doulos*, Isa. 49:3 LXX) in the accomplishment of this task. At Rom. 2:19 Paul alludes to Israel's awareness of this mission. In Isaiah 53 the Servant of the Lord is described as a harassed sufferer who is ultimately vindicated. Paul took seriously his responsibility as an Israelite and understood himself in the role of Israel as God's servant to Israel and to the world (cf. Rom. 1:14). In Rom. 15:21 he identifies his evangelistic task with that of the Suffering Servant by citing Isa. 52:13 in its Septuagint form: "They shall see who have never been told of him; and they shall understand who have never heard of him." It is from this perspective that Paul places so much emphasis on light in connection with the proclamation of the gospel (*euangelion*, 2 Cor. 4:4). Paul's use of the term *euangelion* is a further indicator of his interest in the book of Isaiah, which uses the verb *euangelizein* (proclaim) in reference to God's good news (Isa. 40:9; 52:7; 60:6; 61:1). In keeping with the Servant's sense of responsibility to God as *kyrios* or master (see, e.g., Isa. 49:5, in connection with identification of the Servant as God's "slave," v. 3) Paul identifies himself as the Corinthians' slave (v. 5), with the qualification **for Jesus' sake,** a phrase that is further qualified by the concluding words of v. 6, **in the face of Christ.** An important feature of Isaiah's Servant is his receipt of God's Spirit (Isa. 42:1). This presence of the Spirit is associated in Isa. 61:1 with anointment for an evangelistic task. The Septuagint here uses the verb *chriō* (anoint), from which the term *Christos* (Christ, Anointed One) is derived. Especially significant is Paul's use of the word *doxa* (**glory**) precisely at this point. The phrase in which it occurs, **knowledge of the glory of**

God, means "knowledge of the glorious God." Of the 19 uses of the word *glory* in 2 Corinthians, all but 6 appear in the brief span of 3:7 to 4:6. It appears that Paul was conscious of Isaiah's emphasis on God's glory in Isaiah 40–66 and its association with the Servant's responsibility relative to the evangelistic task. Ultimately it is God's glory that is to be advanced. That goal is achieved when God's beneficent action in and through Jesus Christ is recognized. Paul's reference to **knowledge** (*gnōsis*) relates to Isaiah's repeated emphasis on the knowledge of God's saving intentions (see, e.g., 45:3,6; 49:23; 52:6; 60:16).

Credentials Confirmed (4:7—5:10)

7-12—In keeping with his all-pervading theme of human weakness as the staging ground for God's beneficent triumph, Paul states that he and his colleagues who share in Israel's mission **have this treasure in earthen vessels.** The term **treasure** again calls attention to God's munificent philanthropy, which is entrusted for its distribution to such insignificant instruments as the apostle and his colleagues. The reference to earthenware in this particular context suggests fragility and relatively trivial worth. It is true that many ancient vessels of earthenware were *objets d' art* (Martin, p. 85), but numerous writers, including especially social critics and moral philosophers, do not ordinarily think of them in such a sense. Wettstein cites, among other ancient authors, Artemidoros, interpreter of dreams, and Epictetus. Artemidoros (5.25) says that "to a woman, being in an earthen vessel probably signifies death." Epictetus (3.19.18) states that one who thinks gold plate is everything has rational processes of earthenware quality. In a different vein, Horace boasts that he prefers plain cups to delicate goblets (*Odes* 1.20; cf. 2.15,16,18; 3.1). The term **power** (*dynamis*) in this context refers to function or performance rather than dominance. Despite his detractors' criticisms (see on v. 3), Paul is proud of the success that has attended his proclamation of the gospel (cf. 3:2; Rom. 15:14-21). Indeed, the results were phenomenal (**transcendent**). But the credit for such outstanding performance belongs to God, not to the apostle and his colleagues. In modern parlance the result clause can be rendered: "So that credit for success of the operation might be God's, not ours."

That Paul's point was not remote from Hellenic thinking, even though its orientation was different, is clear from Windisch's citation of a Platonic text (*Ion* 533b-d: "The poet is a light and fleeting thing. . . . Therefore God uses them as helpers . . . so that we who hear might perceive that it is not these, who have no sense, who utter such notable words, but that it is God who verily is reciting them").

The picture of the Suffering Servant in Isaiah 53 may have provided Paul the model for his own commitment in the face of trials and tribulations (cf. 2 Cor. 13:4; Rom. 8:17, 31-39; 1 Cor. 15:31; Phil. 3:10). At all times Paul is theocentric. His reverses are God's opportunities for demonstrating divine power. In vv. 8-12 Paul makes use of the formal device known as *peristasis*, that is, a recital of hazards. Greco-Roman heads of state and other holders of public office would on occasion emphasize the personal difficulties that they incurred on behalf of their publics. When Nero went to Hellas to treat the Hellenes to his musical accomplishments, he expressed his appreciation to the deities of Hellas for their protection of his person "on land and sea" (*Benefactor,* no. 44). In reference to the truly wise person, Seneca (*Essays* 2.10.4) wrote: "There are things that impinge on the wise person but do not upset him, such as bodily pain and weakness, or loss of friends and children, and dreadful reverses for one's country in wartime." The balanced structure follows a rhetorical pattern that finds expression also in Epictetus 2.19.24: "Show me a person who when sick is content, when in danger is content, when dying is content, when condemned to exile is content, when dishonored is content." One of the pairs of terms in v. 8 shows Paul's fondness for wordplay: *aporoumenoi all' ouk exaporoumenoi* (**perplexed but not driven to despair**). To express the assonance one can translate: "Sometimes at a loss, but not a loser." When he considers his own resources, he admits that there was an occasion when he was oppressed so far beyond (*hyperbolē*) his functional ability (*dynamis*) that he despaired (*exaporoumai*) even of living (2 Cor. 1:8), but, as he observed in 4:7, there were resources (*dynamis*) that exceeded any obstacle to his success, and they came from God in abundance (*hyperbolē*), hence he never really despaired.

The verb **afflicted** in v. 8 echoes the noun affliction in 1:4. The association signals that Paul is about to explore further the power of God in overcoming obstacles that confront Paul. The verb **crushed** (*stenochōreō*), v. 8, shapes a metaphor that suggests Paul is being hemmed in. Together with the verb **afflicted** (*thlibō*) it forms a word-pair that is paralleled by cognate nouns in Rom. 2:9 and 8:35. The verb *stenochōreō* is again used in 2 Cor. 6:12 in connection with Paul's relation to the Corinthians and is there rendered "restricted" by the RSV. With the verb **persecuted** (*diōkō*), 2 Cor. 4:9, Paul prepares his addresses for the noun "persecution" (*diōgmos*) in 2 Cor. 12:10, where it is paired with the word "calamity" (*stenochōria*). God does not abandon the apostle.

Although the apostle's source for his strength in trials and tribulations is understood from a Christian perspective, some of his Greco-Roman auditors would appreciate his autobiographical account all the more because of their acquaintance with traditions that extolled similar virtues, especially *constantia* and *fortitudo*, among the Romans, and *andreia* among the Hellenes. The importance of these virtues is dramatically illustrated by an ode that Horace (*Odes* 3.3) addressed to Caesar Augustus, in which he lauds Pollux (Polydeuces, brother of Castor), Heracles, and Bacchus for their courage in adversity.

Through this recital, which derives from the same reservoir used by Paul at 2 Cor. 6:4-11 and Rom. 8:35-39, Paul expands on his theme of dedication to the interests of the Corinthians. He is their benefactor. Far from being embarrassed by the apostle's difficulties, they should rejoice, because his constant exposure to death is accompanied by a sequence of survivals that exhibit his constant reliance on the resurrection life of Jesus. The phrase **mortal flesh** (v. 11) suggests that Paul is not primarily thinking along the lines of Rom. 6:4, in which the implications of "burial with Christ" are explored from an ethical perspective, but rather ponders his own mortality.

12—At this point Paul anticipates his more detailed discussion of the meaning of the death of Jesus Christ (see 5:11-20). Since Paul functions in the role of Israel as Servant of the Lord, it is a foregone conclusion that he must suffer (cf. Isaiah 53). But his sufferings, associated as they are with the sufferings of Christ (cf. Col. 1:24), redound to the benefit of the recipients of his message, in this case the Corinthians. If Paul's death means life for the Corinthians, it is only because the death of Jesus Christ is life for all, and through Paul the Corinthians are beneficiaries of that good news. Barrett puts it succinctly: "The destruction of the earthenware vessel (v. 7) reveals more clearly the treasure it contains" (p. 140).

13-15—Emphasizing his continuity with the history and the traditions of Israel, Paul says that he shares the faith of the psalmist who said, **"I believe and so I spoke"** (Psalm 115:1 LXX = 116:10 MT). The citation of this one verse might well have prompted some Corinthians to ask what else the psalmist said. Then they would have heard one of their members recite: "The snares of death encompassed me; the pangs of Sheol laid hold on me; I suffered distress and anguish" (Ps. 116:3).

Evidently the themes of hazard and death are derived from this psalm, and Paul's words in this fourth chapter are a commentary on Psalm 116. God demonstrated power over death by raising Jesus from the dead. And God will raise up Paul and will take him, together with the Corinthians, into the divine presence. The words **with you** make a strong impact. This ultimate benefit, the resurrection, is Paul's gift to the Corinthians through the proclamation of the gospel. Hence he concludes, **it is all for your sake.** The result? The beneficiaries should render thanks. To whom? To God for his many benefactions. Thus Paul's passion for proclaiming the gospel is again theocentric. The more he proclaims the beneficence of God, the more thanksgivings will go up from more people in praise of God. Thus the glory of God that once made the face of Moses shine and which made Jesus the likeness of God is increasingly celebrated.

16-18—Coming full circle to the thought expressed in v. 1, Paul says, **So we do not lose heart** (v. 16). Paul acknowledges that his person as viewed from the outside (**outer nature**), bears all the marks of mortal frailty as described in vv. 7-11, but the real Paul is to be seen from the inside (**inner nature**), as one who experiences daily renewal. Far from experiencing deterioration of his identity as one who is responsible to God for the manner in which he conducts himself in his body, Paul experiences constant personal renovation.

John Adams, when asked in his old age how he was doing, likened his body to a decrepit old house whose roof was leaking and the shutters falling off, but he assured his interlocutor that John Adams was doing fine. Nothing can compare with the glory that awaits Paul. This is the language of one who is aware of being dedicated to the greatest service a human being can render to humanity, the proclamation of the glory of God, that is, of God's philanthropic intentions for humanity. Ordinarily one would speak of the weight of suffering, but Paul views matters differently. The suffering is light, and is far outweighed (*kath' hyperbolēn eis hyperbolēn*, in echo of 4:7 and 1:8) by **an eternal weight of glory.** In short, Paul is not concerned about winning cheap laurels from human beings in the present time. As he will state in 5:9, his constant aim is to "please" God. And it is God who will reward him amply for his labors. Everything connected with the present is transitory. Paul wants to possess the things that abide forever. But the anticipation becomes reality only for those whose sights are fixed not on things that are now visible and then fade away, but on those that have not yet become apparent but will abide forever. The writer to the Hebrews (11:1) explored the thought in a classic roll call of Israel's most valiant witnesses to divine fidelity. The more sophisticated Hellenes among Paul's addressees might have noted that Plato (*Phaedo* 79a) had taken a different route in arriving at a similar conclusion: "The things that are unchangeable can be perceived only by the mind for they are invisible and cannot be seen." Seneca (*Epistles* 58.27), as noted by Wettstein, observed that many things which titillate the senses "lack reality and for a time assume a certain form, but there is nothing durable or firm about them. . . . Let us rather turn our minds to the things that are eternal."

There is no suggestion in 2 Cor. 4:17 that one can improve a relationship with God through virtuous performance. Such a perception would have nullified Paul's strong protest against attempts to make bargains with God (cf. Rom. 3:20), for reconciliation is God's gift to the world (2 Cor. 5:19). Rather, Paul's experience of divine beneficence incorporates the gifts of the Spirit which include the apostle's ability to function with total dedication to the plans and purposes of God, and the Supreme Benefactor climaxes all displays of beneficence with a generous bonus for a task well done. Indeed, to know God's goodness in Jesus Christ apart from any benefits beyond this mortal life is itself a gift beyond calculation. But to have this benefit crowned with the glories of an eternal future staggers the imagination. Thus the Lord himself had spoken (Matt. 5:11-12) in words that echoed the utterance of numerous courageous Jews, such as the sons of Eleazar who faced the tortures of Antiochus with confident assurance of divine requital: "After enduring this time of suffering, we shall receive the prize for valor and we shall enjoy the very presence of God, on whose account we suffer" (4 Macc. 9:8). In addition to these passages, Windisch notes that Seneca came very close to this line of thought when he recalled the virtues of Heracles, Regulus, and Cato: "They discovered in a brief expenditure of time how they might defy the ages, and by dying they achieved immortality" (*Tranquillity of Mind* 16.4).

St. Paul's Greco-Roman auditors were well acquainted with ways in which one might gain immortality. The most well-known route was heralded in every marketplace and temple precinct— zealous concern for the well-being of one's city. One would live forever enshrined in the memory of a grateful citizenry. So spoke Pericles centuries earlier in a public address to fathers and mothers who were mourning their sons who gave all for Athens in the Peloponnesian War (Thucydides 2.43.3). Others, as Pindar's eighth Isthmian ode attests, to cite but one ancient witness, found immortality through poets who celebrated their prowess in battle or on the athletic field. The Boeotian bard more than once warns miserly athletes that without a poet's commemoration their names and deeds would be lost to eternal memory. To die without glory is a miserable fate (*Isthmian Odes* 1.68). Also there were those who found comfort in promises of an afterlife associated with certain mystery rites.

5:1-4—Paul is after much more. He pictures the body functioning as a tentlike shelter. Facing the fact that death may take place before the return of Jesus Christ, he states that God will remedy the problem of present dissolution with a dwelling that is not subject to the vicissitudes of time. To say that something is made without hands (v. 1) means that it is of extraordinary and enduring quality. This unique quality captivates Paul and he informs his addressees that there is more involved than merely getting rid of the present weak body and replacing it with one of celestial strength. The imagery used by Paul is complex. On the one hand he thinks in terms of dissolution and replacement, and on the other in terms of taking off one garment and putting on another. The reason for this shift is Paul's concern about continuity between Spirit-life in the present body and the Spirit-directed life of the resurrected body. To be **naked** means that during the present time spent in the body one displays no marks of the kind of life that is appropriate to the resurrected body. Old Testament background for Paul's line of thought concerning "nakedness" vis-à-vis God is provided in Ezekiel 16. God found Israel naked and clothed her. Paul has, of course, in his own case discovered the antidote to such a dreadful possibility but, as the pleading tone of v. 20 indicates, he is anxious that the Corinthians do not fail to find it for themselves. Verse 3 is then to be understood as a monitory statement: "Of course, we wouldn't want to be found naked after putting off the body, would we?" But how do we avoid nakedness? Verse 4 answers by accentuating the act of putting on, so that **what is mortal may be swallowed up** or gulped down (*katapotheō*) by life. How does this take place? As always, at the threshold of mystery, Paul focuses on the Supreme Benefactor: God **has given us the Spirit as a guarantee.** In other words, the Spirit is the connecting link between the future and the present. The life of resurrected body is in continuity with the Spirit-life in the mortal body. Therefore, when the body dies, the person is not found "naked," for the Spirit-life is not doffed in the process. Rather, there is more to put on; that is, God guarantees that we will be **further clothed.** Through the rhetorical figure known as "derivation" (Latin, *derivatio*), composed of terms that are similar in sound but not in sense, Paul emphasizes the problem that he explores. For Paul sin is the basic destructive factor. Through sin death entered into the world (Rom. 5:12). Salvation means that the problem of sin is overcome and that life becomes operative in its place. God begins now to display in and through Paul's present poor weak body the life of the age to come. Death will not interrupt that process. Rather, death is gulped down by life that is characterized totally by the activity of the Spirit. Thus resurrection is not mere resuscitation.

Paul is a charismatic person; he puts great emphasis on the role of the Holy Spirit. The prospect of a life that is completely under the control of the Holy Spirit is so captivating that the delay in realizing it is a source of misery. And it prompts the apostle to say that he "groans" (RSV: **sigh,** cf. Rom. 8:23, the only other passage in which Paul uses the word *stenazō*, "groan") while he waits for the fulfillment of the glorious expectation. Paul's double reference to groaning (vv. 2 and 4) suggests how deeply he felt about the theme under discussion. In v. 4 he emphasizes that his groaning comes from the depths, but not from a dissatisfaction with life as such, for he is not looking for an escape from a miserable existence. Therefore he does not share the sentiments of the poet Theognis (425-428), who wrote:

> 'Twere best of all for earthlings never to be born
> nor even to behold the sun's bright rays; but if
> one's born, to pass with full dispatch through Hade's gates
> and lie beneath a heavy mound of earth.

This morose sentiment is, of course, not to be viewed as typical of Hellenic thought. Indeed, most traditional generalizations about the Greco-Roman world are to be avoided, and especially so the view that most Hellenes looked forward to death. Like those from Theognis cited above, lines from Sophocles' *Oedipus at Colonos* (1224-1226) are frequently mentioned in favor of such a view, but it is essential to note that the dramatist illustrates the truth of Solon's word to Croesus: "Call no one happy until the day that person dies." The dramatist's point is that a current pattern of good fortune may change for the worse, as was the case with King Oedipus, who found himself at the pinnacle of success and then wrought such ruin on himself that it was well said:

> "Not to be born" is the wisest saying;
> next best, "Once born to go from hence with
> quick dispatch."

Certainly those who had a hope of immortality would be inclined to view the body as a limiting experience, but this was a perception shared by a very elite group, including especially philosophers. They and some others probably found solace in death as a solution to the miseries in which they found themselves. Others, as Socrates points out in Plato's *Cratylus* (403b), do not appear to have looked forward to dying, for they are terrified by the prospect that their soul will go to the realm of the dead denuded (*gymnē*) of the body. Much of the lamentation documented in Greek literature is in fact a protest against the dissolution of values that life in its brief span provides. Indeed, the many epitaphs that protest death's interruption of cherished times and moments, such as youth and marriage, point in an opposite direction from that taken by philosophers. In his drama *Agamemnon* (434-443) Aeschylus honors the tears of a countless multitude who have felt the pitiless maw of war:

> In place of men,
> urns full of ashes make their way
> to each one's home.
> Barterer of bodies, Ares
> holds the scales in battle
> and sends from Troy
> a dusty weight that calls
> for bitter tears, for thus he fills
> the pretty jars with ashes
> that before were men.

An epitaph for a woman incorporates this lament (*Sammelbuch Griechischer Urkunden* 1267):

> One who died through violence, inglorious victim of
> capricious death that spurned her goodness.

5—Confident that God will not be remiss in generosity, Paul goes on to explain that God "equips" (**has prepared**) us for the very goal of realizing the glorious expectation of fullness of life in the Spirit. Life in the most complete sense of the word is to characterize Christian identity in the resurrected phase. To that end God gives **the Spirit as a guarantee** or downpayment for the future. That is, the Holy Spirit begins now with the renovation of the believer's life. And this present experience, partial though it is because of the co-existence of the "flesh," serves as a promissory note which guarantees delivery of the full package that spells complete and abiding fulfillment of the will of God without interference from the sinful flesh. When that fulfillment takes place, death will verily be swallowed or "gulped down," as Paul's verb *katapotheō* puts it (v. 4).

It cannot be established that Paul dreads the possibility of facing an intermediate state for his soul.

6-10—Thoughts about the wonderful phase to come prompt Paul to shift in his expression of emotion. A few sentences earlier he wrote about groaning. Now he writes about **courage,** as he ponders the significance of one of the most important words in his vocabulary—**faith.** In Paul's thought faith or commitment is intimately linked with uprightness. Commitment to God's beneficence in Jesus Christ secures acquittal from all legal indictment, and the way is cleared for the Holy Spirit to create the new life of uprightness. Therefore Paul is **of good courage.** He knows that it will not be long before the fulfillment of his heart's desire takes place, namely, to be with the Lord Jesus, who is the fount and source of all uprightness. Expressed in theological parlance, Paul's pneumatology is intimately connected with his Christology. His thoughts about the Spirit-filled and Spirit-permeated life are dictated by his understanding of the role of Jesus Christ in salvation.

In v. 3 the apostle had expressed anxiety about "being found naked." But the assurance of God's commitment to the divine promise, as exhibited in the giving of the Spirit as a downpayment on things to come, releases him from all anxiety about leaving his body. One thing dominates him, namely, to **please** (*euarestos,* "pleasing") the Lord. This term is used, for example, in *Priene* 114.15 of a public servant named Zosimos, who is praised for honesty in all his financial transactions. The expression **make it**

our aim (*philotimeō*) marks a further draft on Greco-Roman culture (cf. Rom. 15:20; 1 Thess. 4:11). The term was frequently used in reference to civic-minded people who vied for recognition as people of exceptional quality. By combining the adjective *euarestos* with the verb *philotimeō*, Paul affirms that he desires to pass audit as a person of exceptional integrity.

Paul's repetition of the thematic pair, "being at home" and "being away," is especially significant because of the cultural baggage suggested by these terms in association with the word *philotimeō*. When the subject is a public official, such as a city's envoy or a circuit judge who has temporary quarters in a town, it may be mentioned that the public servant in question displayed laudable decorum while he was away from home. For example, the public assembly of Iasos passed a decree in honor of a judge named Herocrates and a clerk named Hegepolis, who were sent from the judicial center Priene, a city to the south of Ephesus. Among the accolades are the following:

> Whereas, the people of Priene have in time past continually displayed their friendship and goodwill toward us; and recently, when we requested a judge, they sent us a fine and noble man, Herokrates, the son of Andrios, who upon his arrival resolved a number of suits by using his untiring efforts in assisting the litigants to effect an amicable settlement, and in others he himself rendered impartial verdicts; and in all other respects he spent his time among us in most exemplary fashion and in a way that speaks well for both our cities; therefore . . . (be it resolved) to commend the People of Priene . . . [for sending] us a man exceptionally qualified to try cases; and (be it also resolved) to commend the judge who was sent . . . for his arete [exceptional merit] and for his unimpeachable conduct of the judicial proceedings and of the (amicable) settlements, all of which he handled in equity and fairness; and (be it also resolved) to commend the clerk who was dispatched with him, namely Hegepolis, the son of Hegios, for the conscientious way in which he carried out his duties, and for the fine manner in which he comported himself during his stay in our city.
>
> (*Benefactor*, no. 16)

Paul aspires to be a person of exceptional merit, not to curry favor with God but simply because the privilege of being such a person is the great gift that God offers him and every Christian. In the Greco-Roman world, people of exceptional merit are recognized by public assemblies. Christians will have the privilege one day to stand in the presence of Christ himself with resurrected bodies. And all will have the opportunity to be treated on the basis of their performance as persons of distinction while they were away from the Lord. This democratization of awards for excellence in the world to come certainly made a dramatic impact on Paul's world, where immortality was ordinarily associated with enshrinement in human memory. The following epitaph (*IG* 3.1380) in memory of an unknown woman is typical of such paltry consolation:

> Lady divine, yours the renown of deity on earth.
> Therefore you live forever with unravaged name,
> for time shall ne'er debase your treasured life.

The Greek word that underlies the phrase "what they have done" connotes policy. The term **good** (*agathon*) refers to quality performance that in some way benefits others. The term **evil** (*phaulon*) denotes that which is substandard. Paul in effect says that Christ will judge whether one's conduct was first or second class, of value to the public or self-centered. And the body is the instrument for production. Once the body has served that purpose, there is no need to mourn departure from it, for God will raise it up to be totally motivated and impelled by the Spirit (see 1 Corinthians 15).

In view of their familiarity with the Greco-Roman custom of recognition of public-spirited citizens, Paul's Corinthian addressees would feel the persuasive force of the apostle's line of argument, and they would agree, "We certainly do not want to appear before Christ as second-class performers," but as people who are pleasing or acceptable to him.

Along related lines Pindar had sketched the two main roads for humanity, one leading to the Islands of the Blessed and the other to punishment (*Olympian Odes* 2.56-66):

> Those who have their treasure linked with knowledge
> of the future know that those of lawless mind must

pay the fee for sin when death has struck—
for there is One who sits as judge
and speaks the sentence for those crimes
that cry for vengeance here in Zeus's realm.
But those of noble mind
behold the sun in days
that are no fewer than the nights, and spend their life
in softened toil. Their hands will force no clod,
nor will they press the sea
to eke a paltry livelihood, .
but in the circle of the honored Gods,
who take delight in well-kept oaths, they bask
in endless tearless time. But none can look
upon the sufferings of those with lawless mind.
And all who keep their souls free from sin will go . . .
where ocean breezes float around the Blessed Isle,
where blooms of gold are ablaze, some on the shore
from radiant trees, and others nurtured in the sea.
Chaplets and crowns from these enwreath their hands
according to the good decrees of Rhadamanthus,
whose mighty seat the Father shares with him.

Such was the "larger hope" of some who dreamed the future in antiquity. Paul's conclusion echoes thoughts expressed in Rom. 2:6, 29; 14:12; 1 Cor. 3:8, 13-15; 4:5; 6:7-9; 2 Cor. 9:6. Ultimately, says Paul, God rewards the Holy Spirit's own production. All is the product of divine beneficence.

Some of Paul's diction concerning departure from the body appears at first sight to express thoughts similar to those found in Philo's work *On Virtues* (76 [387-88]): "When Moses had ended his hymns that were composed in a devout and humane spirit, he began to transfer from this mortal life to an immortal state . . . in the course of which his body was detached like a seashell and his soul, which longed for its natural migration, was laid bare." Philo's thought reflects the body-soul dichotomy popularized by Plato, who also takes up the theme of "nakedness" in two passages cited by Wettstein. In the *Cratylus* (403b), Socrates says that people have fears about going to Hades denuded of their bodies. The fact is, he says in the *Gorgias* (523-524), that judgment can be more fairly executed without the impediment of misleading earthly circumstances. Paul, of course does not think in terms of a body-soul dichotomy. For him, as 2 Cor. 5:10 declares, the body is the essential locale for determination of a person's future.

Appeal for Reconciliation (5:11—7:16)

God's Reconciling Effort as Motivation for Paul (5:11-21)

11-15—Considerations of such moment as are recited in vv. 5:1-10 are the propelling force for Paul's urgent outreach to people. God can attest that; for, says Paul, "I am well known to God. My life is an open book to God; and I hope that deep within your hearts also you Corinthians know what I really am. I am not trying to curry favor with you. On the contrary, I am giving you an opportunity to be proud of me, so that you have an answer for those to whom appearances are more important than character."

At this point Paul acknowledges that he is not a model of self-containment and poise. To people brought up in Greco-Roman traditions of observance of the "Golden Mean" (*mēden agan*) Paul's emotionalism appeared to tip in the direction of imbalance and fanaticism, and to some who did not share his enthusiasm he appeared to parade like a rooster in a barnyard manor. Deftly deflecting the criticism, the apostle says, "If I appear to be daft and religion seems to have gone to my head, charge it up to devotion to God. If I manifest any sobriety and moderation, it's out of consideration for you." These words set the stage for the succeeding line of thought in which Paul explains, first, why he appears to have gone overboard in devotion to God and, second, what the implications of God's act in Jesus Christ are for Paul's ministry and for the Christians who are exposed to his message.

The love of Christ controls us, he says. From his succeeding words it is clear that this love of Christ embraces Paul and especially the addressees. So intense is Christ's love that he was willing to die **for,** on behalf of (*hyper*) humanity. The preposition *hyper* is used also by Gentile writers to express a deity's interest in devotees. For example, a worshiper of Isis, whose eyesight had been restored by this deity, remarked near the beginning of the recital of her virtues: "You came to me, when I called upon

you, for my salvation (*hyper tēs emēs sōtērias*, 'for my healing')"
(cf. *Benefactor*, no. 26, p. 180).

But especially the Corinthians must ponder the significance of
that death. It was a death for all of them, without exceptions.
Jesus Christ is here presented as an endangered benefactor, who
went to the outer limits of beneficence on behalf of humanity.
And the apostle emphasizes that he did it **for all.** This is the
pandemic or universal motif that Hellenes would readily appreciate, for numerous honorary decrees take note of the unlimited
generosity displayed by the honorand. Thus a philanthropist
named Menas is praised for taking cognizance not only of his
compatriots and other inhabitants of his city, but also of the temporary residents, and for giving to strangers a share of the offer-
ings at public celebrations. The birth of Caesar Augustus, "benefactor of all," was observed as a "piece of good fortune that
redounds to all." Tiberius Julius Alexander, Galba's legate, boasted that his emperor beamed salvation for the benefit of all humanity (*Benefactor*, pp. 336-37). And Epictetus (3.24.64) asks
whether there was anyone who was denied the love of the Cynic
Diogenes, who was so "kind and philanthropic that he gladly
assumed on behalf of the general mass of humanity all those
troubles and hardships that befell him."

To die for the benefit of the general public was considered the
ultimate in virtue. Dio Cassius (63.13) reports that Emperor
Otho, upon receiving the news of his impending defeat at the
hand of Vitellius, told his soldiers:

> You will agree that it is far better and far more upright that one die
> for all rather than many die for one, and that I make the decision
> not to involve the Roman people in civil war and for the sake of one
> person destroy so great a multitude of people. . . . You have chosen
> as your emperor one who who does not offer you up to spare himself,
> but gives himself on your behalf.

According to John 11:49-50, the high priest Caiaphas knew well
the sentiment, and Vergil (5.815) decades earlier had put it in
poetic form:

> One destined head alone
> shall perish, and for multitudes atone.
> (Dryden)

In his *Symposium* (179b), Plato narrows the perspective: "Only lovers, whether men or women, are willing to die for one another. And Alcestis, the daughter of Pelias, renders a fine witness to this fact, for she alone was willing to die for her husband, although he had a father and a mother, and thus demonstrated that they were merely sharing a name with him and lacked any real relationship with him."

If the death of Jesus was for the benefit of all humanity (cf. Mark 10:45), it is necessary to infer that the Corinthians, along with all the rest of humanity, were victims of death. As Rom. 5:12 clearly states, "death came to all people" because of sin. In short, Christ's death is designed to solve the problem of humanity's common malady—death in alienation from God. On the other hand, believers are taken into Christ's death and therefore also into his resurrected life (cf. Rom. 6:3-4; 1 Cor. 15:22). Hence Paul says that **those who live,** meaning the believers, are no longer committed to the self-centered kind of living that is in opposition to the "good" behavior described in v. 10. Rather, they live for Christ who died and rose for them. As Windisch points out, Philo had expressed a similar thought about devotion to God: "What could be better than living with all parts of one's being dedicated to God rather than to oneself?" (*Who Is the Heir of Divine Things?* 11 [488]). In typical Jewish fashion Paul praises God by acknowledging the uniqueness of God's beneficence as exhibited in Jesus Christ, the Great Benefactor. And the Corinthians are to share Paul's enthusiasm and devotion, for they have experienced the same extraordinary love that he has been shown. As in Paul's case, they have the down payment of the Spirit, the guarantee of things to come, and as Paul will shortly specify, they are to live upright lives in accordance with that expectation.

16-17—It is now clear why Paul refuses to truckle. He measures everything from the perspective of God's action in Christ. Once he viewed others the way human beings ordinarily do, that is, in terms of their supportive value. At this point he begins to play on the double sense of the term **Christ** (*Christos*, Anointed One) which can refer to the Messiah as an anticipated figure or to Jesus as the recognized Messiah. **Once** he viewed the Messiah (*Christos*) from a purely human perspective, that is, as a national hero who would endorse the traditional interests of Israel. But it is no longer possible to take such a viewpoint. Paul expresses the shocking revolutionary reality in crisp syntax: "If anyone belongs to Christ, it's new creation!" To be **in Christ** means to be under the control of Christ. It is not a mystical immersion, but the believer's condition of being totally dominated by the mind of Christ. This line of thinking accounts for Paul's and what is to be every believer's "fanaticism."

The RSV does not translate the word *idou* ("behold"), which introduces the words "new creation." The word *idou* is ordinarily used by biblical writers to mark an unusual moment or deed. Paul uses this interjection with profound effect in v. 17. Paul's exclamatory mode in v. 17 is typical of the "crazy," excited manner for which he was criticized by some of his detractors at Corinth: "The old is no more. Look! The new is here." It is the language of one who knows what it means to die and then to be dazzled by the future.

18-19—In vv. 18-19 Paul spells out the monumental implications of his Christian experience. God is the source and power behind it all. A profound personal confession underlies Paul's affirmation concerning God's action. Despite all his zeal for Israel's traditions, he was at odds with God, an unwitting enemy of the Creator. Paul admits that the problem did not lie with God but with himself, and he is grateful that God took the initiative to reverse his headlong plunge to ruin. God does not need to be reconciled to human beings, for God is always on the search for humanity. Human beings need to be reconciled to God. But such is our burial in sin that the very attempts we make on our own to reconcile ourselves to God become routes to further estrangement (Rom. 5:20-21). Coming to the rescue, God does the reconciling that Saul cannot do. God tugs at Paul and hugs him via the gift of Jesus Christ, who, says Paul at another time, "loved me and gave himself for me" (Gal. 2:20). But the climactic display of God's utterly fantastic display of affection was the assignment given to Paul as proclaimer of the message of reconciliation. Far from being a source of pride and feelings of arrogant supremacy, as some of his detractors charged, the fact of Paul's apostleship is a vivid reminder of his total unworthiness (see 1 Cor. 15:9) and at the same time a constant affirmation of the immense love of Christ.

What God did for Paul God desires to do for every human being, except for the unique apostleship that Paul exercised. There is no need for anyone to think that God bears a grudge. Far from waiting for human beings to bridge the gap, God moves to reconcile the world to their Creator, and it is done through Christ. Paul does not say that "God was in Christ and then reconciled the world," but that "in connection with Christ (RSV: **through Christ**) God was reconciling the world." The reconciliation is an objective reality that was undertaken on God's own initiative (cf. Rom. 6:10-11). The gift of Jesus to the point of death is God's definitive statement of goodwill. In this context, the term rendered **message** (*logos*) has an accounting connotation. The way back to God is cleared of all obstructions, for God has discarded all the arithmetic that has to do with humanity's sins. Instead, says Paul as he expands on the mathematical imagery, God entrusted me with the "balance sheet" of reconciliation.

It is evident from what Paul said about God in the earlier chapters of his letter that his image of God as Supreme Benefactor here finds its ultimate expression. A primary indicator is the pandemic theme. God makes no exceptions. All humanity is reconciled: the sins of every one are forgiven. This is tantamount to a declaration of amnesty. Pronouncement of amnesty is one of the marks of a benevolent head of state. Such was Caesar Augustus, who boasts in his *Res Gestae*, the equivalent of a state of the union message, that he extinguished the fires of civil war by overwhelming his opposition and then sparing all citizens who begged for mercy (cf.3 and 34). Since God is the ultimate expression of excellence, Paul takes very seriously his responsibility as personal envoy to the Supreme Reconciler, who gives him the opportunity to proclaim benefits to humanity that exceed anything that was ever done since the beginning of time. Much of his apparently fanatic and reproving language receives elucidation from the Greco-Roman social and cultural context in which the Corinthians lived, for they were accustomed to stories about generals and heads of state who tried to win laurels for upstaging predecessors. Thus Caesar Augustus boasted (*Res Gestae* 15.26-27): "Others before me had planted colonies in Italy and in the provinces, but my contemporaries could recall no one who matched me in such concern for veterans." And in an imperial decree delivered in person at Corinth in the year 66, the emperor Nero proclaimed freedom to the Hellenes. He concluded his prefatory declaration with these words: "Other commanders have liberated cities, [but Nero] an entire province" (*Benefactor*, no. 44). Alas, Nero was not aware that an action taken a decade earlier had already expanded the concept of liberation to its limits. Nero might liberate an entire province, but God had already delivered the entire world from confinement to a destiny of death (cf. Rom. 11:15; Col. 1:20). Besides, history records that Nero's decree was repealed by Vespasian. God's is valid for all time.

In addition to the pandemic note, Paul's emphasis on God's reconciling action per se would convey to Greco-Romans a philanthropic tone. Thus, a judge named Herocrates was considered worthy of special recognition because of his ability to adjudicate cases in private conference with the litigants (*Benefactor*, pp. 89-91), thereby avoiding a punitive legal procedure. In Paul's script, God, who is both judge and plaintiff, endeavors to effect a reconciliation without resorting to legal processes.

20-21—As God's personal envoy, Paul addresses the Corinthians directly. So authoritative is his message, that Paul views himself as God's mouthpiece and as Christ's delegate and urges the Corinthians to *be reconciled to God*. These words seem odd and even contradictory after Paul's emphasis on the divine initiative. To understand Paul's line of thought, it is necessary to note the concluding sentence of the chapter, whose last phrase emphasizes the reason for all of God's action in Christ. God went to extreme lengths to save us. Using an extraordinary metaphor, Paul says that God made Christ the essence of sin for our benefit. That is, God accepts the responsibility for exposing Christ to the situation in which sinners, who comprise all human beings, could appear to be just, whereas Christ became identified through the crucifixion as the ultimate sinner. But God did it for humanity's sake. And God did it not only to clear humanity of sin, but to make possible the opposite type of conduct—uprightness. To heed the call to be reconciled to God means then that we understand the reason for God reaching out to us, namely, to reflect the beneficent character of God, which finds expression in the new life that was described in v. 15. Dramatic indeed is the mystery of faith expressed in these last two verses. The One who has been made sin for us becomes the means for the Corinthians' ability to practice uprightness. As Paul puts it in another letter, "It is no longer I who live, but Christ who lives in me" (Gal. 2:20).

Of special interest is Paul's theological tactic in getting the Corinthians to resolve some of the problems relating to their life together. As noted in connection with v. 19, the ability to effect reconciliation was one of the prized marks of a benefactor. According to Plutarch (*On the Fortunes of Alexander* 6, 329c), cited by Windisch, Alexander the Great believed that he "came from God as the governor and mediator for the whole world." And in his Fourth *Eclogue*, Vergil celebrates the virtues of an unidentifiable future ruler, under whose leadership the earth was to prosper in peace and harmony amid the splendor of a millennial dream. In the case of the Corinthians, uprightness especially involves their efforts to improve relations with the apostle Paul and to resolve their internal difficulties.

Price for Paul's Proclamation of Reconciliation (6:1-10)

Paul proceeds to undergird his line of argument with a detailed inventory of his credentials as an apostle.

1—He first emphasizes his partnership with God and Christ. We are **working together,** he declares (cf. 1 Cor. 3:9). It is from this perspective that the Corinthians are to understand the urgency with which Paul writes.

"We are all fellow workers for one objective," wrote Emperor Marcus Aurelius, "some of us in full awareness and others simply going along with the rest. . . . And the One who is responsible for the entire Universe will make profitable use of you and will make it possible for you to cooperate with God's coworkers" (6.42).

With the term **grace** Paul announces that everything he has said in the paragraphs that immediately precede this appeal is a description of divine beneficence. It would be a shame not to realize the full benefits of that beneficence, namely, the new life of uprightness in Christ. Therefore the Corinthians must be fully attentive to what the apostle says.

2—Paul writes his own footnote to his winsome invitation in v. 1. Paul is here applying to himself the words addressed by God to Israel in Isa. 49:8, a passage which is part of the context in which the Servant of the Lord is addressed (49:1-6). The Servant of the Lord appears in the book of Isaiah at times as a corporate figure, Israel (see especially chaps. 42–43), but also as an idealized individual. One of the primary functions of the Servant in Isaiah is to recall Israel to her covenant obligations. In Luke-Acts, the Servant serves as primary model for Jesus and secondarily for Paul. Paul himself understands the imagery of the Servant in application to his own role as one who invites Israel to share in the benefits of the new age and at the same time proclaims the grace of God to the Gentiles.

Some of Paul's addressees might have read themselves into Paul's statement about partnership and identified with the corporate figure addressed in Isa. 49:8, but Paul's concern up to this point has been to establish his credentials as one totally dedicated to God's program and the interests of the Corinthians. The question of their involvement in the mission of Israel remains to be developed in 6:14—7:1. At this point Paul makes an opening for his autobiographical recital in 6:3-13.

Paul's intensive missionary effort, ignited by God's gift of Jesus as the Messiah, is the living demonstration that Isaiah's vision of salvation has found fulfillment. Hence the apostle emphasizes the point with the word **behold** and underscores it with the emphatic adverb **now.** The very fact of his ministry among the Corinthians is proof of the extraordinary experience that is theirs.

The apostle's contemporary application of Isa. 49:8 is expressed in diction that would be readily grasped by Greco-Romans. As can be seen from Seneca's parallel statement in *Medea* 1017 ("Do not miss your opportunity . . . now the day is yours, yours the opportunity"), the thought had become a transcultural cliché.

Some of Paul's addressees might well have thought that Paul was expressing himself in the manner of a field general. Upon the eve of the battle of Cannae, Hannibal endeavored to stimulate his soldiers to feats of heroism with these words: "Just as I assured you, through many perils you gained control of the countryside, with all its produce. Indeed, everything we told you has come to pass. But the great struggle immediately before us has to do with the cities and their wealth. Be victorious, and forthwith you will find yourselves masters of all Italy" (Polybius, 3.111.8-9).

Paul's sense of destiny in being at the service of the Supreme Politician in an enterprise of extraordinary significance could not fail to make an impression in a society where service to the state, which necessarily involved pious regard for deity, had been traditionally held in high esteem. Emperor Marcus Aurelius (6:30) admonished, "Show reverence to deity and save humanity." In his speech *On the Crown*, Demosthenes frequently calls attention to his own piety in reinforcement of his patriotic commitment to the interests of Athens. And Plato (*Laws* 12.955c-e) connects fiscal integrity with religious devotion.

With the gradual diminution of the prestige of the city-state as a dominant political and cultural factor, it was natural that philosophers would think of the deity as the ultimate recipient of service. Hence Epictetus advises that God's true herald or scout should not be hampered by a network of familial concerns (3.22.69-71). In keeping with such perspective is St. Paul's renunciation of relationships that were taken for granted by others (cf. 1 Cor. 7:7; 9:5).

3-10—Since personal identity was intimately connected with one's social usefulness, embarrassment to one's home city was considered a cardinal sin in the Hellenic world. Public servants cherished the recognition of blameless service that is recorded on numerous Hellenic inscriptions. For example, Moschion II, a priest of Heracles, was praised for having rendered services "blamelessly" (*Benefactor*, pp. 354-355). It is understandable therefore that Paul would be very anxious to have the record show that his own service was beyond reproach. Ordinarily one would receive a recommendation from others for a public position. Paul, already engaged as a servant (*diakonos*) of God, himself states his credentials for the task. Along similar lines Epictetus (3.24.65) stated concerning God's servants that they ought to be under subjection to God while they express their care for people.

That Paul should here and elsewhere engage in self-praise has seemed to many readers an unbecoming stance for an apostle. But would Paul's first addressees have so perceived it? Data from the ancient world suggest that the circumstances in which Paul found himself actually demanded the type of approach that Paul takes in this letter. That Paul thinks in terms of his cultural situation is further apparent from his concerted effort to make as favorable a rhetorical impression as possible. As Windisch notes, the sequence of words beginning with the letter *m* in v. 3 is calculated to arrest the Hellenic ear.

The poet Pindar's indulgence in self-praise is a primary case in point. On the one hand, he declares that "an untimely boast plays in tune with madness" (*Olympian Odes* 9.38-39). But he has little hesitation about celebrating his own powers of song (see *Olympian Odes* 1.115-116; *Pythian Odes* 8.34; *Nemean Odes* 3.80-82), for he desired to shoot his darts of verse close to the mark of the Muses (*Nemean* 9.55). The reason for such pride in his poetic task is not far to seek. Great deeds will be remembered only if the poet is equal to the task. Because of Homer's extraordinary poetic skill, Odysseus is remembered as a far better man than he really was. Likewise Pindar's athletic clients can be certain of immortality because they have the best poet of their time to sing their praises. As for his critics—they are but chattering daws who fly far below the soaring eagle (*Olympian Odes* 2.83-87; 95-97; *Nemean* 3.80-82). Along related lines, Paul is the instrument through whom the mighty deeds of God and Christ are celebrated. And it is important that he defend his credentials, not for his own sake, but on behalf of the gospel to whose prestige he is committed. As Plutarch observed in his essay *On Inoffensive Self-Praise*, the defense of one's good name or the refutation of an accusation does not elicit resentment. "One cannot term it bragging, vanity, or pride," he argues, "when in such a situation one speaks about oneself in lofty tones. . . . Rather, it displays good judgment and a superiority of merit (*aretē*) that humbles and reduces envy by itself refusing to be humbled" (540c-d). In support, he cites from Thucydides (2.60.5) words addressed by Pericles in a funeral oration at Athens: "Yet you are angry with me, a person who, I am convinced, is second to none in determining and then presenting measures that must be taken—a patriot, who cannot be bought." Plutarch goes on to say of Themistocles that the illustrious naval commander "neither said nor did anything offensive at the peak of his success, but when he perceived that the Athenians were tired of him and were ignoring him, he did not hesitate to say, 'My good people, are you so weary of the benefits you have enjoyed from the same source?' And also, 'In a storm you find in me a tree for cover, but when the sun comes out you pluck the leaves and pass me by' " (541d-e).

Even in the absence of denigration by others, one may indulge in self-praise so as to encourage excellence in others. Emperor Marcus Aurelius Antoninus (6:30) advises that aspirants to virtue should not think of what might please Caesar, but rather consider themselves disciples of Antoninus, their moral teacher, and follow his example, including such virtues as devoutness, piety, pleasant disposition, disinterest in fame, refusal to requite injury for injury, forbearance, patience, and fear of God without fanaticism.

Apart from such considerations, it does appear at first sight that Paul is violating his own disclaimer of self-commendation (3:1; 5:12; 10:18). But sympathetic addressees would note that he was on solid cultural ground. Throughout Greek literature one encounters the motif of deeds matching or failing to match one's words. Homer (*Iliad* 9.443) has Phoenix expressing the expectation for Achilles that he "be an orator and a man of action." The historians Thucydides and Polybius are especially fond of exploring the combination in connection with the performance of states and their functionaries. Numerous inscriptions display accolades voted for people who combined performance with their oratory. Typical is the recognition given to Hermaius, a loyal member of an association dedicated to the Great Mother. Not only did he offer best words of counsel, but he proved himself generous in a number of ways (see *Benefactor:* 340). By appealing to his performance, Paul is in effect saying that he has put his life on the line with his mouth. Let his detractors do the same.

Among the principal Roman virtues celebrated by philosophers were: ability to endure suffering (*patientia*); justice (*iustitia*); fidelity to a trust (*fides*); steadfastness of purpose (*constantia*); wisdom and deliberation in action (*consilium*); simplicity of living (*frugalitas*); unflinching performance in the face of difficulties and hazards (*fortitudo*); reverence for deity and authority figures (*pietas*); and morality (*castitas*), with special emphasis on honoring marital responsibilities. Greeks emphasized uprightness (*dikaiosynē*), self-control (*sōphrosynē*), endurance (*hypomonē*), and courage (*andreia*).

One of the topical presentations attributed to the philosopher Teles (*Peristaseis*) contains words to this effect:

> As poets are wont to do, Fortune creates a variety of roles, such as the shipwrecked one, the poor, the exile, the reputable, and the disreputable. Therefore any person of merit ought to play well whatever role she assigns. You're shipwrecked? Play the part well. You've suffered financial reverses? Be the best in poverty.

In a related round of questions, Epictetus (1.18.22) asks fledgling philosophers whether they will remain as committed as athletes, undaunted in the face of temptation, whether it comes in the form of money, a young woman, honor, calumny, praise, or even death.

Ability to hold up under pressure was evidently highly prized. Therefore, in view of the fact that some of Paul's life's experiences and the charges of his opponents might appear to nullify the self-assessment made in the first two verses, Paul shows in vv. 3-10 (see also on 12:10 and cf. 1 Cor. 3:22; 4:11-13; Phil. 4:11-13) how his apparent liabilities actually endorse his identity as Servant of the Lord. Obstacles that might cause others to detour from their obligations have only intensified Paul's sense of responsibility. Heading his list, therefore, are terms that denote Paul's ability to survive any storms that come his way. Ancient rhetoricians applied the term *peristasis*, "experience of a crisis," to this type of recital. An elaborated form of a presentation, including one of this species, was termed a *diaskeuē*. Paul's self-affirmation appears in numerous recitals relating to exceptional personalities in Greco-Roman times. Antiochus I of Commagene, to cite but one of the more illustrious, recorded the following on his mausoleum:

> I considered piety not only the most secure possession but also the
> most pleasurable enjoyment for human beings, and the same judg-
> ment I held to be the cause of of my prosperous power and of its
> most blessed use; and for my entire life I appeared to all as one
> who considered reverence the most faithful guardian of my reign
> and an inimitable source of delight; in consequence of which I was
> able to survive hazards and achieved remarkable mastery of hopeless
> situations and in the fulness of my many years found blessedness.
>
> > (*Benefactor*, p. 238)

In a letter of acceptance to Ionians who had voted him a gold
crown of valor and a statue, Eumenes II repeats their references
to the "many great struggles" that he had undertaken in their
behalf against non-Greeks, struggles that were in harmony with
his policy of indifference "against approaching danger" (*OGI*
763.8-14).

As Plutarch points out in his essay *On Inoffensive Self-Praise*
(544d), audiences are not inclined to resent those who have
earned their reputations at quite some cost to themselves.

Since Paul is God's envoy to the nations, the association of
hazards with his diplomatic mission would readily lead the Corinthians to interpret him as an endangered benefactor. The topic
is international. Of a public official named Menas, who was honored by the city of Sestos for his ambassadorial services, it was
acknowleged that he "spares no expense or public service, avoids
no personal inconvenience or danger, nor gives thought to any
hazards threatening his own interest, when he leaves on embas-
sies in behalf of" Sestos. Of a priest and envoy named Acornion,
of Dionysopolis, it was said that he "achieves the very best for
his home city through his powerful words and counsel . . . and
in all other matters he gives himself unsparingly in his repeated
role as envoy for our city, and shrinks from no danger . . . to
accomplish whatever might be advantageous to the city" (*Benefactor,* p. 363). As far away as Istros, on the Black Sea, an envoy
named Dioscourides, was described as "a good man in matters
that concerned the welfare of Istros and her citizens—one who
was eager to assist the people, and when the city was imperiled,

in the interest of peace he served as envoy, to Hellenes and non-Hellenes, without giving a thought to personal jeopardy" (D. M. Pippidi, "Decret Histrian inedit din epocha ellenistica," *Studia Classica* 21 [1983] 23).

In view of the sociocultural patterns of the time, Paul's recital may be said to serve as a mini-*Res Gestae*, but with emphasis on his troubles as foil for his claim to exceptional performance. By formulating his presentation as he does, Paul's Greco-Roman-oriented addressees would be able to translate the Jewish figure of the Servant into their own cultural experience. And they could be expected to condone the apostle's self-adulation, since a person of Paul's distinction as God's envoy would be expected to refute the charges of detractors through a recital of virtues. To ward off any diminution of his accomplishments by future generations, Caesar Augustus asserted of himself that he had been honored with an inscription above his portal that attested his "arete (exceptional merit), forbearance, uprightness, and piety" (*Res Gestae* 6.34.19-20).

6-7—In the second part (vv. 6-7) of the triad Paul parades personal virtues that would have the effect of marking him in the ears of the Corinthians as a man of exceptional merit and distinction. **Purity** (*hagnotēs*), that is, personal integrity, is the counterpart of blameless conduct and was highly prized in the Greco-Roman world. In one of his many playful moods, the Roman poet Horace (*Odes* 1.22.1) described himself as "integer vitae scelerisque purus," that is, a model of virtue. His phrase well translates the concluding words of a decree in honor of Moschion II, who is praised for having rendered public services "with integrity and without a blemish to his name" (*hagnōs kai amemptōs* [*Benefactor*, p. 354]), two characteristics that are expressed in cognate terms in 2 Cor. 6:3,6. An inscription in the British Museum (*IG* 588.15), which couples the term with uprightness (*dikaiosynē*) reveals the close association of the term with one of Paul's favorite nouns, which closes the list of virtues in v. 7 (**righteousness**).

Integrity finds a powerful ally in **knowledge,** which in this context denotes the ability to size up a situation and adopt appropriate measures. **Forbearance** means that one is tolerant in the face of opposition and patient in dealing with those who are disagreeable. **Kindness** is a synonym of beneficence, and the Greek word underlying it is used in honorary inscriptions. For example, an associate of Julius Caesar named Callistus was recognized for the "kind services" he rendered to Cnidus, his home city, through his hospitality and generous assistance to both needy individuals and the general public (*SIG*[3] 761). In brief, Paul describes himself as a concerned, caring person.

Much reference has been made in this commentary to Paul's ability to reach the ear of a Greco-Roman oriented public. But Windisch's observation concerning Paul's Jewish sensitivities, as expressed especially in vv. 4b-7a, deserves to be heeded by citing what he terms a "wonderful parallel" in 2 Enoch 66:6: "Walk, my children, in patience, in meekness, in honesty, in provocation, in misery, in distress, in fidelity, in uprightness, in hope, in illness, in derision, in wounds, in temptations, in nakedness, in privation, loving one another, so that you may leave this aeon of pain and become heirs of the eternal age to come" (composite translation). Paul has an ancestry well acquainted with grief.

With his reference to the **Holy Spirit** Paul aims at emphasizing the dominant control element in his life. Far from seeking accolades for personal achievements, Paul embeds the source of all his virtues at the center of his list. At the same time, this reference to the Holy Spirit serves to introduce a series of expressions that emphasize Paul's purity of motive in all his dealings with the Corinthians. Unlike many partisan politicians, Paul does not exploit his constituency for personal advantage. His **love** is **genuine.** If his hand is glad, it is because the joy of the Lord runs deep in his heart. In concert with the genuineness of his love is Paul's **truthful speech.** As he said at the beginning of the letter, the Corinthians can count on his yes being yes and his no being no. Unlike many public figures, Paul does not test language for its deceptive possibilities. Nor does he rely on his own resources, but puts his trust in **the power of God.** With this last phrase he introduces the third section of his triad, in which he sketches the paradox of success in apparent failure.

Conflicts suggest the need for **weapons.** In his encounters with opposition forces Paul's weapons are forged out of **righteousness,** one of his favorite terms and one of the cardinal virtues in both

Greek and Roman society. The topic of uprightness is a major feature in Plato's dialogues. And to be committed in a just cause was every good Roman's dream. The term is standard in descriptions of ancient public-spirited persons, who are praised for their just and equitable conduct. The fact that the weapons are **for the right hand and for the left** suggests that uprightness is applicable to every situation, and Paul features it in all his personal relations. He does not cater to one at the expense of another.

8-10—In this unit Paul presents a series of contrasts. To be held in **honor,** that is, to be recognized for personal merit, was a goal highly prized in Greco-Roman society. The underlying Greek term, *doxa* (glory) denotes the reputation one reaps for extraordinary performance. Its opposite is **dishonor.** By calling attention to the glory he has enjoyed, Paul declares in effect that he has been the Corinthians' benefactor. The phrase **in ill repute and good repute** is synonymous with the paired expression that precedes it. The inverted order is known in rhetoric as chiasmus, a mode of phrasing in the form *a-b-b-a.* Since Greco-Romans respected people of extraordinary rhetorical ability as well as performance, Paul frequently displays his facility with words, especially when he is under attack for alleged misuse of language, and this chiasmus is but one of a number of elegant turns of expression in the triad that is developed in vv. 4-10. A laudatory inscription from Greece displays the close association of the term *euphēmia* (good repute) with the Greco-Roman concept of meritorious public service, for it links the word with *aretē,* the Greek term for exceptional personal endowment (*SIG*[3] 711.11). Paul has enjoyed such recognition, but he is also the recipient of denigrating criticism, which he will refute in devastating fashion especially in chaps. 10–13.

Paul's rhetorical skill is readily apparent in his use of *anaphora* (repetition of initial words or phrases) and *homoioptoton* (similar inflections of grammatical forms) in vv. 2-8. The Greek prepositions *en* (rendered "in" and "by" in vv. 3-6) and *dia* (rendered "with" and "in" in vv. 7b-8a) respectively dominated two series of terms. In vv. 8b-10 the adverb *hōs,* consistently rendered by RSV with **as,** is the prevailing rhetorical feature and marks a movement from abstract qualitative terms to personal substantives.

We are treated as impostors, and yet are true embraces the first pair of the series begun by "as." Since Paul was not one of the twelve apostles, his enemies charged him with falsely assuming such prerogatives. In chaps. 11–12 he unleashes a full-scale refutation of the calumny, and emphasizes his truth-claim (11:10; 12:6; 13:8).

The phrase **as unknown** (*agnoeō*), **and yet well known** (*epiginōskō*) connotes a claim to exceptional merit, despite the fact that one is not generally recognized as such. The first term, as Windisch notes, finds a parallel in Epictetus 4.8.35-36, where budding philosophers are told to practice concealment of their identity as seekers of truth in the initial stage of their study. As Marcus Aurelius (7.67) observed, "One can be a divine man (*theios anēr*, an exceptional person) and yet be known (*gnōrizō*) by no one." Along similar lines Philo (*On the Migration of Abraham* 86[449]) points out that being good and having the reputation of being so is a double benefit, but one must face the fact that virtue may on occasion encounter hostility. The second of Paul's two terms (*epiginōskō*) is a common expression for recognition of public service. A decree published by a guild of actors concludes a description of the faithful and generous priestly services of a member named Solon with these words: "In recognition (*epignontes*) of which our guild considered him worthy of honor and awarded him a crown" (*SIG*³ 1101.22).

With the phrase **as dying and behold we live** Paul makes an especially impressive impact on his addressees. The Greek word rendered by **live** means quality of life as opposed to mere existence. It was said of Caesar Augustus that his birth meant the end of regrets to any one for having been born. In place of the misery that had prevailed, Augustus ushered in a new age that made real living possible. Paul has experienced such a new age in connection with God's reconciling act (2 Cor. 5:17). In consequence, apparently negative aspects of Paul's experience become surprising avenues for appreciation of Paul's new Christian identity. Although the kinds of sufferings he described in 6:5 are equivalent to constant dying and appear to be signs of divine disfavor, Paul survives them and is thus confirmed as an exceptional person.

The words **as punished and yet not killed** continue the thought expressed in the preceding phrase. In certain criminal cases it was customary to give the accused a beating, that is, "teach a lesson." This was a light whipping of the type used on juvenile gangs and accompanied by a stern warning. Pilate suggested such a whipping as an alternative to the harsh demands of Jesus' opponents (Luke 23:16). Paul himself refers to three whippings that he had absorbed (2 Cor. 11:25; cf. Acts 16:22). Since in vv. 3-4 he firmly maintained his innocence of any activity that could legitimately provoke censure, Paul is clearly reinforcing his self-portrait as a person who is noted for endurance as well as being innocent of all charges. About 12 years after Paul's letter had been written, Emperor Nero convened an assembly of all Hellas at Corinth and in his public message boasted that the gods had attested his exceptional merit by bringing him to Greece safely through perils on land and sea (*Benefactor,* p. 284). Paul's survival potential in the face of unjust charges attests the divine support that undergirds all his ministry.

As the inscription at Priene in celebration of the Augustan era attests (*Benefactor,* p. 216), joy is of a piece with real living. In similar fashion Paul affirms the quality of the new age by emphasizing its power to generate joy as relief for sorrow. Sorrow comes repeatedly, but it is outmatched by experience of joy: **as sorrowful, yet always rejoicing.** Paul always comes up a winner.

Although Paul has no status as a man of exceptional means—he is no Herodes Atticus—he makes **many rich.** That is, despite his poverty he is a benefactor. The wealth he dispenses is the riches of God's gifts in the new age (8:9; 9:11; cf. 1 Cor. 1:5; 4:8; Rom. 9:23; 10:12; 11:12,33; Phil. 4:19; Col. 1:27; 2:2). He can lay claim to nothing—his assets are meager. Yet he posesses **everything,** that is, he claims title to everything. Thus he excels the Caesars in his claim to exceptional merit. The world is his province, and the heavens are his domain, for he is the ambassador of Jesus Christ (2 Cor. 5:19-20).

Epictetus (2.19,24) expresses a parallel thought on being true to one's principles:

Show me a person who when sick is content, when in danger is content, when dying is content, when in exile is content, when in disrepute is content. Show me such a person. By God, I would just like to see a real Stoic. The truth is, you can't show me a person who is shaped like that. Well, then, show me one who is in the process of being shaped, who has taken a move in that direction. Please do me the favor. Don't begrudge such a sight to an old man, who up till now has not seen anything like it.

At a later point in his discourses, Epictetus (3.22.45-48) asks:

And how is it possible for one who has nothing, who is naked, without home or hearth, in squalor, and without a slave or city, to fare well. Look, God has sent (*apostellō*) you one who will demonstrate in practice that it is possible to do so. "Take a look at me," he says. "I am without a home, a city, property, or slave. I use the ground as my bed. I have no wife, no children, no small-scale executive mansion, but only the earth, the sky, and one little rough cloak. Well, then, what do I lack? I am without pain and fear, and I am free, am I not?"

Transition (6:11-13)

11-13—If 6:14—7:1 is an interpolation, the early editors of what is now 2 Corinthians did a skillful job in mending the seams, for vv. 11-13 constitute an appropriate transition. In these and the following verses, Paul pleads with the Corinthians to practice in their relations with him the kind of reciprocity that is deeply embedded in Greco-Roman culture. All Hellenes know the basic social rule: beneficence merits recognition. And since children especially are sensitive to fairness, Paul says, **I speak as to children,** a theme that will be picked up again at 12:14. We have poured out our very selves to you, he writes. With the words **You are not restricted** (*stenochōreō*, as in 4:8; cf. the noun, *stenochōria,* 6:4) **by us** Paul means that his addressees are not boxed off in a narrow section of his affections. They have total access to him. That is, his whole being is involved in the way they think and act. He cares unreservedly. They have no cause for complaint. If anything, it is they who have put boundaries on their own emotional outreach. Along similar lines Epictetus (1.25.26-33) admonishes those who envy the rich and famous: "In general, note that we are responsible for our own confinement, for we tend to box ourselves in (*stenochōreō*); that is, the (erroneous) opinions we hold restrict us and box us in."

Paul has been honest with the Corinthians. He has told them how he feels, and he will have still more to say. In this very ability to share feelings, Paul treads on common ground with his addressees, for Hellenes as a people from the time of Homer have, as their literature attests, displayed uncommon resources for emotional expression. This is true of both males and females. In the United States many consider it unmanly for males to weep. But in Homer's world it was not considered odd that Telemachus, for example, should drop a tear when he dashed his scepter to the ground after his plaintive plea to the assembled elders, who in turn were filled with grief (*Odyssey* 2:80-82). And it was said of Scipio Aemilianus that he wept after his own destruction of the city of Carthage, when he reflected that his own city of Rome would one day fall victim to the inevitable fate of great empires (Appian, *Punic Wars* 132).

Personal Appeal (6:14—7:1)

Ancient orators recognized the importance of interlacing self-praise with exhortations to emulation. The purpose, wrote Plutarch in his essay *On Inoffensive Self-Praise* (544d), is to show that one is not greedy for adulation but anxious to inspire others. In illustration of the point he references Homer, whose Nestor recites his own feats in battle so as to incite Patroclus and others to heights of courage (*Iliad* 7:124-160). So highly does Paul value his relationship with the Corinthians that he cannot endure any suggestion of a shift of affection on their part. Having climaxed his own tale of devotion on behalf of others with a declaration of passionate love for the Corinthians, he pleads for reciprocity (vv. 11-13) and without explictly saying so urges imitation of his own total commitment. He therefore begins his impassioned exhortation, 6:14—7:1, with the plea, **Do not be mismated with unbelievers.** Those among Paul's addressees who were familiar with the Greek Bible might well have recalled Deut. 22:10: "You shall not plow with an ox and an ass together," but the apostle's meaning could be readily grasped without recollection of that passage. According to 4:4, "the god of this world," who is apparently identified as Beliar (RSV: **Belial**) in 6:15, "has blinded the minds of the unbelievers." From the nature of the argument in chap. 4, it is clear that the "unbelievers" are people who have proved disloyal to their avowed interest in the God of Israel and have reneged on their allegiance to the claims of Christ. Paul is very desirous that the faith of the Corinthians display growth (10:15), and in 13:5 he cautions them to "examine" themselves to see whether they are "holding" to their faith. Therefore Paul appears to be saying in 6:14 that the Corinthians should demonstrate their loyalty to Paul and to Jesus Christ by refusing to identify with the positions of those who challenge Paul's apostolic authority and his counsels for growth in the faith.

Since faith and righteousness are inseparable in the apostle's mind, Paul asks, **What partnership have righteousness and iniquity?** The form of the question is at least as old as Euripides: "What do herders have in common with the sea?" asks a tender of oxen (*Iphigeneia in Taurica* 254). Good and evil are poles apart, says Paul. In other words, lack of righteousness displays lack of faith or commitment to God.

To Corinthian ears the contrast between "righteousness" and "iniquity" would sound a strong Hellenic note (see, e.g., Herodotos 1.96-97). Similarly, the contrast of **light** and **darkness** was well established in a part of the world that could not escape the impact, for example, of Sophocles' *Oedipus Tyrannos*. To be a believer in God's redemptive action means to enter into a partnership with God and Jesus Christ and with one's associates in such commitment. Greco-Roman society placed a high priority on strict fulfillment of covenantal obligations.

6:15—7:1—For ears that had been attuned to Jewish traditions, Paul sharpens the point by introducing the terms **Christ** and **Belial**. Belial is here equivalent to Satan. The transition from the darkness-light pair is readily understandable in view of a later statement by Paul that Satan can disguise himself as an "angel of light" (11:14). The adversarial nature of Belial is confirmed by literature found at Qumran. Also, it was common practice to include the names of domestic and foreign deities in magical formulations, and Paul may well have used the term **Belial** instead of Satan to add a dash of satire to his array of absurd alliances.

Since the common factor in all the rhetorical questions is loyalty and commitment, it is logical to ask, **What has a believer in common with an unbeliever?** In vv. 14-16 Paul uses six different terms to express the concept of association. This could not fail to impress his Hellenic addressees, who lived in a world of clubs and associations, whose members prided themselves on loyalty. Thus Paul's plea enunciated in vv. 11-13 is intensified through this appeal to cultural awareness. The fact that these verses include several words used only once by Paul (hapax legomena) may be an indication of the rhetorical power exhibited in the passage rather than a proof of pseudonymous origin as is frequently alleged. In any case, this particular rhetorical feature has been singularly left unexplored in discussions of the passage. Demosthenes similarly uses for special effect in his speech *On the Crown* (see, e.g., 35,49,97,119,152) terms that are found only once in all his speeches.

As Paul notes in 1 Cor. 6:8, the Corinthians made a hobby of litigation. They would therefore readily grasp his point when at 2 Cor. 6:15 he satirically asks, "Does any one seriously think that God would sign a contract with idols?" Inference: how can a Christian engage in any activity that compromises God's interests? In answer to his own query, Paul submits the kind of sharp theological conclusion for which he distinguished himself in 1 Corinthians. Most akin to the present passage are the lines of argument in 1 Cor. 5:6-13; 6:9-11 and chap. 10, but see also other examples in 1 Cor. 5-12. At 1 Cor. 5:7 Paul used the metaphor of unleavened dough to describe Christians. Here he uses the metaphor of the divine temple. In both passages the metaphors serve to establish intimate connections between the Corinthians and their redemptive experience.

The chain of Scripture passages cited by Paul in vv. 16-18 must surely have made a profound impression on the addressees, for they carried a heavy weight of sacral sanction. Many Greco-Roman prescriptions relating to ritual purity bear a close resemblance to Levitic regulations cited in the OT. In his *Metamorphoses* (23), Apuleius reflects a broadly held view concerning the importance of ritual purity. An ordinance from Lindos (*SIG*³ 983), dating from the time of Hadrian, displays a trend in antiquity toward a moral consciousness in cultic contexts with its exhortation that "it is necessary to enter the temple with due reverence; above all, with pure and sound mind and intention." The kind of thought expressed, for example, in Plato's *Laws* (4.716d) hastened such development. Epictetus (3.21.14-15) lectures thus on the pedagogical function of religious ceremony: One must approach sacred rites with appropriate intentions, for "only in this way can the Mysteries be helpful, and only in this way can we realize that all these were established by our ancestors for the improvement of our lives."

Equally impressive was the reference to God as **father.** As indicated in BAGD (s.v. *patēr*), paternal attribution to God was common in the Greco-Roman world. Epictetus (1.9.7) dramatically asks whether earthly associations will make for greater security than to "have God as creator, father, and guardian, to rescue us from griefs and fears."

The sequence of scriptural quotations in vv. 16-18 is formulated in a contractual form that is in keeping with the legalese that precedes in vv. 14-16 and with the plea for maintenance of reciprocity that was expressed in vv. 11-13. In effect it is a decree in which Israel's beneficent God offers privileged status and anticipates appropriate response. This conclusion is reinforced by the apostle's choice of the term **promises** in 7:1. Beneficiaries ought to respond to manifestations of generosity by actions that do honor to their place of residence. In this case the Corinthians are urged to respond in such a way that they may be recognized as people of distinguished merit, who carry out the obligations that they have assumed. The expression **make perfect** translates the Greek word *epiteleō*. This term is frequently used in Greek inscriptions concerning civic-minded persons who have accepted a "liturgy," that is, a public obligation, such as the repair of a temple, sponsorship of a gymnastic contest, or assumption of expenses for a choral production. In recognition of such service a citation might read that so-and-so had "completely discharged" said services on behalf of the public. In effect, Paul implies that

God has called the Corinthians to be liturgists in the Greco-Roman sense. Their task is **to make holiness perfect,** that is, to be such models of holiness that one would be inclined to call upon the city to give them public recognition. If the Corinthians behave in such fashion, they can be assured that the divine favor as described in vv. 16-18 will rest upon them. The reference to *flesh* is no indication of non-Pauline usage. It is true that in Paul's writings "flesh" (*sarx*) frequently denotes a human being in self-centered rebellion against God, but Paul's usage is flexible, and in 2 Cor. 10:3 he refers to himself as one who walks "in flesh" (*en sarki*), that is, in the frail bodily condition of humanity, but he does not permit that condition to determine (*kata sarka*) his decisions.

An especially striking illustration of the use of the term *epiteleō* (**make perfect**) and the association of ideas in 6:14—7:1 appears in an inscription from the first century B.C.E. recording the regulations of a private religious association in the ancient city of Philadelphia, Asia Minor (*SIG*³ 985). Among the commandments that Zeus gave to Dionysus were instructions to "observe (*epiteleō*) purifications, cleansing ceremonials, and sacrifices in accordance with ancestral and contemporary custom." Indicative of the high moral standards that were upheld in various parts of the Greco-Roman world are the following specific requirements: "The men and women, whether free or slaves, who enter this house are to bind themselves by oath that they have no malicious intent towards any man or woman and that they neither know of nor prepare any potion for use (*epiteleō*) against people or engage in recitation of evil spells; that they themselves are not guilty of robbery or murder and prepare no drugs for love charms, or to induce abortions, or to prevent conception, and that they neither advise nor consort with others in such enterprises, but instead are resolved to exercise all goodwill towards this house and that, in the event any one in the house does or encourages any of these things, they will neither ignore it nor be silent about it but rather expose it and take appropriate measures." The inscription continues with indictments of adulterous behavior. Terrible curses rest upon violators, but to the obedient "the gods will be gracious and continually bestow on them all the good things that they are wont to bestow on those whom they love, but they hate transgressors and will impose great penalties upon them."

As in Paul's exhortation, this inscription shows (1) the incompatibility of allegiance to the deity with connivance in the immoral practices of others within the religious group; (2) earnest moral exhortation; and (3) assurance of divine favor to those who maintain their commitment to the deity.

As the text now stands, far from introducing what appears at first sight to be an interruption of the movement from 6:13 to 7:2, Paul dilutes any suggestion that his plea in 6:11-13 is purely personal. Rather, it is God's own interests that are at stake in connection with the manner in which the Corinthians respond to Paul's ministerial approach. Hence, as one might also be led to expect from acquaintance with Greco-Roman religious practice, Paul was obligated to remind his group at Corinth of their moral and spiritual responsibilities as worshipers of God. At the same time, by stressing the theme of association, he prepares the way for his affirmation of association in dying and living in 7:3. The paragraph also serves as a buffer between the passages (6:3-10 and 7:2) that emphasize his integrity, which contrasts with the possibilities for defilement to which the Corinthians have exposed themselves.

Having scored points through his application of the reciprocity metaphor to the Corinthians' redemptive experience, Paul can now continue his personal appeal.

Paul's Anxiety about the "Sorrowful Letter" and his Joy over the Return of Titus (7:2-16)

The first phrase of v. 2, **Open your hearts to us,** contrasts with the imagery of constriction in 6:12 and picks up the plea for openness in 6:11-13. An ancient rhetorician would have termed 6:14—7:1 a digression and would have viewed 7:2 as an *epanalepsis* or resumption of the point made at 6:13. The triple *anaphora* (repetition) in the clause "*no one* have we harmed, *no one* have we corrupted, *no one* have we defrauded" suggests that Paul is intent on maintaining rhetorical momentum.

2—In all his dealings with the Corinthians Paul has given priority to their well-being. Therefore he is not interested in merely berating them. To Greco-Romans these remarks would be profoundly meaningful, for they come to grips with a basic social concern about shame. By casting himself as he did in the role of a distinguished benefactor (6:1-10), he showed that his credentials were of the highest order, and that there was nothing in his conduct that could possibly cause shame either to himself or to the Corinthians. The summary declaration, "We have wronged no one, we have bribed (RSV: **corrupted**) no one, we have exploited no one," reinforces the point.

Paul may well be anticipating his later more detailed refutation of allegations concerning his stewardship (12:14-18). If not, he here endeavors to meet any and all slanders by selecting extremely damaging diction for immediate refutation. So also Demosthenes defended his conduct before the Athenian assembly. After alleging that all other officeholders had been corrupted, he declared that "no attractive opportunity, no smooth talk, no magnified promises, no hope, no fear, nor anything else intrigued me or beguiled me to betray anything that I deemed just and advantageous to the state" (*On the Crown* 297-98). About to face his judges, Socrates was advised to make appropriate preparations, and he replied that he had spent his entire life in making preparations. "I have never," he said, "engaged in anything that was contrary to justice and the public interest" (Epictetus 2.2.9). Fair-minded people at Corinth would expect the apostle to express himself along similar lines.

3—Paul adds that it is not his intention to cause the Corinthians shame in the eyes of others by writing as he does. On the contrary, when he told them at 3:3 that they were his "epistle written in his heart," he assured them of his commitment to them. And his Greco-Roman auditors, who could not fail to be familiar with the emphasis that Greco-Roman society placed on the obligations of friendship, would recognize the depth of his feelings for the Corinthians from the words that close his sentence: "to die together and to live together." The formulation is of the type used in 2 Sam. 15:21. Those of Paul's auditors who were acquainted with dramatic tradition might have recalled the words of Electra to Orestes: "I am prepared to join you in death or life" (Euripides,

Orestes 307-8, cited by Bultmann), or Lydia's protestation to her lover: "I would love to live with you, and would freely join you in death" (Horace, *Odes* 3.9.24). But some of Paul's addressees could not have avoided thinking about the fidelity of a Pythagorean philosopher named Phintias to his friend Damon. Even a century after Paul, the literary savant Lucian included his own version of the story in an essay on friendship (*Toxaris* 20):

> What firmer display of goodwill could one make to a friend who has fallen overboard into a raging sea at night than to share his death? Let your eyes take in for a moment the awful cresting of the waves, the crashing roar of the waters, the rolling boiling spume, the darkness, the despair. Then behold the one man, his lungs filling with water, scarcely holding up his head, hands reaching out for his friend; now see the other frantically plunging toward him and swimming with him, fearful that his Damon should perish first.

This story suggests the importance of hearing Paul's protestations in connection with the recital of his life-threatening hazards. In Paul's mouth, of course, there is a dimension of meaning that no pre-Christian Greco-Roman ever entertained, for the apostle is linked with his beloved Corinthians through the death and resurrection of Christ (cf. Rom. 12:5). "We who are many are one body," he declared in 1 Cor. 10:7. The fortunes of Jesus are his and theirs. Hence Paul repeatedly emphasizes his own sufferings so that the Corinthians may recognize in him their comrade as they identify with the destiny of Jesus.

4—To undergird his assurance that he has no intention of shaming the Corinthians, Paul expresses pride in their performance, especially in their acceptance of obligation to sympathize in the tribulations that Paul has experienced because of certain unpleasant developments among the Christians at Corinth. Because he is their friend, he writes frankly, without weighing every word. As noted in BAGD (s.v. *parrēsia*, 3a), Philo takes up the subject of freedom of speech in *Who Is the Heir?* (6): "Under what circumstances does a household slave speak frankly to the master? Surely when he is conscious of having done nothing wrong, but has looked out for the interests of his owner in all his speech and action." Paul is not subservient to the Corinthians, but he is certainly concerned about their welfare, and his freedom of speech is at the same time a compliment to their sense of responsibility in the relationship.

Paul's language also bears all the marks of a response to a benefactor whose generosity knows no bounds. Greco-Roman benefactors prided themselves on being the cause of joy to their beneficiaries. Preeminent among them was Caesar Augustus, whose birthday was celebrated as the beginning of joy for all humanity. Numerous inscriptions record the appreciation of city councils, who applaud benefactors for their assistance in time of tribulations.

Paul makes use of commercial metaphors in expressing his appreciation. Far from wronging the congregation, he has expended much of himself on their behalf, but he is **filled with comfort.** That is, he has been paid in full through the consolation they have given him. (For discussion of the term *plēroō* in Paul's correspondence, see F. W. Danker, "A Form-Critical Study," [see bibliography], p. 96). Indeed, he comes up with a profit (*hyper-perisseumai*), **I am overjoyed.** (For the monetary association of the simplex form *perisseuō*, used in the sense of "show a profit," see *SIG*[3] 672.19; *Festschrift Gingrich*, p. 100.) Through the compound form, Paul heightens the effect: "I have a super profit in the joy that tops all our troubles." That is, "the interest rate I pay in troubles is outweighed by all the profit I experience in joy."

5—In contrast to the long list of tribulations that he had recited in 6:1-10, Paul now demonstrates how much the Corinthians' affection meant to him. At 2:12-13 he had indicated how apprehensive he was when he took his leave at Troas and headed for Macedonia. That recollection of his travels led to the long recital of 2:14—7:4. Now he expresses the turmoil within him when he arrived in Macedonia. This inventory of his feelings introduces his climactic expression of joy in 7:8-15 over the good news brought by Titus. How important Macedonia was in Paul's thinking relative to the spiritual needs of God's people at Corinth will be seen in the exposition of chaps. 8–9.

The balanced structure of vv. 5-7 and the evident personal relief that Paul describes in vv. 6-7 relative to the negative experiences related in v. 5 suggest that the **fighting without and fear within** had to do with anxiety over affairs at Corinth. Wettstein calls attention to Deut. 32:25: "In the open the sword shall bereave, and in the chambers shall be terror." But it is more probable that Paul is repeating a sententious cliché, a variation of which appears, as Wettstein noted, in Thucydides 8.71.1: "disturbance within and without" (the city). In any event, deductions concerning the apostle's state of mind (e.g., depression) or hostility that he might have encountered in Macedonia have no scientific standing.

6-7—Paul acknowledges God as the primary source of comfort. Some of Paul's addressees might have recollected Isa. 49:13, especially since Isa. 49:19-21 refers to constraint and a plea for space (cf. 2 Cor. 6:12; 7:2). Just as Timothy had brought good news about the Thessalonians' strength in the faith (1 Thess. 3:6), so Titus cheers the apostle with a favorable report about affairs in Corinth. For further details about Titus, see on 2:13.

Titus's presence and the encouraging news that he had brought doubled the divine consolation. And this was tripled because of the Corinthians' responsiveness, expressed in their **longing, mourning,** and **zeal.** The triad is generated by the apostle's perception of their ultimate sense of commitment to God. Their "longing" is tantamount to regret ("mourning") for their failure to deal properly with the issue that had aroused Paul's concern for them. To such a pass had matters come that he had delayed a visit because of the distressing circumstances (see on 1:23) and in its place wrote a painful letter (see on 2:4). Now they would like to see the apostle, so that they could assure him of their repentance and commitment (*zēlos*). This last term is frequently found in public documents in the cognate form *zēlōtēs*, to express an honorand's fidelity to lofty principles. For example, an organization of youths in Athens was praised "because of their ardor for the finest character from their earliest youth" (*SIG*³ 717.33; cf. *OGI* 339.90). The apostle is not interested in forming a "party" for himself, but by siding with him in the matter that was at issue the Corinthians demonstrated that they were zealous for God's interests (cf. v. 12). The joy generated by this good news exceeded even what he felt at the arrival of Titus, and at the same time it outweighed the apostle's grief and anxieties over conditions in Corinth.

In short, a mutiny was quelled. This was the kind of devotion that Julius Caesar enjoyed. After his troops had lost their only battle before the conflict at Dyrrachium, they felt such shame that they demanded some kind of punishment from Caesar. But he was so impressed by their valiant performance that instead of rebuking them he offered his condolences (Suetonius, *Julius Caesar* 68).

Like a lover who is apprehensive over the kind of response his sweetheart will make to communications in a crisis, Paul was worried about the Corinthians' reaction to his admonitions and counsel. How cheered he was when Titus told him how responsive the Corinthians were to the apostle's distress! Not only were they longing to see him, but they were in mourning over the circumstances that had provoked his concern for their welfare. Not to be overlooked are the words **your zeal for me.** This expression is a further clue to the importance of 6:14-7:2 in the context. The Greek term *zēlos* frequently denotes partisanship. Instead of giving in to the temptation to side with the faithless (6:14-15), the Corinthians as a whole are siding with God—as Paul is quick to point out in 7:10-11—and therefore with the apostle. With the words **so that I rejoiced the more** Paul concludes his qualification of the term "joy" in v. 4.

8-10—**Regrets** over remarks made orally or by letter have in various societies generated recommendations for repairing relationships. The sophist Libanius suggested as a model the following epistolary formulation: "I did not give a second thought to words that I had said to you, for I never suspected that they could have caused you pain. But if you were offended by them, please know, most excellent of all men, that I shall never repeat one of them, for I am interested only in being of service to my friends and not to cause them pain" (*Epistles* 15). Paul had some misgivings about the Sorrowful Letter that he had sent them. But whatever regrets he might have had about sending the letter were dissipated by the joy that the Corinthians' response had given him. Paul's excitement bubbles through a colloquial portion of syntax that contrasts with the polished rhetoric in much of chaps. 6 and 7: "As for that letter, even if it grieved you for a time, . . . I now rejoice." The important thing was that their grief was synonymous with repentance before God. Paul here disclaims interest in a mere apology by the Corinthians for tolerating disparagement of Paul's apostolic function. That would be a human-oriented repentance. Instead the Corinthians have displayed a God-oriented change of heart, one that derives out of awareness of having violated divine prestige. Once again the apostle draws on the theme of partnership that was expressed in 6:14—7:2. The Corinthians have an intimate association with Paul, but an even more intimate one with God.

Translators and commentators advocate a variety of renderings for v. 8 and the first words (*nyn chairō*) of v. 9. But the syntax of the Greek is unnecessarily alleged to be difficult. The negative verdict primarily derives from a failure to recognize that Paul expected his letter to be heard by the Corinthians. Modern auditors of extemporaneous presentations are accustomed to the phenomenon of a speaker's utterances making perfectly good sense when heard but lacking in literary polish when seen in print. The latter results from the fact that the speaker's gestures, manner of vocalization, audience response, and other factors that create meaning in a specific situation cannot be included in the written text. The result is an overloading of the language circuit for the reader, or surprise that the speaker appeared somewhat inarticulate. Participles dangle, sentences break off and are restarted in fresh syntactical directions. Frequently the speaker, conscious of the fact that words are not keeping up with the thought, may punctuate with "I mean." But this is of the nature of colloquial communication. It is the way most people ordinarily talk. In more formal publication such utterance will be edited for greater clarity. Similarly, in the translation of a personal letter, especially one that is written with intense feeling, an attempt to compress the original utterance within the confines of a rendering that aims at reproducing as much as possible the word order of the original can be disastrous, for the translated statement is overloaded. To avoid the effect of such compression, it is necessary to paraphrase, a procedure that upgrades a translation from a wooden rendering into literary pleasure. In the case of an ancient letter, the bearer who was delegated by the writer would inform the recipients of additional information not included in the letter and could interpret whatever was not readily grasped by the auditors at the receiving end. Ancient orators would have their speeches edited for publication. Similarly, copyists of biblical documents frequently improved the grammar of evangelists and apostles, and attempts of this kind were made in connection with 2 Cor. 7:8. The verse makes good sense if it is read as follows, with the understanding that the apostle takes a new syntactical direction after the first clause: "For even if I did grieve you in the letter, I do not regret it—even if I was inclined to regret [*metemelomēn,* imperfect tense, with conative force] the writing of it in view of the fact that, if indeed only for a time, it caused you grief, I now rejoice. . . ." But the Greek text is clearer than most attempts—including the preceding rendering—to reproduce it. A more polished translation is therefore required, and to that end it is necessary to recognize that Paul's statement is a condensation of several thoughts: (1) Even if I did cause you grief, I do not regret it. (2) I was, I must admit, inclined to regret it because of the grief, even though only temporary, that you went through. (3) But, even though I was inclined toward regrets, I now rejoice. Translation: "I know I grieved you with my earlier letter. Yet I have no regrets. I must confess that I did have some second thoughts when I saw that it caused you even a bit of temporary grief. But that's all over now, for I am filled with joy. Please understand me: not joy over the grief itself, but joy because you grieved so penitently."

In grammatical analyses, colloquialisms of the source language are dignified with prestigious titles, including "anacolouthon" for a sentence structure that takes a new direction midstream, as in this passage and two verses earlier (2 Cor. 7:5). For related examples of such colloquial syntax, see 2 Cor. 7:5; 5:12; 6:3-10; 8:18-20; Rom. 2:17-21; Gal. 2:3-5.

The phrase **so that you suffered no loss through us** forms a contrast with the first clause of v. 10. The point is that the Corinthians cannot legitimately charge the apostle with any unhappiness they have experienced. On the contrary, it is God with whom they have had to do, as the term **godly** (*kata theon*) indicates, and their sincere remorse (*metanoia*) clears the way for **salvation,** that is, a repentant life. In English usage the term "repentance" denotes the resolve to alter one's conduct, whereas the Greek term *metanoia* is ordinarily used to denote remorse over one's wrong conduct and then to connote the resolve to change it.

The term *metanoia* receives extended discussion in Philo's essay *On the Virtues* (175-186, pp. 405-407) and it is frequently used by philosophers in the Greco-Roman world. Wettstein refers to Plutarch (*On Tranquillity of the Soul* 476f.), who argues that "reason can relieve many pains, but reason is itself responsible for remorse (*metanoia*) when the soul is stung with shame and chastised by it." A moral treatise called *Tabula*, attributed to a member of the Socratic circle named Cebes and cited by Windisch, contains an allegory about a spendthrift who encounters four prostitutes named Wantonness, Profligacy, Greed, and Flattery. After his life falls into ruins, he encounters Repentance. The narrator describes her function to Cebes: "She rescues him from all his sins and commends to him another Perspective [Desire], who in turn conducts to true Education, but at the same time she commends him to still another Perspective, who conducts to False Education." Cebes asks, "What happens then?" "Well," he says, "if he welcomes this Perspective that will conduct him to true Education, he will be cleansed and saved by it, and lead a blessed and prosperous life; otherwise he is led astray again by False Perception" (Cebes, *Tabula* 11). Because of his distinctive approach to Christology and ethics, the term *metanoia* is not one of Paul's favorite expressions. Paul prefers to emphasize the new life that God begins through the Holy Spirit's activity in association with the death and resurrection of Jesus Christ. Apart from 2 Cor. 7, the noun *metanoia* occurs elsewhere only in Rom. 2:4 and 2 Tim. 2:25, and the cognate verb *metanoeō* appears only in 2 Cor. 12:21. "Salvation" for Paul is the full realization of the Spirit-directed life in the resurrected body. Reconciliation is a present reality, and the Christians can be assured of God's total forgiveness by virtue of the redemption provided in Jesus Christ, but full salvation lies in the future. On the other hand, in the present context, the use of the term *metanoia* would communicate well to Paul's Greco-Roman oriented public. Similarly, his line of thought in his use of the adjective *ametamēletos* (**brings no regret**) runs transculturally. The kind of salvation Paul proclaims will be no cause for "regret" (*ametamelēton*). In his comment on the Pythagorean *Golden Poem*, cited by Windisch, Hierocles (14) observes: "Repentance itself is the beginning of philosophy, and escape from foolish deeds and words is the first step toward a life that is subject to no regret." Similarly, Cebes (32.2) said of true knowledge concerning what is beneficial, that it is a "safe and reliable gift, and not subject to regret." Since salvation is a key word in the Greco-Roman political vocabulary, signifying rescue of people from a variety of real or threatening perils, Paul's addressees would readily grasp the benefactor imagery in Paul's contrasting statement.

By stating that regretful **grief** as ordinarily understood produces death, the apostle aims at emphasizing the life-giving aspects of **godly** (*kata theon*), that is, God-approved, repentance. "True God-approved repentance," according to the *Testament of Gad* (5:7) puts darkness to flight, enlightens the eyes, furnishes knowledge for the soul, and guides the pondering mind to salvation." The close association of divine standards and salvation is marked in 4 Macc. 15:2-3, in which we are told that the mother of seven martyred brothers was confronted with the choice of being true to her religious scruples or saving the lives of her sons, "but she chose the course of piety that in line with God (*kata theon*) spells eternal salvation." In effect, Paul says that the Corinthians are fortunate that he expressed such concern for them. Far from causing his addressees loss, Paul has been the instrument for their experience of divine philanthropy.

11—Dominant in manifestation of new life is the earnestness or **eagerness** (*spoudē*) that the Corinthians are displaying. This commendatory term is one of the most common expressions in descriptions of Greco-Roman benefactors, who are praised for the alacrity with which they assume responsibility for actions that involve the public welfare. Paul implies that the Corinthians wished to avoid all suggestion of liability for shame and have made every effort upon receipt of the apostle's latest admonitions to

clear themselves (*apologia*) of connivance in other people's sins. How they did it is described in the words of approbation that follow. Instead of continuing to overlook deviations from Christian practice, they expressed their **indignation** (*aganaktēsis*). It is probable that the apostle is here thinking of the problem aired at 2:1-11. The standard word for fear (*phobos*) is here rendered **alarm,** which expresses the seriousness with which they have now faced the problems in their midst. The terms **longing** (*epipothēsis*) and **zeal** (*zēlos*) reinforce the thought in v. 7, where the same terms are used. That is, they have seen matters from the apostle's perspective and have taken his side against the instigator or instigators of resistance to apostolic authority. The RSV's rendering, **What punishment!** (*ekdikēsis*) for the last term in the series appears to be inappropriate in the context, for it suggests that Paul is delighted about punishment as such. The thought is not "Three cheers for punishment," but rather, "What sense of justice!" Instead of further sitting idly by while apostolic ministry was being undermined, they proceeded to exercise discipline, which is one aspect of justice, and at the same time vindicated the apostle, who was responsible for the well-being of God's people at Corinth.

The term *synistēmi,* **proved yourselves,** is one of Paul's favorite expressions. Through actions some indication is given to others as to one's character and intentions. Echoing v. 1, Paul says of the Corinthians that they were **guiltless** (acted without reproach, *hagnos*) **in the matter** (*pragma*). The term *hagnos* appears frequently in Greco-Roman bureaucratic documents. For example, of a public servant in Asia Minor it was said that he carried out numerous functions without reproach and blamelessly (*hagnōs kai amemptōs, OGI* 485. 13-14). Paul's use of the term in the present context is in keeping with the bureaucratic tone that pervades the rest of 2 Corinthians. Indeed, the diction of v. 11 would suggest to the rank and file of the addressees that they were people of distinction, superstars in their own right, and an implied contrast is here developed between most of the addressees and the dissident faction at Corinth. Paul's pastoral procedure here is but one of his numerous approaches to encouragement and is in keeping with his general practice of helping addressees think positively of themselves as the redeemed of God. He who wrote so fervidly about reconciliation in chap. 5 knows how to practice it.

The term *pragma* refers to "the affair," the "business" that jeopardized relations between Paul and the Corinthians (see on 2:1-11). The reference to blamelessness is therefore not a clean bill of health for all the conduct of the Corinthians, but a commendation for the way they conducted themselves in handling the matter after Paul called its seriousness to their attention.

12—The initial phrase, **So although I wrote to you,** is another of Paul's colloquial structures. He means to say, "Even though I wrote as I did. . . ." From what is said in 2 Cor. 2:5, it is quite probable that the apostle is referring to himself in the reference to the one **who suffered the wrong.** But despite uncertainty about the identification, the main thrust of the sentence is clear. Far from being concerned about only the two principals in the case, Paul had the interests of all the people of God at Corinth in mind. Therefore he wrote as he did so that their **zeal** (*spoudē*, as in v. 11) on behalf of the apostle and the position that he represented might ultimately be disclosed (**revealed**) to them in the very presence of God. In short, the painful letter made the members at Corinth face themselves and their problem, with the result that they repented. The combination of the Greek terms *phaneroō* ("revealed") and *spoudē* ("zeal") would evoke for the Corinthians the image of a public ceremony in which an individual or a group would be recognized for distinguished service. For example, a synod of poets located in Athens was honored by Delphi with a memorial, "so that the ambition and the goodwill of such people might be exposed ('become evident,' *phanera*) to all who shall come after us" (*SIG*³ 699.13-14); and the importance of the religious factor is noted in the directive that the honorary decree be inscribed on the Athenians' treasury in the temple of Apollo (lines 14-15). In the case of the Corinthians it was important that they recognize the zeal of which they were capable through God's mercy. Paul therefore celebrates it with them and assures them that since it was done in full awareness of God's presence they can be assured of reconciliation also with God.

13—Because their zeal has divine approval, Paul is thoroughly consoled. And he cannot praise the Corinthians enough. Their own beneficence knows no bounds. Besides the joy they have caused Paul directly, the Corinthians have given him the additional joy of knowing that Titus was similarly filled with joy over the reception accorded Titus when he carried out his errand at Corinth. It is important again to note the cultural context. Ancient international protocol, then as now, presumed hospitable treatment of official envoys. A decree issued by the deme of Oropos commended Hieron of Aigira for "displaying his goodwill and generosity in welcoming any Oropians who came to him" (*SIG*[3] 675.14-16). By writing as he does about the role of Titus, Paul suggests the extraordinary responsibility that he himself has as God's delegate to the Corinthians. Paul is God's envoy, and Titus is Paul's envoy, but both men are totally in service to God.

14—Evidently Paul had assured Titus that he could count on the Corinthians to do the right thing, whatever the situation. The fact that Paul expresses such pride in them must have made them feel all the more sheepish about some of their earlier lack of appreciation for his valued services. Shame is an omnipresent cultural factor in any society, but especially so in the Mediterranean world, and the Corinthians can be happy over the fact that their reception of Titus did not make a liar out of Paul. Paul desires an honest and open relationship with the Corinthians. Such a relationship is an impossibility if the partners do not share their feelings about things done or said. The alternatives to openness are a polite playing of social games, an armed truce, or a parting of the ways. But just as Paul deals with negative aspects in a forthright manner, so he lays his heart on the table in expression of admiration for all that is positive. Nor can they interpret such approach on his part as mere public relations. If that were the case, he would not have confronted the Corinthians as he did. Paul refuses to be a mere master of the glad hand.

15—Paul is proud of the Corinthians. He had assured Titus that the Corinthians could be counted on, and they did not cause the apostle to lose any face. Paul's reputation for telling the truth remains untainted. But he does not want the Corinthians' repentance to fade. Therefore he emphasizes that Titus's joy was not a fleeting matter. He was effusive in his praise of the Corinthians when in the presence of the apostle he related his recent experiences. Far from feeling elated over winning what might be construed by some as a diplomatic victory, Titus developed a feeling of closeness to the Corinthians because of the way in which they responded. In his "tear-filled letter" (2:4) Paul had written about obedience (2:9). That this obedience is not a matter of submission to Paul as an earthly authority figure, is clear from the words **fear and trembling.** These terms suggest extraordinary and majestic status of the entity that elicits such responses (e.g., of God, Exod. 15:16; of Israel, 11:25). Here they relate to awareness of the divine presence (cf. Ps. 2:11), and the thought echoes the phrase, "in the sight of God," in v. 12. In effect, the Corinthians have done what Paul had counseled in a general way in 7:1: they had "made holiness perfect in the fear of God."

From 1 Cor. 2:3 it is clear that Paul approaches his own responsibilities with the same attitudes that he anticipated from the Corinthians. In his letter to the Philippians, Paul also uses the phrase "with fear and trembling."

Paul concludes the paragraph with expression of joy over the fact that he can depend on them, no matter what the problem or the circumstance may be. He has made numerous boasts about the Corinthians, and in the very next two chapters he will have something to say about one of them (cf. 9:1). In any case, he is about to give the Corinthians an opportunity to cash in on their reputation for zeal. He is above-board with them in every way. Now they will have an opportunity to show whether they in turn will match deed with word. Because of the apostle's boasts about them they have a far-flung *reputation* for philanthropy. But will they really *be* what they are reputed to be?

Through this presentation Paul succeeds in balancing his own philanthropic self with that of the Corinthians. He is not ashamed of them. This leads him to the Macedonian collection. On the one hand, he wants them to carry out their pledge. Then he will not be ashamed. On the other hand, he wants them to carry it out so that they can verify their credentials as philanthropists. Thus chaps. 8–9 are conceived as integral parts of the document by the early editors of 2 Corinthians. Hence 8:11 echoes 7:1, which had anticipated also this completion of a promise.

■ The Collection: A Statement of Unity in the Gospel (8:1—9:15)

Description of the Project (8:1-24)

The syntax and diction of chaps. 8–9 bears so much of the aroma of bureaucracies and houses of commerce that Hans Windisch, followed by Hans Dieter Betz, referred to them as "business letters." Whether they were written at different times and then incorporated into the rest of what is now 2 Corinthians cannot be determined with certainty, but Betz has offered the most detailed discussion of the question, with emphasis on the rhetorical techniques exhibited in these chapters. Many of his observations incorporate explorations of bureaucratic language discussed in *Benefactor* (1982) and BAGD, and the following commentary on 2 Corinthians 8–9 in turn reflects his advancement of the inquiry.

In his letter to Rome, written after 2 Corinthians, Paul refers to a resolution of the Macedonians and Achaians (Rom. 15:26-27) to send relief money for the poor in Jerusalem. According to 2 Cor. 8:6, Titus had accepted responsibility for organizing the process. But the very first reference to the collection described in chaps. 8–9 is in 1 Cor. 16:1-4, in which Paul advised each member to lay aside a certain amount each week, and promised that on his next visit he would attend to the delivery of the collection.

As has been repeatedly noted, beneficence and reciprocity are dominant structural motifs in Paul's second letter to the Corinthians. His discussion of the collection, which by its very nature presupposes these structural elements as constitutive factors, therefore appears, despite some dissonances, to be integrated with the entire presentation that precedes it. And whatever the time of origin of these chapters on Paul's itinerary, the reference to Macedonia in 7:5 cleared the way for an overt link of chaps. 8–9 with chaps. 1–7. Since Macedonia is not a single city, Paul uses the plural, **churches,** in reference to the various groupings of the people of God in that area.

116

Thoroughly ingrained in the thinking of Greco-Romans on the subject of rewards for excellence is the understanding that such recognition may well evoke further exceptional performance by the honorand and encourage others to follow an exceptional distinguished example. In a decree formulated between 230-220 in honor of a banker named Athenodoros, the people of Histiaia, on the island of Delos, declared that they made the award "so that all may know that the people of Histiaia understand how to honor their benefactors, and that more may be responsive to the best interests of the city, as they see worthy people in receipt of honors." Similarly, the people of Miletus granted honors to Antiochus, the son of Seleucus, "so that others also might make it their policy to be concerned about the temple in Didyma and about the people of Miletus, as they observe the benefactors of the temple being honored by the people" (*Benefactor*, p. 437).

According to traditional Jewish understanding and also Greco-Roman perception, the ultimate manifestation of beneficence is associated with deity. Psalm 34 is typical of the Hebrew perspective; and the recognition accorded, for example, to Isis is characteristic of devotion in the Greco-Roman world. In Apuleius's *Metamorphoses*, the initiate Lucius concludes a celebration of the beneficence of Isis with this doxology:

> Yet my own skill is far too weak to register your praise, and my estate too poor to satisfy your altar's meed of sacrifice. I feel to the depths your majesty but lack full-throated utterance. And truth to tell, a thousand mouths and thousand tongues to fill the same with endless file of unwearied words would not suffice. In beggarment one course is left to me, devoted as I am: deeply engraved within my heart, I shall forever hold in store your countenance divine and treasure your most holy Godhead.
>
> (*Benefactor*, pp. 178-79)

1—In keeping, then, with universally recognized piety, Paul begins by stressing God's beneficence (**grace**, *charis*), which has generated a phenomenal performance in Macedonia. The term *charis* is also used of generosity displayed by administrators in the Greco-Roman world. Antiochus I of Commagene, who aspired to divinity, referred to the works of his own "grace" (*OGI*

117

383.9; see also lines 136,154). The actions taken by Tiberius Claudius Balbillus as Nero's governor in Egypt are termed "godlike deeds of grace" (*isotheoi charites*, *OGI* 666.22; cf. lines 7-8). Similarly, the "grace" or favor of "divine Claudius," manifested of course in imperial generosity, receives recognition from a grateful public (*OGI* 669.29). Paul's use of the term in v. 1 anticipates the usage in 2 Cor. 8:4, 6, 7, 19.

The opening phrase, **We want you to know,** parallels usage in Gal. 1:11; 1 Cor. 12:3; 15:1 and initiates Paul's exordium or introduction, whose core consists of the example set by the Macedonians. In place of the RSV's **brothers,** it is more accurate to read "brothers and sisters" in a document ostensibly addressed to the total membership of an association (the philological data are laid out in BAGD, s.v. *adelphos*).

2—The link between chap. 8 and what precedes is strongly forged by the **affliction-joy** contrast. This combination is in continuity with the description in 2 Cor. 4:17-18 of Paul's own experience (cf. 1:3-11) and with the polarities of grief-repentance and anxiety-joy expressed in chap. 7. Moreover, the term "joy" (*chara*) echoes the repeated use in chap. 7 of the Greek cognate terms for the verb *chairō*, rejoice (7:7, 9, 13, 16) and the noun *chara* (7:4, 13). Likewise, the increase (expressed adverbially, *perissoterōs*, at 7:15) of good feeling on the part of Titus is the background for Paul's reference to the Macedonians' abundance (*perisseia*) of joy.

Amplifying his use of the term *peresseia*, Paul points out that divine beneficence evoked such joy that the Macedonians' pathetic poverty abounded (*eperisseusen*) in a "wealth of heartfelt concern." The RSV renders **wealth of liberality,** but the Greek term rendered "liberality" is *haplotēs*, which expresses the unsophisticated good breeding of the *petite noblesse*, those openhearted folk whose annals, in the words of Thomas Gray, are "short and simple." The best commentary on the term is *Test. Issachar* 3–4, in which Issachar expresses the very type of contrast used in 2 Cor. 8:2 (*thlipsis-haplotēs*): "In the simplicity (*haplotēs*) of my heart I supplied the poor and the troubled (*thlibō*) with the produce of the earth." Test. Issachar 4 goes on to outline a number of moral characteristics, among which display of monetary generosity is but one item, under the rubric of *haplotēs*. The point is that such a person's life is an open book. "Simple" people are people whose interior does not contradict their exterior. Hence a person who makes a donation may be called "openhearted" if the gift is made ungrudgingly and without guile or hidden agenda. The fact that Paul qualifies this characteristic of openness with the term "wealth" indicates that the term *haplotēs* is not used in the bare sense of "liberality." Rather, the Macedonians have shown a "wealth of open-heartedness," a quality that will receive definition in vv. 3-6. In short, they construed the privilege to participate in beneficent activity as being itself a generous gift from God. And, like the Corinthians, who experienced and contributed joy in a time of great stress, the Macedonians found their abysmal or **extreme poverty** turning into a huge profit of openheartedness. The Greek verb *perisseuō*, rendered **overflowed** by the RSV, has here a commercial connotation and means the opposite of showing a loss (see on v. 14). In other words, they discovered themselves capable of far more generosity than they had dreamed possible. By thus heaping up commercial terminology Paul develops an image of Macedonian Christians as benefactors in the ranks of a Croesus and a Herodes Atticus— the Rockefellers of the ancient world. On the traditional poverty of Macedonia, see Betz, pp. 50-51.

3—Ability to pay is an important consideration, and the words **according to their means . . . and beyond their means** express, as the evidence in BAGD indicates, a type of commercial formulation found in business and official documents of the time. The people of Halasarnai, e.g., praised a public-spirited citizen named Theucles for "doing everything within his power (*kata dynamin*) that was advantageous to his city (*SIG*[3] 569.32-33).

The phrase "beyond one's means" is as old as Homer (*Iliad* 13.787) and the motif is transcultural. Marcus Porcius Cato argued against repeal of the "Oppian Law," a wartime measure that forbade women to wear more than half an ounce of gold or dresses with purple trim, or to ride in a two-horse carriage in Rome (Livy, 34.1.3). Livy noted that the "poor, out of fear of being despised, tend to extend themselves beyond their means" (Livy, 34.4.15).

Through such expressions Paul celebrates the magnitude of the Macedonians' generosity. They have exceeded the normal bounds of liberality. What Aristotle said in his *Nicomachean Ethics* 4.1.18 was true of the Macedonians. "Liberal persons," the Greek philospher wrote, "in fact are inclined to be so generous that they have comparatively little left for themselves. Indeed, it is characteristic of liberal people to have no eye for their personal interests." He then went on to state: "Resources are to be taken into account in making a judgment about a person's liberality. For liberality does not depend on the amount of the gift, but on the attitude of the giver. . . . Indeed, one who gives out of rather limited means may be considered quite liberal" (4.1.19). "It is not easy," he continued, "for generous people to remain rich . . . for they are lavish in expenditure and esteem wealth not for itself but as an instrument of donation" (4.1.20).

Antiquity is replete with evidence of lavish givers. Of a public-spirited citizen named Menas, in the ancient city of Sestos, it was said that he spared no expense in meeting numerous needs (*Benefactor,* p. 332). Among the accolades accorded Emperor Nerva's coregent, Gaius Popillius Python, was the recognition of his generosity in selling grain below cost to undercut profiteers in disastrous times (*Benefactor,* p. 76; see also *SIG*³ 304.9-10; 708.40). Commenting on the purpose of wealth, Herodes Atticus, builder of a theater that still stands in Athens, took a dim view of safe-deposit boxes, considering them "detention centers for cash." Wealth, he said, was to be distributed to deserving people of wealth, so that they might not experience the embarrassment of want and to people in need so that they might be relieved of the burden of poverty (*Benefactor,* p. 375). In a world accustomed to such types of philanthropic expression, Paul's diction would have had a meaning that transcended the surface message of the commercial terminology: Paul was elevating the Macedonians to the status of public-spirited philanthropists.

Of a public-spirited citizen named Adrastos it is said that he served as a gymnasiarch "freely and of his own accord" (*dōrean kai authairetos, OGI* 583.8), that is, he accepted no fee for his services, and he did not wait to be asked. There were many people with such dedication to the public interest, but it is also true that many wealthy citizens were simply drafted for public philanthropies. As for the Macedonians, they are like Adrastus and undertake the collection **of their own free will** (*authairetos*), that is, "on their own initiative"; cf. the contrast expressed in 9:5). The word *authairetos* is used only here and, of Titus, in v. 17.

4—The Macedonians did not want to miss out on the opportunity to help the poor in Jerusalem. Therefore they pleaded with Paul to grant them the favor (*charis*, in echo of v. 1) of participating in the relief collection. The RSV's phrase **taking part** is a correct rendering, but tunes out an obvious echo of 6:14 in which the same Greek term (*koinōnia*, fellowship) is used. Paul had warned the Corinthians about condoning lack of commitment to Jesus; now he shows the Corinthians how to establish broader association with others who are committed in the faith. As noted by Betz, the entire statement has a bureaucratic tone. The phrase **begging us earnestly** (*meta pollēs paraklēseōs deomenoi hēmōn*) suggests an official demand, and the terms *charis* and *koinōnia* are characteristic of administrative and business documents.

5-6—So thrilled is Paul over the Macedonians' response that his thought bubbles over the boundaries of his syntax. In effect, he says that the Macedonians threw themselves so wholeheartedly into the cause and experienced such exhilaration in the venture that Paul himself was heartened to urge (*parakaleō*) Titus to secure the Corinthians' commitment for execution of their pledged contribution. Betz correctly chides Plummer for stating that as a result of the Macedonians' display of generosity Paul got the idea of sending Titus. Rather, Paul focuses on the completion of the project. The apostle's relationship with the Corinthians had, after all, been rather fragile, and the question of diplomatic propriety in bringing up the matter of the collection must at times have appeared to Paul somewhat inadvisable. But he overcomes the problem by drawing on the Corinthians' familiarity with a dominant Greco-Roman phenomenon.

Besides the explicit diction used in praise of the Macedonians, the very form of the description would arouse the Corinthians' awareness of their cultural traditions in which the celebration of a public-spirited citizen is designed to stimulate others to similar activity. For example, the people of Miletus gave this as the primary reason for the award they granted to Antiochus the son of Seleucus: "So that others also might make it their policy to be concerned about the temple in Didyma and about the people of Miletus, as they observe the benefactors of the temple being honored by the people" (*Benefactor,* p. 437).

Self-donation is a recurring theme in Greco-Roman documents. For example, of Menas it was said that he "gave himself" wholeheartedly on behalf of the interests of his city Sestos (*OGI* 339. 19-20). Similarly, Protogenes of Olbia, a city on the Black Sea, volunteered to assume the entire cost for the city's walls, "when no one else came forward to render such services either in entirety or in part" (*SIG*³ 495.125). Therefore, when Paul writes that the Macedonians first gave themselves to the Lord and to us, he means that the Macedonians not only undertook a project, but viewed their participation as partnership in enterprise along with the Lord and Paul. To Greco-Roman understanding this statement would further imply that the Macedonians are making an appropriate response to divine beneficence by imitating it within the realm of their own possibilties. God has set an example. In honor of Menas of Sestos it was said that "through his personal dedication he impressed on the young men the importance of cultivating discipline and tolerance of hardship" (*OGI* 339.70-71). God's grant of the ultimate gift, Jesus Christ, is the ground out of which the Macedonians' crop of beneficence flourishes.

The term **complete** (*epiteleō*) echoes the usage in 2 Cor. 7:1. It is common in honorary inscriptions and evokes the image of a benefactor who completes an obligation, whether assigned or self-assumed. Thus it was said of a Thessalian religious administrator named Nicostratus that he "completed (*epetelesen*) everything that was to the interest and advantage of the (Amphictyonic) League" (*SIG*³ 613.17; cf. *Benefactor,* pp. 332, 374 n. 70). In Rom. 15:28 Paul refers to his own completion of the assignment given him in connection with the collection.

Through the use of the past tense in the verb **urged,** the RSV expresses the result of the Macedonians' own insistence. Paul does not say that he was asked to appoint Titus as a fund-raiser, for Titus had been active in that capacity at least a year earlier (cf. v. 10). Rather, Titus is directed (*parakaleō*) to secure completion of the project. The verb *parakaleō* is used to give a less peremptory tone to the orders of a head of state or bureaucrat. Thus Ptolemy II "urges" the people of Miletus to "practice the same policy of goodwill" toward Ptolemy's administration as they have in the past (Schroeter, no. 13 = Welles, no. 14.12-13). Paul, as God's bureaucrat, transmits instructions to his colleague Titus, who is mysteriously absent from Paul's earlier outline of plans for the collection (1 Cor. 16:1-4). The word **also** in the concluding clause connotes an additional accolade for Titus. Besides other services Titus has rendered, this supervision of the final stages of the collection is an additional benefit he confers on the Corinthians. They, in turn, are privileged to become benefactors of others through their participation in the venture.

7—Greco-Roman honorands ought not rest on their laurels. Hence numerous inscriptions include encouragement to further acts of generosity. About a century after Paul wrote to the Corinthians, a billionaire named Opramoas was said to be so generous that he appeared to consider his own funds as public property. Once, after subscribing a substantial portion of the cost of a portico for the city of Patara, he was persuaded to assume the entire expense. And the city of Myra hesitated, after an earthquake, to accept his offer of 100,000 denarii, unless he also supervised the work of reconstruction (*Benefactor*, p. 132).

On top of all their other marks of excellence, the apostle is hopeful that the Corinthians will show a surplus of beneficent assistance by way of the collection for the people of God in Jersualem.

Paul's use of the theme of escalated beneficence in v. 7 helps explain what the RSV evidently considers a rough patch of syntax. The Greek text concludes this verse with a clause introduced by the conjunction *hina*. This clause parallels the *hina* clause of v. 6. Between these two clauses Paul inserts in colloquial fashion the accolade that serves as the basis for the conclusion expressed in the second purpose clause. Thus v. 7 is in effect an amplification of the *hina* ("that") clause of v. 6 and completes the thought initiated by the verb *parakaleō* ("urged") in v. 6.

The verse may therefore be rendered: "Yes, indeed, just as

123

[*hōsper,* as in 1 Thess. 5:3] you abound in everything else—including faith, word, knowledge, all zeal, and our love for you—we anticipate that you will abound also in this opportunity to show your beneficence." Paul's reference to the abundance of gifts at Corinth parallels the congratulations he offered in 1 Cor. 1:5-7) and echoes the series of gifts recited in 1 Cor. 12:7-8.

The first four terms are linked chiastically, in such a way that the related terms **faith** (*pistis*) and **earnestness** (*spoudē*) frame the words **utterance** (*logos*) and **knowledge** (*gnōsis*). In many Greco-Roman honorary documents "faith" generally refers to the honorand's sense of honor in carrying out an assignment and is frequently found in association with other virtues, including especially uprightness (see *Benefactor,* pp. 352-54). Since the term **faith** is applicable to contractual obligations, Paul appropriately uses it to introduce his exhortation concerning their participation in the collection. Through their positive response to the apostle's tearful letter (cf. 2 Cor. 7:11) they have demonstrated their reliance on, and commitment to, God. They now have opportunity to further demonstrate the depth of that commitment through fulfillment of their pledge. Allied to faith is *spoudē* (earnestness, zeal). This term appears five times in 2 Corinthians (7:11, 12; 8:7, 8, 16) and only two other times in the rest of his correspondence (Rom. 12:8, 11). Indeed, the entire word-family relating to zeal is represented 7 times in 2 Corinthians 7–8 and 11 times in all the rest of the Pauline correspondence. To a Greco-Roman person, the impact of this term in association with all the other bureaucractic diction in this portion of the letter would suggest that Paul was approaching the Corinthians as people of exceptional merit, as superstars in their own right. A further semantic signal would be the adjective **all,** which is one of the most common terms used to qualify virtues.

The terms **faith** and **earnestness** suggest positive response. This pairing in effect constitutes the first of the two components in the association of deed and word that is so common in Greco-Roman literature. The second component, word, is covered in the two terms **utterance** (*logos*) and **knowledge** (*gnōsis*), a formulation that echoes 1 Cor. 1:5. Among the Christians at Corinth are people who have extraordinary gifts and skills in structuring theological arguments. But the products were not always spiritually wholesome. Hence Paul had to rebuke the Corinthians for their rationalized permissiveness respecting an illicit marital relationship (1 Cor. 5:1-8), their distorted understanding of the Lord's Supper (1 Cor. 11:17-34), and their divisive reasoning about spiritual gifts (chaps. 12–14), among other things.

As Paul observes in 1 Cor. 8:1, knowledge without affection puffs one up. Therefore Paul takes note of the virtue that forms the climax in his celebrated evaluation in 1 Cor. 13:13. The Corinthians abound in Paul's affection for them (cf. 1 Cor. 4:14; 10:14; 15:58; 16:24; 2 Cor. 2:4; 7:1; 12:19). This interpretation is more probable than the view that Paul here refers to the capacity for love on the part of the Corinthians. Paul takes that matter up in v. 8. It may appear strange to latter-day readers that Paul should here call attention to his own affection, but this is part of Paul's strategy for stimulating the addressees to exceptional performance. Instead of relying on legal formulations for moral and ethical counsel, Christians have living exemplars in the Lord (1 Thess. 1:6); Christian congregations (1 Thess. 2:14); Paul (2 Thess. 3:6-9; 1 Cor. 4:16; 11:1; Phil. 3:17). Similarly, Greek and Roman moralists or historians (or both) cultivated virtue by calling attention to the heroic exploits of national heroes such as Heracles and Horatius and the virtues of a Cato or a Diogenes.

The climactic touch is Paul's paronomasia or play on the word *charis*, here rendered **gracious work.** Faith, utterance, knowledge, zeal, and affection are divinely bestowed gifts. The present challenge to participate in the collection is also a gift, an additional benefit bestowed by God.

8—In keeping with the principle he had expressed in 2 Cor. 1:24, Paul assures his addressees that sanction for their participation is not connected with an official order (*epitagē*). Rather, the example of the Macedonians is the gauge for the Corinthians' response. Here again Paul draws on the "boiler plate" used time and again in honorary inscriptions. Through the publication of an award others are to be stimulated by the splendid example set by the honorand. For example, a club known as the Sarapiastai honored its treasurer, clerk, and trustee, "so that the members might be prompted to emulate one another in generous service to the membership" (*Benefactor*, no. 21). Through their response to the appeal for funds, the Corinthians will demonstrate the quality of their own capacity for generous affection. They will have the opportunity to prove that they are people of honor.

9—As capstone for his appeal, Paul cites the example of Jesus Christ himself, benefactor of benefactors. Greco-Roman benefactors could generally rely on reserves. But Jesus, wealthy beyond conception, became poor so that others might be enriched through his beneficence. The celebration of such magnitude of grace provides an extraordinary stimulus to imitation. Precisely what Paul had in mind by the reference to Jesus' poverty is not stated. But one can confidently infer that the context of 2 Corinthians 8 elicits a variation of the thought in Phil. 2:6-11, in which the status of Jesus as Son of God is contrasted with his experience of a slave's death. In a discussion concerning relief of the poor it was only natural to translate the theology of the cross into "rich/poor" terminology.

10—Since Paul stated in v. 8 that he was not issuing an order, he modestly expresses his own judgment (**advice**) in the matter. Of many honorands in the Greco-Roman world it is said that they have considered and done "what is best" (*sympherō*) for the recipients of their beneficence (see *Benefactor*, pp. 362; 390, n. 212). Demosthenes repeatedly makes the point about his own good performance for the welfare of Athens in rebuttal of Aeschines' negative allegations (e.g., *On the Crown* 298, cf. 295). As God's instrument of beneficence to the Corinthians, Paul says that the advice he gives is best for them, namely, the prompt discharge of their self-chosen responsibility toward the poor in Jerusalem.

The words **you began not only to do** (*poiein*) **but to desire** (*thelō*) is a phrase of approbation. It is one thing to undertake a project in word, but another to be serious about carrying it out in deed. Paul praises the Corinthians on both counts. According to an inscription found at Ilium (*SIG*[3] 330), a philanthropist from Gargara asked the council of Ilium to inform him of its expenses for a theater and other purposes. He said that he "was willing" (*thelō*) upon arrival of their representatives, to "give the entire amount." In effect Paul says that he did not have to twist the Corinthians' arms to secure their participation, but now the time has come to make good on their IOU.

With the phrase **a year ago,** which may cover an interval of 3 to 18 months, Paul apparently refers to the occasion of Titus's second visit to Corinth (cf. 2 Cor. 8:6).

11—It is apparent from the usage in Plato, *Laws* 3.697d, that the expression **readiness in desiring,** that is, showing fervent willingness to undertake the project, is firmly embedded in Greek usage. The term for readiness (*prothymia*) is a commonplace in honorary documents and is frequently linked with such synonyms as *spoudē*, which is found in 2 Cor. 7:11, 12: 8:7, 8, 16. In the *Nicomachean Ethics* (4.1.12-18), Aristotle devotes an entire paragraph to the theme. "The liberal person," he states, "gives gladly or without pain, for arete or excellence is scarcely fraught with pain. But one who gives . . . not for nobility's sake, but for some other reason, is not a liberal person." But enthusiasm without production can lay no claim to public recognition. As in 7:1 and 8:6 the verb **complete** (*epiteleō*, see on v. 6) has the bureaucractic connotation of carrying out a public obligation, whether assigned or voluntarily assumed. Failure to match words with deeds is a commonplace in Greco-Roman literature, and honorary documents frequently include the thought that the honorand carried out assumed obligations. Of a judge named Herocrates it is said in a decree passed by the people of Iasos that he was "untiring" in carrying out his judicial responsibilities (*Benefactor*, p. 320). And Menas of Sestos was described as filled with "enthusiasm" to "supply something useful to the people" (*Benefactor*, 14.320-21). In the oration *On the Crown* (286, noun; 110, adjective), Demosthenes speaks of "readiness" in the same breath with a common term for generous goodwill (*eunoia* or *eunous*). As would-be benefactors of God's people in Jerusalem, the Corinthians are to implement what they so eagerly accepted as their responsibility and thereby show themselves to be truly liberal people.

To talk out of an empty purse would mean to lay an idle claim to beneficence. The Corinthians are told to align their cash with their words. As v. 12 indicates, they have sent out signals of promised aid through their enthusiastic verbal response and must

127

now deliver the goods. In similar vein 1 Clem. 33:1 admonishes: "Let us show zeal in completing every generous work with eagerness and alacrity."

Far from expecting the Corinthians to mortgage themselves to the hilt, the apostle urges them to discharge their pledge out of what they have. Aristotle (*Nicomachean Ethics* 4.1.19) expressed the principle in these words: "Liberality is to be evaluated on the basis of one's capital. Liberality is not determined by amounts given but on the basis of the donor's disposition, which gives in proportion to capital."

12-15—In politics, observes the Greek historian Polybius (2.39.8), equity (*isotēs*) and philanthropy (*philanthrōpia*) go hand in hand. Aristotle (*Politics* 1263a) thought that certain states served as models in this respect, with "all citizens having their own holdings but having their possessions at the disposal of their friends and in turn treating their friends' possessions as common property" (cf. Acts 2:42-47). Philo (*Who Is the Heir?* 145) thought along similar lines: "Cities are accustomed to follow the principle of equity in times of crisis (*kairos*). They expect all citizens to make equal contributions out of their capital—not, of course, in a numerical sense, but in proportion to holdings—so that one who contributes 100 drachmas would be equated in generosity with one who gives a talent." And the dramatist Menander (*Monostichoi* 259, see BAGD, s.v. *isotēs*) counsels: "Prize equality; don't try to get more from another." Paul affirms the time-honored axiom and assures the Corinthians that he has no intention of burdening them so as to ease the responsibility of others. Rather, the principle of equality must prevail in this philanthropic enterprise. The Corinthians **at the present time** happen to have **abundance,** that is, they are economically better situated than their brothers and sisters in Jerusalem. The people in Jerusualem would in turn reciprocate should conditions be reversed. This is in accordance with the experience of the Israelites in the wilderness, as expressed in Exod. 16:18, a passage cited by Philo (*Who Is the Heir?* 191) in the context of his discussion of equality. The temporal expression, "at the present time," is firmly fixed in Greek parlance, and the term *kairos*, rendered **time** by the RSV, ordinarily in official documents refers to periods of crisis, such as food shortages or military threats. An inscription (*SIG*³ 306.55), dated 324 B.C.E., contains the very phrase used by Paul in reference to returnees from exile. A variation of the expression (*en tōi paronti kairōi*) is used (in *SIG*³ 700.10) in reference to a time of threatening hostilities. As used by Paul in 2 Cor. 8:14, the term *kairos* makes a strong claim on the Corinthians' sympathies—the need of the poor in Jerusalem has reached crisis proportions. To suggest, as some commentators have done, that Paul is thinking along "eschatological" lines is to dilute the apostle's eloquent intercession.

The RSV's sequence of clauses might suggest to some readers that Jerusalem's poor will be able to reciprocate once they have received the Corinthians' contribution. But this is scarcely Paul's thought. And if Paul was here thinking along the lines of Rom. 15:27, he expressed himself so cryptically that it is questionable whether the Corinthians would have caught his meaning. Simple reciprocity, on the other hand, they would readily understand.

16—Always conscious of the Supreme Benefactor, who makes possible all human beneficence, Paul gives **thanks** to God. The content of his thanksgiving relates to the **earnest care** or zeal manifested by Titus. And by praising Titus, Paul is able with one stroke of his pen to toss an accolade in the direction of the Corinthians. Titus's zeal is the **same** as theirs. But he is engaged in more than a fund-raising effort. At every stage, Titus has the best interests of the Corinthians at heart.

17—Paul does not let his own role in the proceedings fall out of sight. He had appointed Titus to complete the collection in Corinth (see v. 6) and now states that Titus had accepted the apostle's **appeal** or appointment. Titus showed himself **very earnest** in his acceptance of the assignment. Such a mission would entail a variety of personal expenses, for which there would be no recompense by way of per diem allowance. Instead of declining or grudgingly accepting the assignment, Titus welcomed it. And with the words **of his own accord,** which echoes the word *authairetos* in v. 3 ("of their own free will"), Paul informs the Corinthians that Titus undertook the responsibility at quite some expense to himself. Through his use of diction that was formulaic in public honorary documents, Paul seeks to project Titus as a model of beneficence for the Corinthians.

18—It was customary in the Greco-Roman world to entrust important missions to envoys, often sent out in groups of two or three (documentary and literary evidence is cited in *Benefactor*, p. 91, n. 37). Since a large sum of money was involved, it was only natural that a company of envoys should be responsible for the collection and delivery. Ancient inscriptions attest the blameless fidelity of envoys in financial matters. For example, the people of Sestos said of one of their distinguished citizens, Menas, that "he completed many diplomatic missions to kings, in the course of which he accomplished, in company with his fellow envoys, everything that was to the best interests of the people and devoutly guarded matters that were entrusted to him" (*Benefactor*, pp. 92-93). In keeping with time-honored practice, and to reinforce the picture of an embassy that is characterized by total probity, Paul makes a similar boast about Titus's partner. From the manner in which Paul describes him, the Corinthians would understand that this envoy is a person of exceptional merit, the type of public servant whom a city would honor for display of arete. Because of his arete, the billionaire Opramoas, who lived in the century after Paul, enjoyed citizenship in the leading cities of Lycia. In related vein Paul notes that Titus's partner was held in honor throughout Christendom because of his efforts on behalf of the good news (cf. Phil. 4.3). That the **brother** was himself a preacher, as the RSV renders the text, cannot be determined with certainty.

19—To disarm detractors (see v. 20), Paul emphasizes that the "brother" was "elected" (RSV, **appointed**) **by the churches.** Evidently the "assemblies" or **churches** that were involved in the elective process followed Hellenic practice. A decree from 289–288 B.C.E. specifies that a "delegation of three men, chosen from the entire Athenian populace," be dispatched to a king named Spartocus with the resolutions passed in his honor (*SIG*[3] 370.42-46). The names of the envoys are not given in this decree. Similarly Paul veils in anonymity the second and third members of the delegation to Corinth.

Paul has a further reason for such effusive praise of Titus's partner. The apostle will be in charge of the caravan that brings the collection to Jerusalem. As he points out in vv. 20-22, it is imperative that no suspicion of misappropriation of funds be directed at Paul. Given the problems that Paul has had with detractors at Corinth, the extra precaution appears to be well taken. Therefore Paul emphasizes that Titus's partner was assigned **by the churches** to be Paul's travel associate during the collection of the money. The phrase **to travel with us** conceals a technical term (*synekdēmos*, see also Acts 19:29) that Paul uses for a member of a delegation (cf. *OGI* 494.13-14). *Comes* is the corresponding Latin term. "The churches" are the various congregations which joined in the selection of this associate. Paul's point is that the Corinthians can trust someone to whom numerous congregations have already entrusted money. The anonymous brother, then, enjoys the apostle's complete confidence for the discharge of the enterprise, which is defined as a **gracious work** (*charis*), in echo of the same term used in v. 6. At the same time, the apostle does not permit the Corinthians to forget that participation in the collection is a distinct benefit mediated for them by the apostle himself. He is in complete accord with the Christian assemblies and shares their objective in appointing the "brother," namely, to promote God's reputation (**the glory of the Lord**) and to communicate the apostle's goodwill. In other words, I am not about to do anything that would destroy the entire objective of my life— to promote God's prestige. Nor would I do anything that would jeopardize my commitment to excellence. The Greek term for "goodwill" is *prothymia*. At 8:11 (cf. v. 12) Paul had used the same term in connection with the Corinthians' resolute purpose. Together with them Paul is a benefactor, and because of the exceptional character of his work as emissary of the gospel, he qualifies in Greco-Roman eyes as a person of exceptional merit and intends to maintain that prestige.

20—Ancient documents are replete with references to the "goodwill" (*prothymia*) of public-spirited people. Since Paul does not want his own reputation for goodwill to be in any way tainted, he takes every precaution to avoid unfavorable publicity. As is the case today, the Greco-Roman world had its share of embezzlers, charlatans, and officials who were free with public moneys. But there were also many officials and administrators who merited high marks for civil service and practiced sound economic policies. Unlike Senator David Obey of Wisconsin, who was roundly criticized in 1987 for his initial defense of a certain appropriation with the comment that "It was a lousy $8 million," a civil servant named Moschion won praise in antiquity at Priene for his fiscal frugality. Although he spent more time and energy on an embassy than was expected of him, he did not submit a bill to the state for his extra expenses (*Priene* 108.172-174).

21—To reinforce his point about probity, Paul makes a personal application of Prov. 3:4 LXX: "Take forethought of what is honorable before the Lord and people," simply by changing the imperative of the LXX version into a first person plural and adding the phrase **not only,** which offers the typical balanced construction of which Hellenes were so fond. The phrase **we intend** renders the verb *pronoeō*, which, together with its cognate *pronoia*, frequently appears in honorary documents. Of Menas, the city of Sestos declared that he "displayed forethought (*pronoeō*) in respect to the discipline of the youths and the young men" (*OGI* 339.31). In Acts 24:2, Tertullus praises Felix for his forethought.

Underlying the RSV's rendering **honorable** is the Greek neuter adjective *kalon*. This term is common in honorary documents and is used as a referent for conduct or performance that merits high marks for contributions to the public welfare. A decree concerning a veterinarian named Metrodoros proclaimed that he was a "model citizen" (*Benefactor,* p. 63; literally, he "conducted himself as befits a man who is honorable and good").

Paul's emphasis on good conduct in the presence of people as well as of God would be especially meaningful to Hellenes who were accustomed to hear their honorands praised for piety displayed toward deity and uprightness expressed in society. Caesar Augustus summarized these two aspects of his imperial service by reciting in his *Res Gestae* the words that were inscribed by order of the Roman people on a golden shield displayed in the Senate House: "A man of arete and forbearance, of upright and reverent character" (*Benefactor,* p. 269).

Wettstein took note of Cicero's appraisal of the theme: "One's chief concern in private business and public service ought to be the avoidance of even the least suspicion of self-service" (*De Officiis* 2.21.75).

22—Besides Titus and Paul's traveling associate, Paul has also dispatched in their company another brother. Paul has found him earnest or dedicated (*spoudaios*) in a variety of obligations at various times (*en pollois pollakis*). Through this choice of diction Paul classes the envoy as a benefactor. So also Diodoros of Sicily (1.51.4) describes the legendary king Aigyptos as "generous and upright, and in general dedicated in everything." Paul's envoy has passed the test. And using the opportunity once more to praise the Corinthians, Paul says that this "brother" is especially eager (*spoudaioteros*, as in v. 17) to participate **because of his great confidence** in the Corinthians.

To send an envoy of exceptional character was considered a special boon in antiquity. Nero, for example, receives the following accolade: "In addition to all the good benefits that he conferred in the past on Egypt, he has once again exercised his most brilliant foresight (*pronoia!*) and sent to us Tiberius Claudius Balbillus as governor" (*OGI* 666.4-7; cf. *Benefactor,* p. 35).

23—Paul now climaxes his endorsement of the envoys. Should any question be raised about **Titus,** let it be known that he is Paul's partner and coworker for the benefit of the Corinthians. As for the brothers who were mentioned, they are, like the apostle himself, envoys (*apostoloi*), not of one individual, but of assemblies (**churches**), that is, they have official status. Moreover, they are **the glory of Christ,** that is, they contribute to the prestige that Christ enjoys as the Great Benefactor. The Greco-Roman world was noted for heads of state and public-spirited individuals who enhanced their own reputations (*doxa*) or those of a city or organization through munificent gifts or magnanimous actions. For example, the minutes of a religious society devoted to Dionysus record that the vice-priest Nicomachus magnanimously resigned his office in favor of another member, and all "for the honor and glory of the Bacchic Society" (*Benefactor,* p. 157). In a letter inscribed for posterity by Antiochus III, a priest is assured of receiving "all that will enhance his honor and prestige" (Welles, *Royal Correspondence* 44.19-20). The Corinthians can be assured that Titus and his company belong in the category of those who enhance the glory and prestige of others, in this instance, Christ. At the same time, Paul has enhanced the reputations of the envoys through his generous accolades.

24—Paul concludes this section of his exhortation on the collection with a plea that the Corinthians demonstrate to the churches their affection for the apostle and the quality of his boast about them. The expression **give proof** renders a term (*endeiknymi*) that is frequently used in official documents in reference to one's demonstration of goodwill, zeal, or friendship. Such response is a testimonial to the exceptional character of the one who displays it. In effect, Paul invites the Corinthians to collaborate with himself and the envoys in the pursuit and expression of the highest excellence.

Motivation for Completion (9:1-15)

Numerous commentators have called attention to what appears to be an abrupt transition from chap. 8 to chap. 9. Supported by other considerations, Betz considers it startling enough to suggest that chap. 9 is a fragment of a second "business letter" dealing with the same project, but directed to a broader Achaian constituency than chap. 8, which he thinks was addressed specifically to Corinth. Whatever the circumstances surrounding the production of these chapters, the early editor(s) of 2 Corinthians have again succeeded in showing a minimum of seam work.

1—With the two words **Now . . . about,** which translate a phrase of three words (*peri men gar*), the RSV indicates that chap. 9 is to be understood as a continuation of the argument in chap. 8 and not as a second letter on the subject of the collection. The phrase may also be rendered, "Now, of course," and is, in fact, akin to the phrase *kai peri men* used by Demosthenes to introduce an apologetic observation in his speech *On the Crown* (50), a parallel phenomenon that is overlooked by commentators who see in 2 Corinthians 9 a separate piece of correspondence relating to Paul's fund-raising effort. Hellenic orators knew only too well the truth of what Luke said in Acts 17:21 concerning the passion for hearing "some new thing." The disarming of potential boredom was therefore an essential oratorical tactic, and Demosthenes uses it with dramatic effect in the section introduced by the phrase cited above as he tells the Athenians that it would be ungallant of them not to give a hearing to the measures that he took on their behalf, especially since his industry had put him to a great deal of trouble (see also *On the Crown* 95, 110). In similar fashion Paul grants that the Corinthians are well informed on the matter of the collection, but this rhetorical ploy is designed to facilitate development of the theme of "shame" which was implicit in his reference to boasting at 8:24. In short, Paul has some unfinished business about the collection, and the Corinthians must hear him out. Hence the conjunction *gar* (for) in the phrase *peri men gar* performs the function of connecting chaps. 8 and 9.

2—Corinth was located in **Achaia,** the area of Greece that was defined as a province in 146 B.C.E. Concern for public approbation and fear of humiliation were compelling forces in the highly competitive Hellenic society. It is not surprising therefore that terms denoting and connoting competition frequently appear in documents relating to public service and generous donations. Paul's frequent use of terms that express zeal and intense dedication is part of this semantic field of philanthropic contention. In this verse, the term **readiness** renders the word *prothymia,* which is a dominant word in honorary documents and echoes Paul's usage in 2 Cor. 8:11, 12, 19 (see *Benefactor,* p. 321). Paul states that he had boasted to the Macedonians about the Corinthians' expression of goodwill. This boast was probably made during the visit described in 2 Cor. 1:15-16; 2:13; 7:5-7. Paul had said, "The people in Corinth decided already a year ago to participate" (2 Cor. 8:10). He then refers to their **zeal** (*zēlos*), which echoes usage in 7:7, 11 and is part of a word-family repeatedly used in honorary documents in reference to exceptional generosity.

The exemplary value of a benefactor's performance is a common theme in documents relating to benefactors, and Paul gives it a double edge in the two portions of his exhortation concerning the collection. In chap. 8 he cited the exemplary zeal of the Macedonians to encourage the Corinthians to fulfill the obligation that they had assumed. In chap. 9 he heightens his appeal by affirming the Corinthians as models of zeal for the Macedonians.

135

Evidently the apostle, well aware of the Hellenic competitive spirit, used the enthusiasm of the Corinthians as a stimulus for generosity in other congregations, and with significant results. Paul's appeal to the Hellenic sense of shame is now firmly grounded. Would the Corinthians want to have a reputation for reneging on promises? In such case, it were better never to have made them.

3-4—Having just stated that the Corinthians require no further instruction about the collection itself, Paul explains why he is dispatching the "brothers" who were mentioned in chap. 8. Since some of Paul's detractors in Corinth might well have been critical of Paul for sending these representatives, the apostle must treat the rationale for their dispatch with some delicacy. At the same time, he prepares the ground for the theological instruction and motivation he is about to offer in vv. 6-14.

The envoys, says Paul, are being dispatched out of concern for the Corinthians' prestige as well as his own. Paul will be coming later, accompanied by some of the Macedonians. It would be very embarrassing for the Corinthians and for Paul if the collection at Corinth were not completed when Paul arrived with his entourage.

The words **for being so confident** are an incorrect translation of the phrase *en tē hyopostasei tautē*, which should be rendered, "in this project" or "undertaking." The cognate verb for "undertake" (*hyphistēmi*) is frequently used in honorary texts in reference to philanthropic enterprise. For example, it is said of a certain Claudius Rufinus that he should be appropriately rewarded for undertaking service in behalf of the state (*SIG*[3] 876.6). Similarly, a Milesian named Claudius Chionis undertook the office of prophet in the service of Apollo as well as a civic presidency when no one else was willing to serve in either capacity (*SIG*[3] 494.6-9).

5—From some of Paul's remarks about opponents who criticized the apostle for wielding a big stick in his correspondence while at the same time being weak in presence, one can with strong probability conclude that Paul fears that some of the Corinthians will construe his dispatch of envoys in place of his personal presence as an effort to avoid confrontation. But, as Paul states later (11:28), he bears the burden of responsibility for many assemblies (*ekklēsiai*) of God's people, and to avoid any delay in expediting the collection, he sent his friends on ahead to Corinth to ensure the completion of their pledged responsibility.

The reference to a **promised** (*proepangelomai*) gift is carefully designed. Fulfillment of a promise was considered a primary responsibility in the Hellenic world. Promises are easily made; fulfillment is another matter. Indeed, a Phrygian inscription describes certain politicians as "The Promisers" (*IGR* 4.766, cited by BAGD). Betz notes the parsimonious character, described by Theophrastus in a book titled *Characters*, who makes a discrete exit when a public contribution is under vote in the assembly. In a speech prepared by the ghost writer Isaeus (5.37-38) for one of his clients, a certain Dicaiogenes is censured for failing to fulfill a pledge of three hundred drachmas that he had made "voluntarily," according to the heading that was posted over a list of defaulters. And Dio Chrysostom, in his 31st oration (31.9-10), chastises the people of Rhodes for failing to carry out the provisions of their own decree by engraving the name of an honorand on a statue already standing in the city, which had been erected for someone else. It is therefore patently clear why public documents would make special reference to fulfillment of pledges, for example, by a head of state. Thus, a treaty made by Athenians with Thessalians declares that the people of Thessaly "did commendably and with goodwill (*prothymōs*) everything that their state had promised (*epangelomai*)" (*SIG*[3] 184.35-36). Conscious of such tradition, Demosthenes is proud to state in his speech *On the Crown* (112): "I gave out of my own estate what I pledged to the public." With an elegant bit of wordplay Paul rounds out his appeal: **so that it may be ready not as an exaction** that suggests greed (*pleonexia*), **but as a willing** or generous **gift** that merits praise (*eulogia*).

To capture the numerous plays on words in this verse, the sentence can be translated as follows: "Therefore I considered it essential to instruct the brothers, that they should *pre*cede us on their visit to you and *pre*pare your *pre*announced donation (*eulogia*), so that it might indeed be ready as a donation (*eulogia*) and not as a confiscation (*pleonexia*)." The ordinary meaning of the word *eulogia* is "fame" or "blessing." Frequently fame or blessing result from expressions of liberality. It is then but a short step to identification of the cause with the result, hence the use of the term *eulogia* in the sense of "gift" or "bounty."

Given the intense interest of the Greco-Roman world in reciprocity, Paul's addressees would readily grasp the point. Willingness to participate in the charitable enterprise would manifest a response to divine generosity. Greed is characteristic of an ignoble and unthankful spirit. Socrates observes in the *Memorabilia* written by Xenophon (4.3) that God is the source of all the goods that humanity enjoys. Therefore, he argues, it is one's obligation to observe the law and custom of the state and to show reverence to God. Included in such obligation is the performance of what is useful, that is, of benefit to others. At the very beginning of 2 Corinthians, Paul had eulogized God as the "parent of mercies and of all encouragement" (1:3). Now, in connection with the collection, Paul encourages the Corinthians to show mercy to the poor in Jerusalem. Their response will reflect an understanding of God's generosity towards them.

6—Greco-Romans were fond of crisp counsel that took the form of maxims, for maxims encouraged a balanced view of life and fostered sober judgment based on the experience of a broad segment of humanity. As Betz observes, Paul here uses a proverb, that may have been generated by Prov. 11:24, as a thesis for the line of argument through v. 14. Wettstein notes Cicero's form of the maxim that underlies Paul's formulation: "Expect to reap as you have sown." "Sow sparingly," writes Paul, "and sparingly you shall reap. Sow generously and generously you shall reap." The Greek expression for **bountifully** or "generously" is the phrase *ep' eulogiais*, which echoes the term in v. 5, and here means literally "on top of blessings." The repetition is typical of sententious statements, which frequently play on words, and Paul chooses the phrase precisely because of a common cultural understanding that the more one gives the more one will be recognized for such generosity. It was said of Opramoas of Lycia that the emperor incited him to increase his gifts, and the philanthropist, aroused by the expectation of further glory, persisted in adding to his annual contributions, especially in the nature of public works projects (*Benefactor*, p. 140). He was not one to say, "I already gave." He sowed on top of gifts that helped him reap blessing on blessings from the victims of earthquakes. That Paul may also have had in mind the prudential advice featured in Prov. 11:23-31 is probable, but with his genius for bridging cultures he holds the attention of his Greco-Roman public by giving Semitic tradition a Hellenistic twist.

7—The phrase "make up one's mind," "be committed," renders the Greek verb *proaireō*, the cognate of a noun *proairesis* that is common in honorary documents concerning public-spirited people who have a reputation for commitment to the welfare of others. Thus, an Attic decree declares that "King Ptolemy Philadelphos, in accordance with the commitment of his ancestor and his sister (Arsinoe), is beyond question zealous on behalf of the common freedom of Hellas, and that the Athenian people, after making an alliance with him and the rest of the Hellenes, voted to urge him to maintain the same commitment" (*SIG*[3] 434.16-21).

Heinrici cites Hesiod in connection with the principle of heartfelt giving that is enunciated by Paul. "Those who give willingly, even when they part with a great amount, rejoice in the giving, and their soul is filled with delight" (*Works and Days* 357-358). Aristotle was in complete agreement: "The liberal person, he stated, "will give with pleasure, or in any case without pain. For virtuous performance is a source of pleasure and painless" (*Nicomachean Ethics* 4.1.13). In his study on beneficence, Seneca observes that the most delightful feature of donors is their spontaneous response. One ought to part with a gift without delay lest one appear to be giving it in such a manner that one seems to be extorting from oneself rather than making a donation (*On Benefits* 2.1.2). The same author stated that a certain "Fabius Verrucosus was accustomed to term a gift that was reluctantly given a 'loaf hard as a rock' " (*On Benefits* 2.7.1). Paul's own formulation of the thought suggests Prov. 22:8 LXX (*andra hilaron kai dotēn eulogei ho theos*): "God blesses one who is cheerful and at the same time generous." But Paul enriches the motivation that he had begun to express in v. 6 by highlighting God's affection in response to human generosity.

8—This verse states that God is the source of beneficence and therefore the creator of cheerful givers. God is able to ensure a constant flow of bounty to the Corinthians so that they may be able to engage without interruption in the **good work** of beneficent concern for others.

That God is the source of the bounties (**every** blessing, *pasan charin*) which human beings enjoy was a commonplace in Greco-Roman culture. In its praise of Caesar Augustus, the Asian League states that "Providence . . . orders all our lives" and "has in her display of concern and generosity in our behalf adorned our lives with the highest good: Augustus" (*Benefactor,* p. 217). Xenophon (4.3.3) records that Socrates asked a friend named Euthydemos, "Have you ever reflected how carefully the deities supply human beings with everything that they need?" In his turn, Paul emphasizes the rationale underlying such generous bestowal by God, namely, that human beings may themselves become distributors of benefits.

The term **enough** (*autarkeia*) was favored by the Cynics and Stoics as a referent for self-sufficiency, in the sense of contentment with one's lot, a sense that appears in Phil. 4:11. But here the apostle thinks of material sufficiency.

A **good work** in Greco-Roman parlance ordinarily referred to a philanthropic enterprise, such as the erection of a temple or repair of public buildings. A "good" person is by definition one who renders public service, often at great personal cost. The term **every** would be especially meaningful to Hellenic ears, for numerous documents record that a given honorand performed benefactions far beyond the narrow sphere of his personal acquaintances. For example, a decree in honor of a physician named after the illustrious Hippocrates declares: "WHEREAS [Hippokrates], son of Thessalos and citizen of Kos, constantly renders all [aid] and assistance to the people as a whole and privately to citizens who request his services, be it RESOLVED by the People to commend Hippokrates, citizen of Kos, for his policy of goodwill to the people, and to crown him in the theater . . ." (*Benefactor,* p. 61; see also pp. 336-339).

9—Paul cites Ps. 111:9 (LXX = RSV 112:9), which describes a pious Israelite. In v. 10 the apostle applies the passage to God's philanthropic manner. Especially striking here is the close link that Paul forges between generosity and uprightness (*dikaiosynē*). As the commentary on v. 10 will demonstrate, Greco-Roman thinking frequently linked these two qualities, especially in honorary documents. It is typical also of Greco-Roman thinkers to shift from God to humanity or from humanity to God when reflecting on the practical manifestations of uprightness. Yahweh's uprightness manifests itself especially in concern for the oppressed and the poor. The acme of divine interest in humanity is exhibited, of course, in God's generous forgiveness granted in connection with Jesus Christ. The experience of that righteousness of God is the ground out of which springs Paul's appeal to the Corinthians for participation in the collection for the poor in Jerusalem.

10—Isaiah 55:10 likens the word of the Lord to life-sustaining rain and snow. Paul changes the imagery slightly and connects the benevolent productivity with God, whose action is of course implicit in the prophetic passage. The imagery of a sower and the sowing process is taken from Isa. 55:10 and heightens the impression of bountiful generosity. God **supplies** grain in ample supply for the next planting season as well as for regular eating. The word **supplies** in the RSV does duty for two Greek words, the compound *epichorēgeō* and the simplex *chorēgeō*, from which the word "chorus" is derived. The uncompounded word appears frequently in honorary documents in reference to a philanthropist's willingness to assume expenses for a public project, such as a dramatic contest, which would involve a huge outlay for costumes and provisions for the participants, an athletic program, or restoration of a temple. Thus Menas of Sestos is commended for having supplied (*chorēgeō*) such a basic commodity as body scrapers for athletes. In the inscription known as the "Rosetta Stone," Ptolemy V is praised for "lavishing (*chorēgeō*) many precious decorations of gold and silver on the temple of Apis" (*Benefactor*, p. 331). This same God who is the source of everything in nature that spells security and enjoyment for humanity (cf. Xenophon, *Memorabilia* 4.3.11) is the one who will enable the Corinthians to become ever-increasing sources of beneficence. God will do this by multiplying their "seed" (*sporos*), which echoes the first part of the verse and is rendered **resources** by the RSV. The Corinthians' "seed" is their money. God's righteousness or generosity (v. 9) makes possible their generosity or righteousness. Paul's familiarity with Hos. 10:12 (LXX) and Isa. 61:11 may have been the source of the metaphor, **harvest of your righteousness,** but there is no indication of a direct quotation. Proverbs 3:9-10 expresses related ideas. A remarkable parallel, as noted by Betz, comes from the Hellenic sector. Aelius Aristides (*Panathenaic Oration* 45) observes that "not only the seeds of wheat and barley become the property of humanity, but also the seeds of righteousness and all that goes with life and polity are of divine origin."

As Betz points out, the metaphor of growth under the guidance of a deity would be at home in the Hellenic world. The close connection between righteousness and generosity was noted in trenchant verse by the Greek elegiac poet Theognis (1.149-152) in address to one of his friends:

> In righteousness, to sum it all, is highest virtue,
> and all good persons, Kyrnos, are among the righteous;
> E'en to the basest, God, I ween, gives money,
> but misery will follow few who know such virtue.

About five centuries later, the eminent Roman orator Cicero described righteousness in his work titled *On Ends* (5.23.5) as "that attribute of the soul which apportions what is appropriate for each one, and that which guards the association of human society richly and equitably is termed uprightness, to which are conjoined piety, goodness, generosity, beneficence, courtesy, and all other virtues of the same kind."

Many in the Greco-Roman world were familiar with the pride that Caesar Augustus took in his sense of *iustitia,* the Latin term for *dikaiosynē.* Of Menas it was said that his city of Sestos enjoyed its own coinage because of his "uprightness and generosity" (*dikaiosynē kai philotimia;* see *Benefactor,* p. 345).

11—The purpose for which God has materially blessed the Corinthians is made even more explicit in this verse. Such blessing is designed to make the recipient a source of blessing for others. But God's enrichment of the Corinthians extends beyond the material realm. They are also inwardly enriched so that they can practice the kind of generosity (*haplotēs*) that was characteristic of the Macedonians (8:2). The conjunction of thought here with the opening sentences of chap. 8 is a powerful piece of evidence for the unity of chaps. 8 and 9. From a rhetorical perspective, it is a master stroke. The Corinthians have been given the opportunity to win the type of accolades garnered by the Macedonians. And Paul is their benefactor on this score, for if it were not for him and his associates the Corinthians would not be involved in this extraordinary opportunity for beneficence. But because of his activity on their behalf, thanksgiving will be offered to God. Such assurance would be doubly meaningful to Greco-Romans, first, because the donors gain approval from the deity through the recognition given by the recipients of their bounty. Some idea of the importance that was attached to divine goodwill can be gauged from the awful oath that was recorded by Antiochus I of Commagene against such as might dare to defile his father's burial site:

> Pierced in his base heart, the root of his wicked life, by the unfailing arrows of Apollo and Herakles, let bitter pain possess him in the depths of his being that is so hateful of the good; and through the wrath of Hera let him discover how heavenly justice imposes the penalty that brooks no unrighteousness.
>
> (*Benefactor,* pp. 251-252)

Psalm 10 is the counterpart in Jewish tradition. The statement about thanksgivings would be meaningful, second, because of Greco-Roman emphasis on gratitude for services rendered. Appreciation by the recipients of public or private benefits was itself sufficient and appropriate recompense for the benefactor's services. Especially striking here is the fact that Paul does not say that the Corinthians will be directly thanked, but that God will be thanked. In other words, the beneficence of the Corinthians will heighten the honor and glory of God as the Benefactor of all benefactors. Indeed, to diminish the possibility of augmenting such honoring of God through reluctance to participate wholeheartedly in the collection ought to give one second thoughts.

12—Paul's reference to **service** permitted no doubt concerning the perspective from which the pending collection is to be viewed. His addressees would be well informed on long-standing traditions relating to the rendering of public service, which frequently bore the term *leitourgia* (liturgy). A "liturgy" in the Greco-Roman world meant assumption of a civic obligation. In classical times this involved especially financing of choruses for dramatic productions and maintenance of gymnastic programs. The term was later applied to assumption of a variety of magistracies. The expenses involved in bearing up under the weight of certain honors frequently caused the honorees to plead hardship and thus seek relief from the obligation. Numerous inscriptions record the gratitude of cities for services rendered. By using a term with such traditional associations, Paul transmutes the Corinthians' participation into a grand enterprise. For related usage of *leitourgia* and cognates in Pauline writings, see Rom. 13:6; 15:16, 27; Phil. 2:17, 30.

The apostle goes on to state that their contribution will not only enhance the well-being of the recipients but, even if the contribution should appear in the eyes of some to be insignificant, it will be magnified many times over by the multitude of thanksgivings to God that will be expressed (cf. 1:11). Behind the apostle's phrasing is the understanding that expectation of honor and glory are the primary rewards for beneficence in Greco-Roman society. But again, the emphasis is on the beneficence of God, for God is the recipient of the **many thanksgivings.** Some measure of the importance attached in the Greco-Roman world to recognition of divine benefits can be derived from a devotee's praise of Isis for restoring sight to his eyes:

> I have received [my sight anew; grant that I] may see [how marvelous you are and that] all my words of praise may do justice to the greatness [of your benefactions]; and may my eulogy [reach far beyond] hearing; and may my countenance be inclined to God and humankind.

> (*Benefactor,* p. 180)

13—After all is said and done, the Corinthians will in every way be the gainers. The contribution will be viewed as a validation of the Corinthians' personal Christian claims and of their genuine sense of partnership not only with the poor in Jersualem but with all who display interest in the needs of others. The use of the word **test** (*dokimē*) does not mean that the Corinthians' fidelity to the gospel is in doubt, but that their participation in the collection will provide undeniable proof of their Christian credentials. Through the reference to the glorification of God, Paul once more focuses on divine beneficence as the source of all other beneficence that is to be exhibited. The word **acknowledging** is an inadequate rendering of the Greek term *homologia*, which here means "subscription" to, or "agreement" respecting, **the gospel of Christ** (*eis to euangelion tou Christou*). Paul's terminology suggests Hellenic bureaucratic formulation. The genitival construction of the original, "obedience of your contract," simply means "contractual obedience," that is, "obedience rendered in accordance with contractual obligation." Numerous inscriptions record "agreements" or "contracts" made by heads of state or by cities. As the contract between Eumenes I and his mercenaries indicates (*OGI* 266), such an agreement could project all the force of an oath. In this contract, the mercenaries promise total fealty to Eumenes, even to the death, and Eumenes assures them that if they carry out their part of the contract he will respect their rights. Against the background of Hellenistic covenantal practice, Paul images the Corinthians as having contracted for participation in the task of proclaiming Christ. The RSV's rendering **gospel of Christ** is unnecessarily ambiguous, for it could suggest that the gospel is to be viewed as something that belongs under Christ's jurisdiction. But this is not Paul's point. He thinks of "commitment to the responsibility of proclaiming Christ." This is what the Corinthians obligated themselves to when they became Christians. By participating in the collection, the Corinthians show themselves identified in purpose with the believers or Israelites in Jerusalem. To Israel, as God's servant (see on 6:2), belongs the responsibility of being a light to the nations (Isa. 49:6). God will be glorified in connection with Israel's fulfillment of that task (Isa. 49:3). Paul's envoys represent the vanguard of all those who stream to Zion (Isa. 49:18), that is, Jerusalem. To be sure, the figure of the servant in Paul's imagery becomes a blend of the

145

believers in Jerusalem and the believers in Corinth, but this is precisely Paul's point. All who are engaged in the proclaiming of Christ to the world are carrying out the contract of obedience to God.

For the active force of proclamation concerning **Christ** see also 2:12; 4:4; 10:14; 1 Cor. 9:12; 1 Thess. 3:2; 2 Thess. 1:8; Gal. 1:7; Rom. 1:9; 15:19; Phil. 1:27.

The RSV's rendering of the concluding clause of this verse, **and by the generosity of your contribution for them and for all others,** reinforces the thought of unanimity in an undertaking. At the same time it obscures Paul's evident concern to round out his presentation on the collection with an echo of 8:4, in which the term *koinōnia* (RSV, **taking part**) is used, as here in 9:13, where the RSV renders it with "contribution." In view of the context, which puts the Corinthians' commitment to Christ and to the mission of Israel on the line, the clause is therefore better rendered: "and (glorifying God) over your generous partnership with them and all other (Christians)." The point is that the Corinthians are not to engage in a solo performance at Corinth. They are linked with Christ's people throughout the world. An important nuance of the word here rendered "generosity" (*haplotēs*) is "sincerity." By participating in the collection the Corinthians demonstrate their avowed commitment to the Christ who is Lord of all the people of God. The phrase "for them and for all others" would sound a familiar note for the addressees. The point is not that the Corinthians are presumed to be engaging in a collection that has others besides the poor of Jerusalem in mind. Of such a general collection there is no evidence in the Corinthian correspondence. Rather, the apostle makes use of a motif that is frequently used in praise of philanthropists, who are said to be concerned about people far beyond their own narrow circle (see above on v. 8).

14-15—In the course of praying for the Corinthians, all who know of their generosity will be filled with such affection that they would like to see the Corinthians personally, since they are evidently among God's favorites, for God has bestowed on them such munificent beneficence (**grace,** *charis*). Thus Paul's invitation to the Corinthians to participate in the collection was in itself an outpouring of divine beneficence. In the very deed of giving to the poor in Jerusalem the Corinthians realized an unusual gift from God.

So beneficent is God in every way that Paul concludes his appeal with a thanksgiving. The apostle's penchant for wordplay is again apparent. His word for thanksgiving is *charis*, which appeared in v. 14 in the sense of "grace" or "benefit." Paul had begun his presentation with a reference to the abundant "grace" of God that had been displayed in Macedonia (8:1-2). Now it is the Corinthians who are recipients of God's surpassing grace, which is further described by Paul as an **inexpressible gift.** Paul means that God's beneficence is so bountiful that no recited accolade or aretalogy could do justice to it. Greco-Romans would understand the sentiment (see above on 8:1, Apuleuis, *Metamorphoses*).

■ A Declaration of Loving Concern (10:1—13:13)

As indicated in the introduction, which should be consulted for details, there is a long-standing debate as to the position of these chapters relative to the rest of 2 Corinthians. If these chapters are to be considered a completion of 2 Corinthians, but written after a lapse of time during which Paul received new information about the Corinthians, one can account to some extent for the evident connections with chaps. 1–9 as well as for the discordant features. If these chapters are part of a completely different letter, the early editors have succeeded in erasing some of the dissonances that must certainly have existed between such a letter and chaps. 1–9. On the other hand, modern literary critics are at a disadvantage, since it is impossible to map with desirable accuracy the circumstances that were responsible for the variety of rhetorical and substantive nuances in the various parts of 2 Corinthians.

From various indications in 2 Corinthians (2:1-3; 12:21; 13:1), it is apparent that Paul plans a visit after the dispatch of the letter that includes chaps. 10–13. But from the defense he made in chap. 1, it is also evident that he is under fire for not having carried out a promise to be at Corinth in person before the writing

147

of 2 Corinthians. In chaps. 8–9 he offered some explanation of the fact by directing attention to the envoys he had sent on ahead. At the same time, the topic of beneficence in chaps. 8–9 gave Paul the opportunity to cement relationships between himself and the recipients. But there is still some unfinished business. How will Paul relate to those who denigrate his authority, and how will he deal with the problem of personal attacks occasioned in part by his apparent desire to avoid encounter? In place of a personal appearance, which would expose him to the necessity of answering his critics, his opponents charge that he relies on letters to carry out heavy-handed and intimidating policies. To meet this and other allegations Paul engages in a lengthy ironical defense of his apostolate. Since the collection might also have been misunderstood as part of a project to siphon off money from Corinth in Paul's own interest, the apostle emphasizes in 12:14-18 that he had never enriched himself at their expense. Since the opposition has been so vocal, Paul expresses anxiety concerning the depth of commitment to gospel objectives at Corinth (12:20). Such expression of his fears permits him to urge the Corinthians to work on any problems that remain. Thus, the combination of opposition factors and of anxiety for his beloved Corinthians' long-term commitment to God's gospel program, may to a large extent well account for the vehement tone of these concluding chapters.

Paul's Claim on the Congregation (10:1-18)

Claim to Disciplinary Power (10:1-6)

1—Paul begins by taking up the question of his personal style in dealing with the people of God at Corinth. It is alleged that when the apostle is absent from Corinth he is courageous in addressing the Corinthians, but quite meek when he visits them. But, counters Paul, his opposition had better not test him on his potential for boldness, for he will take the Corinthians' part against any troublemakers.

To meet the charge of arrogance on his part, Paul appeals to the example of Jesus Christ. Christ is the leader of exceptional merit, noted for his **meekness** (*praytēs*) **and gentleness** (*epieikeia*).

The strong cultural current of the reciprocity system and attendant image of the public-spirited benefactor is evident. Plutarch (*Caesar* 57.3) observes that some were of the opinion that the construction of the temple of Clementia (*Epieikeia*) was ordered out of gratitude for Caesar's gentleness (*praotēs* = *praytēs*). The same author says of Pericles that despite demands of office and hostility he preserved his tolerant manner and gentle disposition (Plutarch, *Pericles* 39.1 [173]). The two terms denote one who does not exploit high position to satisfy personal whims or to wage vendettas. Such a person is able to give priority to human interests over legal privilege. Caesar Augustus reflected his father's virtue and he was proud to write concerning his receipt of a gold shield from the Roman people that it defined him as a man of "forbearance" (*clementia*, rendered *epieikeia* in the Greek version of the *Res Gestae*). And of Opramoas, second-century commander of Lycia's guard, it was said that he discharged his office with a sense of equity: desirous of meeting the needs of the people, he did not put the letter of the law above its spirit (*Benefactor*, p. 352). In Phil. 4:5 the apostle uses a variant form of the term *epieikeia* as part of a description of *aretē* or consummate excellence, in order to point out that it is not necessary to do battle for everything that people call their "rights" (*Benefactor*, pp. 351-52).

How this approach to the theme of meekness is to be squared with the vehement tone that at times penetrates Paul's letter has perplexed some interpreters. But from a Jewish perspective, the conjunction is in harmony with God's own display of wrath and power while engaged in the salvation of Israel (cf. Wis. 11:20-26; 12:1-27; Hos. 11:8-9; Pss. of Sol. 8:28-34; 13:6-8). Nor would Greco-Romans with but slight exposure to rhetorical tradition be in the least disconcerted by such apparent shift in mood. Demosthenes' oration *On the Crown* (278) makes detailed commentary on the matter otiose:

> Citizens who are held in high repute ought not to expect a court that is in session for the common interest to gratify any tendency they might have to indulge themselves in anger or hatred or related feelings, nor should they go before you with such end in mind. Indeed, it were best if such feelings were totally foreign to their

disposition; but if that is not possible, they ought to moderate them carefully (*praōs kai metriōs*). But under what circumstances ought the politician and orator to be vehement? Of course, when the city is in any way imperiled and when the public is faced by adversaries. Such is the obligation of a noble and patriotic citizen.

In short, private animosity betrays small-minded people. Heated expression on behalf of others is not only justified but is a sign of magnanimity.

Nor is boldness a negation of the virtue of gentility. On the contrary, Euphrosynos, a citizen of Mantinea, was so zealous in carrying out his vows of service to his home town that he braved the Adriatic Sea twice to further her interests at Rome (*SIG*³ 783. 25-27). This theme of the endangered benefactor was exploited in connection with the experiences of philosophers, and Epictetus (1.24.6-20) offers one of the classic expositions. The threats even of an emperor, he preaches, do not discourage the true philosopher, who can, if need be, sleep on the ground with good courage.

Paul's opposition refuses to recognize Paul as a possessor of lofty virtues and therefore denigrates his function as benefactor of the Corinthians. In self-inflicted irony Paul lays their charge out in the open: "face to face, humble; when away, bold." This mode of statement is a variation of a common charge laid against politicians who fail to deliver on their promises: all words, no performance (see on v. 11). The term **humble** (*tapeinos*) is used by the opposition in the negative sense of "abject" or "servile." Paul, they say, tries to score points by affecting a docile manner when he is present in person, but puts on a tough act in absentia. The charge now becomes the text for the exposition in chaps. 10–13.

Formally considered, this verse presents a dramatic contrast. The positive note on the qualities of Christ precedes Paul's engagement with his adversaries' negative evaluation. In addition to the broad cultural phenomenon that lies behind Paul's choice of language is the more specific portrait of philosophers who were ridiculed for their homely or unkempt appearance, or for their unconventional personal habits. Socrates, as seen especially in Aristophanes' *Clouds*, was the butt of numerous jokes. Cynic philosophers carried the Hellenic thirst for glory to the extreme by denying validity to traditional routes for the measurement of excellence. Among them were those who sought to demonstrate uncommon excellence (*aretē*) by the severest renunciation of riches and ordinary amenities, and denied that exile, death, poverty, slavery, or old age were an index of second-class experience. Because the path from Homeric recognition of military exploits to admiration of moral qualities as encouraged by philosophers had already been paved, Paul could count on understanding for his defense against the allegations of his opponents. Since it is understood in the Greco-Roman world that people of uncommon excellence are to serve as models for others, Paul first exhibits Jesus as the exceptional person and then shows that his own experience at the hands of his opponents is really the product of his acceptance of Jesus as his model for exceptional performance.

2-3—Much of the point of vv. 2-5 is dependent on an understanding of Paul's play on the term "flesh" (*sarx*), which is inadequately rendered **worldly** (as opposed to "spiritually") by the RSV. It is true that Paul frequently opposes "flesh" to "spirit," but the primary point of opposition is one of relative advantage. Flesh is humanity in its frail condition, subject to weakness, including various defects, and ultimately death. This is what it means to "walk in the flesh" (**live in the world**). In such a condition the temptation is strong to express one's ego at all costs. Decisions are then made in terms of what satisfies the ego. Such approach to life and decision-making Paul calls living "according to the flesh" (*kata sarka;* cf. Rom 8:4-5, 13) or being "in flesh" (*en sarki*, Rom. 8:8), and it is not his style, he says. The troublemakers in Corinth, whether from within or from without the membership, can therefore expect to face a Paul who will not play clever diplomatic games. They will find that his toughness in person will match his verbal toughness, of which chaps. 10–13 are an eloquent example.

4—According to Prov. 21:22, a wise man can scale the city of the mighty and bring down the fortress in which they trust. Besides communicating to people familiar with the Jewish Scriptures, Paul's imagery relating to destruction of **strongholds** in an imagistic sense would also be meaningful to those who had been exposed to Greco-Roman preachers. Epictetus (4.1.86-87; cf. 3.22.94-95) wrote:

> How then is a citadel destroyed? Not by metal nor by fire, but by personal judgments. For if we tear down the citadel that is in the city, have we succeeded in capturing the citadel of fever? Of beautiful maidens? In sum, have we subdued the citadel and tyrants that are within us, whom we permit to control everything that involves us daily? No, it is here within us that we must begin. It is here that we must destroy the citadel and cast out these dictators.

Unlike Epictetus, who governs himself through philosophical discipline, Paul derives mastery over his frail humanity from God's action in Christ. We are certainly, he implies, not on "campaign to serve our own interests." And God also gives Paul the power to surmount whatever physical disabilities his opponents decry (see v. 10). Instead of permitting any alleged deficiencies to obstruct fulfillment of his apostolic responsibilities, he serves notice to his opponents that he will topple their syllogistic mountains and citadels of theological contention. David will in the end bring down Goliath.

Along related lines, Philo had written about the offensive tactics of justice, which wars against evil logic. "For," states Philo, "the stronghold that was erected through persuasive reason, was built for no other reason than to divert and deflect the mind from giving honor to God." He goes on to say that the "evil-hating soul is sharpened against the impious to topple every argument that would persuade the mind to divert from holiness. . . . For through stability and serenity of mind, which piety is wont to engender, every argument devised by impiety is overturned" (*The Confusion of Tongues* 129-132).

5-6—The imagery of weaponry is a reminder that the pages of Greco-Roman history were replete with military exploits. Vergil's epic, the *Aeneid*, contains the following words in its introductory lines: "Of arms and the man I sing" (*arma virumque cano*). Every schoolchild knew of Achilles, Hector, Aeneas, Alexander, Hannibal, the Scipios, Demetrios, Pompey, Julius Caesar, and Octavian. All of them were celebrated by their admirers as benefactors of their various countries, as people who gave definition to the Latin word *virtus* and the Greek term *aretē* (excellence of the highest order). But there are those who masquerade as masters of excellence, and Paul apparently knows what a strong appeal the military has for egos that find their chief nourishment in the exploitation and control of others. It was people of this type that Jesus had in mind when he warned some of his disciples against identifying with the ambitions of such as lay false claim to a reputation for beneficence (Luke 22:24-27). In keeping with such counsel, Paul says that he does not use apostolic privilege to control others. God is central in his thinking, and anything that conflicts with divine interests and the claims of Christ is within the range of his artillery. Paul is prepared therefore to **punish** any **disobedience** that lingers in the Corinthian congregations now that the majority have assured him of their **complete obedience** (see 7:15; cf. 2:9). He will not be intimidated by those who suggest that he has influence over a majority because of their passivity but will have neither the nerve nor the acumen to take on the minority of more articulate dissidents.

Paul owes it to the majority who have sided with him to lend support to their assurance of allegiance by stern refutation of the opposition. At the same time, Paul faces the reality of fickleness. Some of those who saw it Paul's way might be swayed by clever arguments from suave leaders or visiting dignitaries. For such Paul has strong words of warning that are frequently punctuated with satire, and at the same time matched by warm affirmations of his affection for the loyal constituency.

Claim to Jurisdiction (10:7-18)

7—The opening clause, **Look at what is before your eyes,** means that the addressees are to look at one another, face by face, one by one, on down the line. The point is that each one must certainly recognize the other as belonging to Christ. Otherwise they could scarcely call themselves a Christian congregation. Had not the apostle called them "epistles of Christ" (3:3), and did he not say that every Christian's face images Christ (3:18)? Let each person, then, ask, "How can I call myself Christ's?" As 1 Cor. 12:3 states, "No one can say 'Jesus is Lord' except by the Holy Spirit." Well, let those who think thus of themselves take account of the fact that he too is **Christ's.** Paul refuses to let anyone draw a circle to shut him out, and he makes anyone's boast of superior alliance his own and thereby democratizes the alleged privilege.

The apostle is, of course making an indirect attack on his adversaries. They claim to supersede Paul in the distinction of belonging to Christ in such a way that they asserted for themselves a prior right to the allegiance of the congregation. The precise nature of their attack cannot be determined from Paul's remarks, but the theological perspective of Paul's imperative, "Look . . . Christ's," permits no doubt as to who is in charge, and the opening theological ploy forecasts a skillfully devised effort at refutation.

8—If the opposition is so foolish as to engage in one-upmanship on the matter of authority, Paul will not shrink from the battle. But because of what is at stake, he may come off sounding more boastful than appears to be appropriate. At the outset, therefore, he wishes to make it clear that he is not interested in winning a debate, but in **building up.** This statement is an illuminating clue to the rhetorical function of chaps. 10–13, whose strong disciplinary tone seems at first glance to be out of tune with the rest of 2 Corinthians. In effect, Paul will function like a second Jeremiah (see Jer. 1:10; 24:6).

Subtle nuances of grammar punctuate Paul's line of argument in vv. 8-11. Verse 8 can be rendered: "Suppose I should boast immoderately about the authority that the Lord has given me—one that has to do with upbuilding and not destroying—you can be sure that I won't have to hide my head in shame because of the outcome." In other words, he is not saying that he refuses to be ashamed about the fact of boasting, whatever its degree. Rather, the exercise of his authority will bring results, and he will not have to take back a single word. For, as he will assert in v. 11, his words are backed up by deeds. As benefactor of the Corinthians, he is at their service for "building" them up. But if occasion calls for it, he may have to do some destroying. The quiet conditional form of the statement is part of the dramatic buildup for the inevitable rhetorical barrage that will shortly follow. Paul *will* engage in some powerful boasting!

9—In this verse Paul states the reason for his declaration of

confidence. The RSV rendition, **I would not seem to be fright-
ening you with letters,** obscures the point through failure to grasp
Paul's colloquial turn of speech: ". . . as though all that we can
do is scare people through letters."

10-11—Paul's opponents charge that he lacks personal presence
as well as the ability to show on the spot why his position is
superior to someone else's. Some measure of the importance of
physical appearance for a communicator can be gauged from Epictetus's requirements (3.22.86-88) for one who preaches in the
public square:

> Such people require a certain kind of body. Suppose they come
> forward resembling consumptives, emaciated and pale, do you think
> their testimony will possess any credibility? On the contrary, while
> discoursing on the things of the spirit, they must prove two things
> to lay people. First, that it is possible to be a person of exceptional
> merit without dependence on the things that most people consider
> important. Second, that the appearance of their bodies demonstrates
> that a plain and simple life spent in the open air in no way injures
> the body. "Behold," Diogenes said, "I myself am a witness of the
> truth of what I have just said. Just look at my body!"

Apparently Epictetus thought that some of the negative criticism
of the moral preachers of his day was homegrown. And he was
not alone in his concern. Four centuries earlier, Aeschines ridiculed Timarchus for appearing in the public assembly, with his
"body so shamefully debilitated by drink and debauchery"
(*Against Timarchus* 26). Lucius Piso came under fire for his un-
couth appearance in hair, eyebrows, and dress. Cicero was taken
to task for his varicose veins (Dio Cassius, 46.18.2). And Pompey
was ridiculed for scratching his head with one finger (Plutarch,
Moralia 89e).

According to one of the accounts in the apocryphal acts of the
apostles, Titus "beheld Paul approaching, rather short for his
weight, bald, bowlegged, healthy, eyebrows joined, with a long
nose, full of charm; for at times he appeared to be only a human
being, but at others, he had the face of an angel" (*Acts of Paul
and Thecla* 3). One cannot vouch for the historical veracity of this
description, but it may well have been stimulated by Paul's text.

In the face of criticism concerning his qualifications, Paul counters: "Let such people know that when I arrive the power of my personal performance will match my words that come by letter." The contrasting expression **what we say** . . . **we do** is a recurring phrase in documents that celebrate exceptional men and women in the Greco-Roman world. Already in Homer's *Iliad* (9:443), Phoenix expresses the expectation for Achilles that he "be an orator and a man of action" (*Benefactor*, p. 339). In Attic Greek the customary formulation is *logǭ kai ergǭ* as in the accolade accorded to a benefactor at Cyzicus named Apollodoros, who is praised for "doing whatever he can in word and deed for the people whom he encounters" (cited in *Benefactor*, p. 339). Since performance does not always match the boastful word, the negative formulation, "not in word but in deed," became common, as in Polybius's descriptions of political figures who fail to deliver on their boasts and promises. Similarly, Epictetus described the disciplined philosopher as "one who is a model of excellence, not in word but in deed" (3.24.110). Paul, who throughout this epistle presents himself as a benefactor of the Corinthians, uses the word-pair ironically. As pointed out in connection with v. 8, he would much prefer to be the kind of person who will be recognized as a benefactor in the true sense of the word, namely, as one who builds up (v. 8). Instead, he fears that he must do some destroying so as to protect the congregation from those whom he later calls pseudo-apostles. The stage is thus further set for much of the irony and satire that is pronounced in the rest of the letter. And those familiar with modes of expression used by Cynic philosophers would recognize that beneath the vehemence there breathed the spirit of a loving parent. As Epictetus (3.22.81-82) put it:

> The Cynic has adopted all humanity. The males are his sons, and the females his daughters. In such manner he approaches them all, and in such wise he cares for them. Or do you suppose that he reviles every one he meets because he has nothing better to do? Nay, he does it as a father, as a brother, and as the assistant to God, the Father of us all.

12-13—The RSV misses the connection between vv. 11 and

12. The timid rendering of the initial phrase in v. 12 (**Not that we venture** . . .) blunts the satirical double-edged thrust of Paul's Greek. Having just referred to his opponents' allegations of phony courage on Paul's part, the apostle proceeds to exploit the criticism: "We do indeed lack courage. We lack the nerve either to put ourselves in the same company with or to compare ourselves with those who recommend themselves." The Greek verb *tolmaō*, rendered **venture** by the RSV, means "to be daring." In a letter written near the end of the first century (*Oxyrhynchus Papyri* 2190), a student named Neilus writes to his father that he had been exposed to a bad teacher named Didymus, who was from the sticks and had the nerve to think that he was on the same level (*eis synchrisen*) with instructors from cosmopolitan Alexandria. This was a restrained way of saying that the teacher was a fool. For an orator to be daring meant that he ventured forth beyond the realm of propriety. Thus Antiphon links the cognate noun with "shamelessness" (3.3.6; see also Plato, *Laches* 193d; 197b; *Apology* 38d). Epictetus discouraged rash enterprise. He argued that "no bull just happening by takes on a lion," but a superior bull might do so (3.1.22).

The kind of invidious comparison that Paul criticizes is cut from the same cloth as the proverbial indictment of those who see the faults of all others but their own. When Thales was asked what was easy, he replied: "Counseling of others." At another time someone asked him how one might conduct oneself in the most appropriate and upright manner. He answered, "Avoid doing what you find blameworthy in others" (Diogenes Laertius, 1.36). Commenting on a general resistance to soul-searching, the Roman satirist Persius wrote: "All are on the march and eye the burden on the other's back" (*Satires* 4.23-24).

Paul's highly rhetoricized condensation in v. 12 has led to some alterations in the textual tradition, but the apostle's thought is quite clear. The path that leads from the opening words, "We do indeed lack courage," to the indictment **they are without understanding** is short, for in 11:21 Paul confesses that the kind of boastful courage ("whatever one dares," *tolmaō*) others manifest is in reality the expression of a "fool." Beginning at 11:1, Paul adopts such a stance for argumentative purposes, after expressing his misgivings in a rhetorical ploy known as *prodiorthōsis* (a precautionary statement). But at 10:12 he opts for sanity as he refuses to compare himself to others. But the same cannot be said of his detractors, who stupidly validate themselves in terms of achievements exhibited by others within their limited group. To heighten the satire in 10:12, Paul makes use of various forms of cognate verbs in different senses, a procedure known in rhetoric as *polyptoton*. Paul's use of this tactic receives further support in the fourfold anaphoric (repetitive) use of the preposition *syn* ("with") in compound verbs. The total effect is one of boastful conspiracy on the part of Paul's opponents.

The tight structure of v. 12 further attests Paul's rhetorical skill. The opening phrase (**Not that we venture**) is balanced, as noted above, by the terminal phrase (**they are without understanding**). The phrase "to class or compare ourselves" is balanced by "compare themselves with one another." At the center comes the full weight of indictment: there are those who **commend** themselves and **measure** themselves by one another. Paul stated in v. 11 that he would demonstrate that his actions were equal to his words. In this and succeeding statements the apostle shows how skillful he can be with words. Thus he leaves to the imagination the comparable weight of action promised in v. 11.

Between the lines of vv. 12-13 Paul says that if he were to follow the course of his opponents, he would be forced to engage in boasting far out of proportion to what he is already charged with. In other words, there would be no contest—so contrary to the purposes of Jesus Christ are these pseudo-apostles (cf. 11:13) that he, with his track record of superior commitment to Christ, would emerge a clear winner. "Rather, we shall evaluate the quality of our performance in the light of our assignment and so avoid engaging in immoderate (**beyond limit**) boasting." God's expectations, not comparative evaluation, will determine his faithfulness and success as an apostle. "In this way we shall keep our boast in line with the direct route (*kanon*) that God has measured out for us, namely, one that proceeds without deviation right to you at Corinth." In other words, we do not meddle in other people's territory and then compare our performance with theirs.

14-16—"In view of our appraisal of responsibility, no one can charge us with **overextending ourselves.** After all, we did come to Corinth, and we were the first ones there with the news about Jesus Christ. We do not select our own areas for labor, that is, those that have not been measured out for us, and then take credit for what others have already begun (**other men's labors**). Rather, we anticipate that, as your commitment to Jesus Christ develops, we shall secure praise (*megalynthēnai*) in connection with you along the route (*kanon*) we take to proclaim the good news in regions beyond you. In this way we shall abundantly realize our anticipation for praise. We refuse to take someone else's route and then boast **of work already done in another's field.**" Paul's approach is in keeping with a proverb quoted by Plutarch (*On Inoffensive Self-Praise, Moralia* 540b): "One who sets foot in someone else's chorus is a meddler and a laughing-stock."

17-18—In the last analysis, as Paul's scripture quotation attests, commendation must come from God, not from oneself. The apostle will echo the thought at Rom. 2:29. Marcus Aurelius (12.1) came at the same idea from another perspective: "One can exercise the right not to do anything that God would not praise." (cf. A. Fridrichsen, *Symbolae Arctoae* 1 [1922] 48).

The first sentence of the paragraph began with the word "commend," and its last sentence ends with it. And its impact could not have been lost on the addressees. A multitude of monuments throughout the Mediterranean world attest the Greco-Roman passion for recognizing distinguished character and performance. The implication is that Paul deserves to be recognized by the Corinthians as their benefactor because of the message of salvation that he has brought them. But Paul looks for more than mere human acknowledgment. He rests his case for recognition with God. This is his answer to the potential for superficial judgment, and in the chapters that follow he will ring changes on the theme.

Since the manner of rendering vv. 12-18 has varied so greatly, the following translation is offered in an endeavor to capture the vigor of the apostle's thought and his arresting wordplay:

> We are not so stupid as to even dare to class or compare ourselves to some of those who commend themselves. They, on the other hand, measure themselves against others within their own group and they compare themselves to one another. Thereby they show that they in fact lack understanding.
>
> As for us, we shall not boast beyond measure, but in line with the measure or distance of the route that our God who controls the measuring has marked out for us, with you included in our destination. For it's not as though we are overextending ourselves and not coming to you first. The fact is that we came to you at the very beginning in connection with the proclamation of the gospel. We were not looking for opportunity to boast without measure at the expense of other people's labors. Rather, we had the hope that as your commitment intensified, we would, in connection with you, win esteem in accordance with our standard for profitable undertaking, namely to proclaim the good news in regions beyond you, and so avoid boasting in connection with ready-made achievements along another's route.

Evidently Paul intended to go to Rome after taking the collection to Jerusalem (cf. Rom. 1:15; 15:28).

In vv. 17-18 Paul terminates a section in which he directs attention away from himself to **the Lord.** Ancient orators were well aware that audiences find self-praise offensive. To ward off hostile reactions they found it advantageous to associate any merit they might have with divine intervention. In this vein, Plutarch informs us (*Self-Praise* 542e), that Achilles told his comrades that through divine beneficence Hector lay dead at his hand (*Iliad* 22.379). And Demosthenes (*On the Crown* 153) tells the Athenians that Philip of Macedonia was restrained, thanks to the goodwill of a deity, but also on account of the orator's efforts.

Illustrative use of the term for "rule" or "standard" is well established in ancient rhetoric. In *Against Ctesiphon* (199-200), Aeschines talks about justice along the following lines:

> Justice is not something vague and undefined, but is bounded by your own laws. In carpentry, when we want to know whether something is straight, we use a ruler (*kanon*) designed for the purpose. So also in the case of indictments for illegal proposals, the guide (*kanon*) for justice is this public posting of the proposal with accompanying statement of the laws that it violates.

"Fool's Speech" (11:1—12:10)

After having stated the theological and socially acceptable perspective, both Jewish and Hellenic, on self-praise, Paul sets the stage for a demonstration of one-upmanship in first-rate credentials. If they want to see a person of exceptional merit, they do not have far to look. Paul is the one. Only a fool would do it, he writes, and with that self-condemnation he carries with him to the depths of folly all who take pride in worldly standards for evaluating success. With exquisite and unerring irony, he makes use of the standard themes and motifs of Greco-Roman adulation in magnifying his office and his contributions to the welfare of the Corinthians, and all with a view to demolishing the value of such indulgence. By himself playing the fool, he shows what fools the Corinthians are in playing up to fools. Ultimately, the only folly worth considering is God's folly—the gift of Jesus Christ, doomed to crucifixion (cf. 1 Cor. 1:25).

Prolog (11:1-4)

1—After having declared at the close of chap. 10 that one's praise ought to come primarily from God, Paul asks his addressees to forgive him some lapses into folly. They are not of his own choosing, he will shortly point out. He is forced into them because of the ill will manifested by detractors at Corinth.

Such an appeal would not come as a surprise to the Corinthians. It was part of rhetorical tradition. At the beginning of his speech *On the Crown*, the Greek orator Demosthenes tells the Athenians that his opponent Aeschines has the advantage, because people would much rather hear invective than self-praise. At the same time, he says, were he to omit recital of his own patriotic deeds, the court might think that he was incapable of clearing himself of charges made against him. Later on in his speech (160), Demosthenes asks the Athenians to "bear" with him as he recites some of the tasks he undertook on behalf of Athens. Indeed, much of Demosthenes' speech is taken up with protestations of the orator's patriotic concern for Athens. Similarly Paul, who uses the same Greek verb (*anechomai*) as did Demosthenes, gives as the reason for his plea the profound partisan affection he feels for the

Corinthians. The thought of "putting up with" a speaker became firmly embedded in rhetorical tradition. Dio Chrysostom noted at the beginning of his 25th discourse (35.1) that his audience was so sophisticated that they refused to put up with (*anechomai*) any but the most skilled speakers.

2—The expression **feel jealousy** (*zēloō;* cf. *zēlos* and see above on 7:7, 11; 9:2) expresses Paul's concern that the Corinthians remain loyal to their initial commitment to Jesus Christ. The word-family to which this verb belongs frequently suggests interest in developing or maintaining an intimate circle of adherents to one's party or point of view.

Paul adopts the imagery used in Rom. 7:5, where Christ is the one to whom the believers are betrothed. Here Paul is the intermediary. According to Jewish custom, it was the responsibility of the father of the bride-to-be to safeguard her virginity until the time that the bridegroom accepted her into his house (Deut. 22:13-21). As noted by Windisch, the imagery of Yahweh betrothed to Israel is not uncommon in the OT (cf. Isaiah 50; 54:5-6; 62:5; Ezekiel 16; Hos. 2:19-20). The traditional Jewish social practice, familiar to the Corinthians through the Greek OT, bore legal overtones that help Paul make a strong appeal for determined allegiance to Christ in the face of detracting efforts. At the same time, Greeks and Romans were at one with Jews on the importance of a monogamous relationship. Of special interest, as Windisch observes, is the application of such imagery to God's people in a single locality. This is in keeping with Paul's view that each congregation is representative of God's people as a whole, a perspective that is fully developed in Ephesians 5 (cf. Rev. 21:2). The bond between Adam and Eve in Eden is a paradigm for the the bond between Christ and the people of God that will be consummated in the paradise to come.

As in 4:4, the verb **present** looks forward to the end of time, when Christ appears. The reference to purity is in keeping with Paul's efforts to prevent moral violations from contaminating the believers (cf. 7:1; 1 Cor. 5:6-8; 1 Cor. 10:1-13).

3—Paul alludes to Gen. 3:13 in the reference to **the serpent** and **Eve.** According to the writer of 1 Enoch, who couples misuse of sexual endowment with military interests, the rebellious angel

Gadreel was the seducer of Eve (1 Enoch 69:6). The same writer states that humanity was made "exactly like the angels, to the intent that they should continue pure and righteous" (trans. R. H. Charles, *APOT* 2:233). The author of 4 Maccabees (18:6-8) alludes to the legend in terms that vividly anticipate Paul's concern for the purity of the Corinthians. In his account, the mother of the seven heroic sons who defied King Antiochus's blasphemous orders recited this aretalogy about herself:

> I was a chaste virgin (*parthenos hagnē*, cf. 2 Cor. 11:2), and I did not wander off beyond my ancestral home, and I faithfully kept watch over the rib that (God) made. Nor did a seducer defile me in a lonely place, nor a debaucher in the open space. Nor did the deceitful serpent despoil me of my virginal purity.

From Paul's perspective, subverters of the gospel are "dirty sophists," clearly in a class with those who violate the virginity of a betrothed woman.

The word **cunning** renders the Greek word *panourgia* and appears to suggest a trenchant attack on those whom Paul construes as seducers of the Corinthians from their virginal commitment. As Betz (*Der Apostel*, p. 105) points out, Plato is followed by a long line of writers who decry the tactics of sophists and clever wordsmiths. Through the substantive *panourgos*, they label them as quacks, mountebanks, charlatans, or swindlers. Such are Paul's opponents.

The term **sincere** renders the Greek word *haplotēs*, which was used in 8:2; 9:11, 13. Paul is worried lest his beloved Corinthians show a lack of thorough commitment to Christ. The very genuineness of their faith is at stake.

4—At several points in a speech given by Demosthenes, the eminent Athenian orator takes the Athenians to task for permitting themselves to be deluded by people who serve their own instead of the national interest:

> I could indict Aeschines for ten thousand other items, but let it pass. . . . I could point to many other instances in which this fellow was discovered to be lending aid and comfort to our enemies and at the same time libeling me. But you have no accurate recollection

of these matters, nor do you display appropriate wrath. Instead, through some bad habit of yours, you have bestowed much authority on one who plots to trip up and libel one who seeks your best interests, and thereby you trade off your city's welfare for the pleasure and gratification of being entertained by invective. No wonder that it is always easier and safer to hire oneself out in the service of your enemies than to hold public office and loyally serve the state on your behalf (138).

A few paragraphs later (159), he chides: "I marvel that you did not immediately turn your backs on him when first you saw him. Or is it that some dense darkness hides the truth from you?"

This Hellenic citation demonstrates that an orator can, as also Paul does in v. 4 and elsewhere in chaps. 11–13, safely engage in criticism of the very audience whose goodwill is solicited. The charge that it is unlikely that Paul would have reopened sores which he tried so hard to heal must therefore be viewed within the larger context of ancient rhetorical technique. Paul's rhetorical approach is further seen in his repetition of the verb "bear with" (*anechomai*), alternately rendered **submit to,** which helps frame 11:1-4 in the same manner that the term "commend" highlights the beginning and end of 10:12-18.

With his customary acuteness, Windisch observed that Paul leaves an impression of fullness and completeness through the triad Jesus-Spirit-gospel (cf. Gal. 1:6).

Declaration of Love, and Protest against Rivals (11:5-15)

5-6—Paul begins with an accounting term, "I reckon" (**I think**). The "super" apostles mentioned in v. 5 are probably leaders at Corinth who managed to secure positions of influence in the Corinthian assembly after Paul's initial contacts. Their points of origin cannot be determined. But their points of view have led to confusion at Corinth, and they have raised serious questions about the apostle's personal merits and his lack of sophistication in theological approach (see on 10:10). In rebuttal, Paul says in effect: "I may be an amateur" (**unskilled,** *idiōtēs*) in public speaking compared to them, but I am not in arrears when it comes to **knowledge,** that is, thoughts and ideas relating to the subject in hand." The combination is a subtle satirical thrust. They may have the words, but Paul has the substance behind whatever words he does use. The Corinthians themselves can attest that, says Paul in the second clause of v. 6. In a related vein, Demosthenes told the Athenian audience of his speech *On the Crown* (280) that skill in oratory was less valuable than seeking the best interests of the state.

Paul's self-denigration is, of course, to be taken with reservations. As Betz points out (*Der Apostel,* p. 66), Paul defends himself in keeping with Socratic tradition. In his 12th oration (15), Dio Chrysostom says of himself that in contrast to the sophists he was an "amateur" (*idiōtēs*), and then goes on to say: "My appearance displays no comeliness nor strength. I am past my prime, and I have no disciples. I have pursued no specific art nor science relating to matters sublime or ordinary. Nor have I any skill as a seer or as a sophist, and certainly no special capacity for rhetoric or flattery. . . ." In *Oration* 32.9, Dio declares that his mode of presentation is quite ordinary, but he does not take a back seat in substance. Yet with the same breath Dio emits a golden stream of brilliant oratory. So also Paul displays masterful control of rhetorical technique in passages within which he embeds his self-depreciation. St. Augustine caught the drift of the passage: "We do not say that the apostle's teaching followed his eloquence, but that his eloquence followed his teaching" (*On Christian Doctrine* 4.7).

From the standpoint of ancient rhetorical conceptions this tack by Paul is quite effective. Plutarch states in his essay *On Inoffensive Self-Praise* that it is appropriate to impress one's auditors, especially if they are imprudent, with one's own qualities. Citing Homer (*Odyssey* 12.209-212), he displays Odysseus calming his comrades when they face the foaming waters of Charybdis:

No greater peril is this than when the Cyclops hemmed us with mighty force within his cave. But thence my merit and my brains wrought our escape.

7-8—In one of his refutations of Aeschines, Demosthenes calls attention to the moneys he expended out of his personal fortune on behalf of the state (111-114) and argues that he should not have to undergo scrutiny as to how such donations were spent but should instead receive praise and thanks. For the most part, Paul argues along similar lines in vv. 7-11.

There is no indication that the opposition charged Paul with moral deficiency. Paul's question is a piece of sharp irony. The expression *hamartēma,* which is rendered **sin** by the RSV, is stated ironically, with Paul in effect asking: "Am I to be charged with a crime because I put your interests ahead of mine?" He addresses the Corinthians at their deepest cultural-political-economic level—the reciprocity system. Throughout the letter he has rung changes on it and uses it to model the beneficence of God as exhibited in and through Jesus Christ. At the same time he has cast himself in the role of benefactor to the Corinthians by emphasizing that they owe the transmission of the message about the divine bounty to his faithful service as an apostle. In turn, he has invited the Corinthians to bolster the reputation they already had throughout the Christian world (see 3:1-3) by completing their pledge to aid the poor in Jerusalem. Now, as he moves into the climactic defense of his apostolate among them, he asks, "How can you be so ungrateful to one who has labored so selflessly in your midst?"

Anyone in the Greco-Roman world knows that the mark of a benefactor is to bestow bounties freely (*dōrean*). In praise of a secretary named Apelles it is stated that he served his superiors without payment. A citizen of Perga named Tiberius Claudius Apollonios Elaibabes served as envoy to Rome, and for his services that were freely rendered three different times he received grateful recognition from his city. Adrastus, a loyal supporter of Tiberius Caesar, not only served without charge as gymnasiarch and priest, but also picked up the tab that his responsibilities entailed (*Benefactor,* p. 333).

According to some traditions, Socrates refused to accept honoraria. In the *Memorabilia* (1.6.10) Xenophon cites Socrates' theological basis for such financial disinterest: "To be in need of nothing, I consider something divine; and to be in need of as little as possible is closest to the divine. Now it is agreed that the divine is the most powerful thing there is. Therefore, that which is closest to the divine is the most powerful." In 1 Cor. 9:18 Paul stated that he had served the Corinthians at no expense to them, that is, beyond the ordinary expressions of hospitality. Through the present reminder Paul reinforces his role as their benefactor.

As Paul noted in 1 Cor. 1:26, not many at Corinth were numbered among the "wise according to worldly standards," nor among the "powerful" and those of "noble birth." For the most part the Corinthian members were made up of slaves and tradespeople. By plying a trade, that of tentmaker (Acts 18:3), Paul identified with the greater part of the constituency. Some of the few members of higher social status might have thought that Paul's engagement in such labor was demeaning and therefore embarrassing to the Christian community. But it is highly questionable whether the majority of the members would have thought ill of Paul on this score. Nor is there any indication in 2 Cor. 10:1 that he had such criticism in mind. Moreover, 2 Cor. 10:8 is a declarative counterpart to the rhetorical question of v. 7, not a second defensive maneuver. With tongue in cheek, he says, **I robbed other churches . . . to serve you.** That is, if you want to charge me with some crime, then make it larceny.

Some commentators have suggested that Paul here takes account of a charge that he has violated customs relating to patron-client relationships. As Furnish states the case (pp. 507-508), patrons are benefactors and have a right to expect expressions of gratitude from their clients. In the case at hand, it is argued, the Corinthians are the patrons and Paul the client, but he fails to honor the relationship, for he refuses to accept gifts from the Corinthians. The basic error in this assessment is the assumption that Paul is the client at Corinth. On the contrary, Paul styles himself as benefactor of the Corinthians. Climaxing a recital of his virtues, together with the crises or "peristaseis" that he had undergone on behalf of the Corinthians, he stated that he enriched many (6:3-10), including of course the Corinthians. Moreover, there is no evidence that the Corinthians pleaded for opportunity to underwrite the apostle's support. On the other hand, to judge from the precautions Paul takes in respect to the collection (8:20), had he accepted such assistance his detractors would probably have been waiting in the wings to pounce on him for alleged greed. Certainly he did not hesitate to express his right to recompense, but he did not do so as a suppliant client (1 Cor. 9:4-7). If anything, the Corinthians are the clients of Paul, and it is they who are guilty of ingratitude, which is at the very least a horrendous faux pas in the Greco-Roman world. In general, it must be observed that all patrons are benefactors, but not all benefactors are patrons with a coterie of the type of client one would find in Rome. It is hazardous to engage in Greco-Roman social exploration without keeping a variety of data in perspective.

The basic fact is that Paul is an envoy of Jesus Christ, and in the Greco-Roman world it is understood that an envoy of a city or head of state ought not to be a burden in the locality that he visits. An inscription from Dionysopolis, modern Baltschik, near Sofia, accurately reflects the cultural aspects relating to the behavior of envoys in the Greco-Roman world. Acornion, a priest of the "Great Deity," may be said to model Paul's own portrait. In the priest's honor it was decreed that he deserved special recognition because

> he gives himself unsparingly in his repeated role as envoy for our city, and shrinks from no danger in his determination to accomplish whatever might be advantageous to the city. . . . And in general, by risking body and soul in every perilous circumstance, and by defraying expenses (for public service) out of his own estate and even contributing money to help the city meet its financial obligations, he continues to demonstrate exceptional zeal for the welfare of his home city.
>
> (*Benefactor*, pp. 77-78)

Acornion is a benefactor par excellence. And the principal features of his exceptional character and performance are his willingness to endure any hazard on behalf of his city and to pay all expenses out of his own estate. These two features highlight Paul's own service as the envoy of Christ (2 Cor. 6:3-10 and 11:5-11).

Paul's word for **support** is *opsōnion*, a reference to the soldier's daily ration. In 1 Cor. 9:7 he had asked, "Who serves as a soldier at his own expense?" Through his military metaphor Paul suggests that he is on campaign for Christ.

9—In view of the satirical vein of most of chap. 11, it is probable that the Greek word *katanarkaō* (used twice in 12:13-14), which underlies the rendering **I did not burden any one,** is to be understood colloquially in the sense of "knock out" or "shake down." Or, to change the figure, Paul did not take the Corinthians to the cleaners. He was no sponger. See also 12:15-16. In the RSV's second sentence for this verse, the word **burdening** renders the Greek adjective *abarēs*, meaning "without being burdensome." Paul's stress on his unwillingness to be a burden reflects a common motif in official documents. For example, in a letter written by a colony of Tyrians at Puteoli, the senders appeal to their home city to assume some of the costs for public services that the Tyrian guild of merchants in Puteoli have assumed; but they assure their compatriots that they will accept responsibility for repair of an office building in time for the celebration of the emperor's birthday, "so that we might not burden the city" (*hina mē tēn polin barōmen*)" (*OGI* 595.15). It is a foregone conclusion that benefactors do not oppress those whom they ostensibly serve. Of Opramoas it was publicized that "he promised to pay out of his own funds for the erection of the statues that were voted him and which were to be set up in cities of his choice; for not even in this matter did he wish to have the province burdened" (*Benefactor,* p. 124; see also pp. 334-345).

Paul's reference to the Macedonians could not fail to bring the addressees up short. Here they were once more faced with the magnanimous poverty-ridden Macedonians (see chaps. 8–9). As in 9:12, Paul refers to the meeting of needs. To a modern reader it might appear that Paul is rubbing salt in wounds. But the Greco-Roman viewpoint is to be kept in mind. It is a mark of good breeding and in accordance with custom to recognize benefactions. This is the flip side of the reciprocity system. Again, the decree in honor of Acornion reflects consensus on this score in the resolution that concludes the document:

> Therefore, in order that all might know that the People (of Dionysopolis) honor such wonderful human beings who prove to be their benefactors, be it resolved by the Council and the Assembly, that Akornion . . . be awarded a golden crown and a bronze likeness. . . .

In and through his reference to the Macedonians, the Corinthians would hear Paul saying that he knows how to express gratitude. And they would be expected to say to themselves, "But do *we* know how?" Appeal to a sense of shame was a telling maneuver in the Mediterranean world, and Paul makes the most of the opportunity that it offers.

Having once again affirmed his unselfish concern for the Corinthians, Paul brings some of his heaviest rhetorical artillery to bear on his opponents in vv. 12-21.

10—At one point in his speech *On the Crown* (141), Demosthenes cries out:

> In your presence, O men of Athens, I invoke all the gods and goddesses who make the land of Attica their own, and also Pythian Apollo . . ., and I beseech them all, if I speak truth to you, . . . to grant me good fortune and salvation; but if out of hatred or personal animosity I am bringing a false charge against him (Aeschines), I pray that they deprive me of acquaintance with any blessings.

Paul does not outswear Demosthenes, but it is significant that oaths are more common in 2 Corinthians, which reflects numerous rhetorical techniques used by the ancient orator, than in any other Pauline letter (see 2 Cor. 1:18, 23; 2:10; 11:11, 31; Rom. 1:9; 9:1; Gal. 1:20; Phil. 1:8; 1 Thess. 2:5, 10).

From time to time Demosthenes punctuates his speech *On the Crown* with boasts about his many services to Athens. Like the ancient Greek orator, Paul knows how to use an incisive boast. To modern ears such indulgence in self-praise is cause for censure, but it is necessary to heed the ancient assessment. As Plutarch pointed out (see above on 6:3-10), the defense of one's good name or the refutation of an accusation does not elicit resentment.

11—Near the end of his speech titled *On the Crown* (322), Demosthenes says to his audience:

> See for yourselves. Not when I was asked to surrender, not when they brought Amphictyonic suits against me, not when they made me proposals, not when they sent these accursed adversaries against me like wild beasts, never for a moment did I betray my loyalty for you.

With no less protestation of concern for the welfare of the Corinthians, Paul's second oath within two verses confirms his loyalty
to the Corinthians.

Such demonstration of Paul's affection would have made a
strong impact on his addressees. Also near the end of the speech
On the Crown (291), Demosthenes criticizes Aeschines for his
lack of passion. "I marveled most of all," he says, "when in the
course of speaking about the misfortunes that had befallen the
city (of Athens) he did not have the attitude that any upright
citizen of goodwill would have manifested: he did not shed a tear;
he did not show so much as a flicker of emotion."

12-15—The governing feature of these verses is Paul's attack
on the integrity of his opposition. But it derives from the intense
affection for the Corinthians that he affirmed at v. 11. Similarly
Demosthenes, who made a fetish of patriotism, stripped his opponents of all prestige. After reciting his extensive contributions
as a benefactor to Athens, Demosthenes denigrates Aeschines by
describing his pitiful attempts at public service. The best he can
do is outfit a third-rate religious association (259-260).

And near the end of his speech Demosthenes climaxes a roll
call of traitors with these words:

> Caught in the mire, parasites who merit swift destruction, mutilators
> of their own homelands, men who have squandered our liberty in
> a toast to Philip and now to Alexander, men who measure happiness
> by their bellies and by all that is most shameful as they dismantle
> liberty and the right of Hellenes to control their own destinies—
> rights that our ancestors knew to be the definitions and standards
> of all that is most highly prized (296).

The dark hues that Demosthenes here uses for the portrait of his
opponents build up into a Vesuvian explosion of volcanic rhetoric
that prepares the gallery for the Athenian orator's picture of his
own patriotic performance (314-323). Comparison of character,
with the tilt in one's own favor, was a common device in ancient
oratory. Writers on rhetorical theory classed it as *sygkrisis* (syncrisis). Paul similarly prepares his addressees for his performance
record in 11:22—12:18.

Paul's opening clause, **And what I do I will continue to do,** refers to his refusal to accept honoraria from the Corinthians. From his concluding statement of purpose one can understand both his many boasts of service to the Corinthians and his attack on the integrity of those who are jeopardizing the apostle's ministry in Corinth.

The RSV's rendering of the second portion of v. 12 does not convey the colloquial tone and wordplay present in Paul's statement: "I'm going to keep on doing what I've been doing. My aim is to cut off the 'assets' of those who would like to have 'assets' so that they can boast about their activities and win credit for being what we claim to be, namely, your benefactors."

The opening clause refers to Paul's total manner of life involving the Corinthians, especially as described in vv. 1-11, where he exposes his innermost feelings for the members. Continuance in such warm concern for them, including his refusal to accept honoraria, is the basis of his boast that no one can more legitimately claim to be their benefactor. Others—and he will describe them shortly—endeavor to project themselves as such. But Paul is determined that no one shall outscore him in beneficence; for, as v. 2 affirmed, he feels "a divine jealousy" for them. By not changing his pattern of zealous interest in the Corinthians, Paul will **undermine** the efforts of his opponents to denigrate him and project themselves as benefactors of the Corinthians. The contrast between Paul and them would tell the tale. The RSV's rendering of the Greek term *aphormē* with **claim** fails to bring out Paul's wordplay. Demosthenes (21.98) used the term in its central sense when he advised the jury to "deprive Meidios of any occasion (*aphormē*) for boasting." Paul's use of the term in application to his opponents is remarkably similar, but in the context of 2 Cor. 11:5-21, with its recurring economic imagery, the term *aphormē* would have been understood in one of its common commercial senses, "assets," as well as in the sense of "opportunity" and "occasion." The "assets" of the opposition include their self-acclaimed apostolic superiority and intellectual-spiritual sophistication. On these they pride themselves and make their boast. The point of comparison, then, is the contribution of assets to the Corinthians. Paul's contribution includes picking up the tab for his expenses at Corinth. The contribution of his opponents consists, as Paul satirically points out, among other things, in hoodwinking and enslaving the Corinthian constituency (11:4, 20). This is the kind of stuff on which they build their boasts of superior apostleship. And they hope to win the same kind of credit for that as the apostle does for his kind of performance. The RSV obscures the point made by the apostle by rendering the Greek word *heuriskō* with the expression **work on . . . terms.** The term *heuriskō* is used frequently by the apostle to express the idea of being subject to scrutiny, frequently with a view to determining genuineness of projected character (cf. 12:20, "find" something out about someone; 1 Cor. 4:2, "found trustworthy"; 15:15, "found to be misrepresenting God"; Gal. 2:17, "found to be sinners"). In sum, Paul claims that he has a right to call himself an apostle of Jesus Christ, for he demonstrates the claim in all his performance relative to the Corinthians. His opponents have no similar right to call themselves apostles. The door is now rhetorically open, first, for the statements in vv. 13-15 concerning the spurious credentials of Paul's opponents, and second, for the rest of Apostle Paul's "Fool's Speech."

The term **false apostles** refers to people who falsely claim to be apostles, that is, who have no right to call themselves apostles. The underlying Greek word (*pseudapostoloi*) follows the form of a term for "false prophets" (*pseudoprophētai*). According to Gal. 1:16, God gave Paul the status of envoy to the nations, and a trio of Christian leaders in Jerusalem—James, Cephas, and John—recognized that jurisdiction (Gal. 2:9), and Paul refuses to budge in claiming his right, especially since, as he had explained in 2 Cor. 10:12-18, he had been the first to bring the gospel to Corinth. In brief, Paul's opposition makes a false claim to administration of the Corinthians' spiritual fortunes. Paul has God and Jerusalem on his side.

Paul further characterizes his opponents as deceitful **workmen;** that is, by interfering in Paul's territory they violate the contractual principles which were recognized at Jerusalem. Instead of being zealous for the best interest of the Corinthians, they seek their own glory. Although the term "workman" (*ergatēs*) is elsewhere applied in a good sense to Christ's envoys (Matt. 9:37, 38; Luke 10:2), it is probable that Paul here uses the term with a

173

satirical bite. They expect remuneration; Paul does not! Also, they appear to claim special credentials from Christ himself, perhaps through visions, and thus bypass the support that Paul received from Jerusalem. Paul labels such effort as an attempt at disguise. Paul himself received revelations, but he does not put them on the top of his curriculum vitae or résumé (12:1-5) for the purpose of accrediting his embassage.

14-15—Since the claims of the bogus apostles apparently include extraordinary communications, which would merit the classification of miracles, Paul caustically observes: "No miracle at all!" (**And no wonder,** *kai ou thauma*) Why? "Satan does it all the time. It's no big trick, then, if his assistants are disguised as upright assistants (**servants**)." But, Apostle Paul concludes, **Their end** *(telos)* **will correspond to their deeds;** that is, "They will get what they deserve" (cf. Phil. 3:19; 1 Thess. 2:16; Rom. 2:6; 3:8; Gal. 5:10). The term **deeds** *(erga)* in part echoes the word for "worker" *(ergatēs)* in v. 13. As Windisch noted, Philo terminates a long list of vices with the verdict that they "result *(hōn ta telē)* in terribly heavy losses to body and soul" *(On the Virtues* 182). The "works" of Paul's opponents comprise especially their specious claims and meddling in Paul's jurisdiction.

The legend of Satan's imitation of an **angel of light** appears in two noncanonical works. According to *The Life of Adam and Eve* (9), Eve was advised by Adam to engage in a penitential rite in the river Tigris. Eighteen days passed. Then Satan, filled with anger, "assumed angelic brightness," came to Eve, and with clever words about divine mercy persuaded her to interrupt her stay in the water. The *Apocalypse of Moses* (17) picks up the same motif. The connecting link between Satan as an "angel" and the "false apostles" is the fact that the Greek words *(angelos* and *apostolos)* underlying both expressions make reference to one who is officially sent on a mission.

Credentials and Crises (11:16-33)

16—The dazzling scope of Paul's wit is exhibited in the concluding portion of the chapter. The false apostles have put on their masks. Now Paul readjusts the fool's mask: **I repeat** (cf.

v. 1). He does not like the role, for engagement in self-praise is a hazardous game, but his opponents, and the readiness of some members to be impressed by their apparent prestige, have forced him to go through with the charade. In this disclaimer about interest in boasting, Paul's addressees would be conscious of popular reaction against such exhibitionism. Pindar proclaimed that "untimely boasting is in tune with madness" (*Olympian* 9.38). At the beginning of his speech titled *On the Crown* (3), Demosthenes declares that he is at a disadvantage compared to Aeschines, because an audience is not appreciative of people who praise themselves. Plutarch expands on the matter in his essay titled *On Inoffensive Self-Praise* (539d):

> First of all, we conclude that those who praise themselves have no sense of shame, for we expect some display of modesty even when they are praised by others. Second, it is not right to take for oneself what one ought to give to others. Finally, if we listen in silence to such praise, we think that we may appear to be resentful and envious; or, fearing that, we compel ourselves, in a manner contrary to our own verdict on the praise, to lend our support and attestation, a procedure that is more appropriate to slavish flattery than to display of esteem.

But the Hellenic sense of balance showed itself also in connection with this social phenomenon by validating a place for self-praise. Plutarch (540a-c) continues:

> Admittedly praise has no merit in the case of those who expect to gain further praise by praising themselves, and it is especially despised when rivalry for honor and earning of untimely glory are behind it. . . . But no one can be blamed for engaging in self-praise when one does it to refute calumny or false accusation.

Then, citing the example of Pericles, who defended himself against detractors by calling attention to his patriotic record, Plutarch (540c-d) goes on to say:

> Not only did Pericles escape a charge of arrogance and vanity and ambition by speaking about himself in such lofty tones, but he demonstrated sound judgment and singular greatness of person.

175

The RSV's rendering of the second part of this verse suggests that Paul contradicts himself in the same sentence. But the colloquial form of Paul's jagged prose must again be taken into account. The entire verse runs along these lines: "I repeat, I would rather not be considered a fool. But whatever your conclusions are, for the moment accept me as one so that I can take my turn at boasting."

Windisch cites a parallel from Plato's *Symposion* (212e). Alcibiades appears on the scene wreathed in ivy and says,

> "Cheers, my friends. Here I am, your drinking companion, and one who is rather drunk. . . . But I have come, wearing fillets on my head so I can put some of them on the head of the wisest and fairest head that's here. You'll probably laugh at me because I'm drunk. Go ahead. But I swear it's true."

17-18—These verses contain the following pattern of thought: "Now, in this boastful undertaking (*hypostasis*), what I am about to say is not to be understood from my stance as a Christian, from the Lord's perspective, but as something spoken from the perspective of folly." The rendering "undertaking" is preferable to the RSV's **confidence** (see on 9:4). In other words, if Paul were to keep the Lord strictly in mind, he would never brag as he is about to do in vv. 22-33. But circumstances have forced him into it.

The phrase **of worldly things** (*kata sarka*), in v. 18, is formally similar to the Greek expression behind the RSV's rendering **with the Lord's authority** (*kata kyrion*), in v. 17, and includes boasting in terms of ancestral values, a point which Paul will pursue at v. 22. The verse may be rendered: "So many others are boasting strictly from a human perspective that I am going to enter the contest."

19-20—Since Paul's addressees are quick to put up with exploiters (cf. v. 4), he had suggested (v. 1) that they could afford to put up with some of his antics. Now he expands on the kinds of exploitation they patiently accept. Ordinarily a speaker would flatter an audience for their intelligence. Thus, Dio Chrysostom (12.14) credits one of his audiences with superior understanding.

Paul gives the familiar rhetorical ploy a twist by injecting an arresting bit of satirical wordplay: "You brainy people (*phronimoi*) are delighted to put up with the brainless (*aphrones*)."

Windisch notes the similarity between the chiding by Paul and Ananus's rebuke of his compatriots during the revolt against Rome. Josephus reports that Ananus berated his compatriots for "putting up (*anechomai*) with seizure and being silent in the face of personal assault" (*War* 4.3.10 [165]).

Paul's fivefold repetition of the conjunction **if** (*ei*) is rendered four times by **or**. The rhetorical effect in the original is devastating: "You people put up with anything and everything!" Paul's diction is dramatically vivid. Paul's description is expressed in verbs, but in corresponding nouns the opposition consists of slavers, gluttons, pocket-stuffers, swaggerers, and face-slappers.

Since Paul is here engaging in the rhetorical sport of invective, it is imprudent to find a specific referent in the Corinthians' congregational experience for each of the verbs. Any policies or approaches that detract from Jesus Christ as the center of God's action in dealing with the people of God spell enslavement. To use the people of God as nourishment for one's own objectives and personal agendas is tantamount to ecclesiastical gluttony. To make others adherents of oneself rather than Christ is to take advantage of, or to grab for oneself, those who seek to serve Christ. To be entranced with one's ecclesiastical importance means to swagger or put on airs. To treat the members of God's family primarily as instruments for achieving institutional goals and objectives is equivalent to slapping them in the face.

By sketching the opposition in this way, Paul leaves it open for the Corinthians to judge his own performance among them. Far from enslaving them, he is *their* slave (4:5). Far from devouring them, he has served without fee (11:7). He does not grab them; he liberates them (4:15). He does not swagger, for all his confidence is in God (1:9). And far from slapping the Corinthians in the face, he carries them in his heart (3:2).

On the whole, Paul's words are a recital of ecclesiastical masochism. But the principal rhetorical feature is the brilliant inverted use that Paul makes of the Corinthians' cultural history. As has been frequently noted in this commentary, the reciprocity

177

system dominates Greco-Roman society. The Corinthians, *mirabile dictu*, wonder of wonders, view their oppressors as benefactors!

21a—The words **to my shame** (*atimia*) suggest that what the apostle is about to say redounds not on the credit side for honorary citation but on the debit. To be held in honor (*timē*) meant that one would be recognized for contributions to the public. A "dishonorable" person in Greco-Roman society is one who contributes nothing of positive value to the city. Paul's self-denigration is, of course, satirical, and rhetorically effective. It is the Corinthians who ought to be ashamed over their ingratitude toward Paul their benefactor.

The entire line of attack in 16-21 is especially effective for its indirect attack on his opposition through description of the Corinthians' tolerance of exploitation and for his satirical self-depreciation as a nonbenefactor figure. From the Corinthians' perspective, he argues, people who exploit others are benefactors. If that is the case, he, Paul, can be no benefactor, for he refuses to exploit those under his care.

The key word in Paul's satire is, "we were too weak for that" (*ēsthenēkamen*), an allusion to the criticism that was recorded at 10:10, but here used with a new twist. The apostle's satirical self-denigration is akin to a thrust delivered by Demosthenes against Aeschines. After attacking him on his alleged traitorous policies, Demosthenes says, "I confess it. I am weak, but all the more loyal than you to my fellow citizens" (*On the Crown* 320). In related vein, Dio Chrysostom (12.13) tells an audience gathered at the Olympic Games in the year 97: "I lack the courage to lie and deceive when I promise something."

Paul's own self-denigration now provides a take-off point for his *peristasis* or description of "weakness" in vv. 23-33.

21b—The Greek term for **boast** (*tolmaō*) echoes usage in 10:12. Paul's use of the term reflects the caution that Demosthenes also uses at a point in his speech *On the Crown* (68), when he sketches, for the sake of argument, an improbable scenario for patriotic Athenians. The apostle continues to speak in the vein of a fool, but his rhetorical ploy makes possible the use of standard topics drawn from his social context.

To demonstrate his rightful claim to the Corinthians' respect, in the middle of v. 21 Paul begins to recite his pedigree in some detail. This rhetorical tack is, of course, taken under the duress described in v. 16.

The rhetorician Hermogenes (*Progymnasmata* 7) called attention to long-standing tradition, when he noted that honorary speeches should include references to distinguished places of birth and ancestry. Pindar makes repeated use of the motif in his praise of athletes (see, e.g., *Pythian* 8.35-42; *Nemean* 6; 11.33-43; *Isthmian* 3.13-14; 4.7-12).

The point is not merely to be able to boast of higher status, but that one's behavior is in keeping with high standards that have been set in time past. As Pericles put it in a funeral oration delivered at Athens in the course of a war with Sparta, "not privilege but the rendering of public service is our city's standard for recognition of merit" (Thucydides 2.37.1). Paul acts in accordance with the model of performance set by his ancestors. This is a common motif in honorary documents. Thus the city of Mantinea commends a citizen named Euphrosynos, who "did not besmirch his ancestors' reputation for excellence, but continally augmented it and daily gave thought as to how he might do something further for his city, all the while displaying gentility in his habits and showing a spaciousness of spirit beyond the gift of nature" (*SIG*[3] 9-12).

Similarly Demosthenes attacks Aeschines for introducing irrelevant matter, such as personal attack, into the proceedings:

Consider, if you will, his libelous portrayal of my private life and see for yourselves how simply and fairly I address the matter. If indeed you know me to be the kind of person he alleges—my life among you has been open for all to see—then by all means refrain from hearing another sound from me, even if you must grant that I have earned the highest marks for my public life among you, and forthwith rise up and pronounce your verdict—now! But if I in your judgment and understanding am a far better person than this fellow and can boast a better lineage, and if I and mine are in no way inferior to our general populace—no offense intended—then do not give credence to this man; and this applies to his other assertions, for it is clear that all have been alike contrived by him (10).

22—Instead of saying, "I am a Jew," which none of his detractors would deny, Paul affirms aspects of Jewishness that run the hazard of being the basis for the arrogance and expression of superiority that he exposed at v. 20. If the detractors claim that he is more Hellenized than Jewish, Paul counters, "I speak Hebrew with the best of them." If they boast of their identity as Israelites, the people of God with a mission to the world, Paul says, "I do not take second place." With the reference to Abraham he trumps all their genetic cards.

23—Paul takes just pride in being a benefactor of the Corinthians but, contrary to his better judgment (v. 16), he is compelled to brag about it. In this verse the main truth comes out. Paul's opponents consider themselves the most qualified to carry out the mission of the Servant of the Lord, as specified, for example, in Isaiah 49. Paul's answer to this is vehement: "That blows my mind. I have to tell you, I outrank them all on that score."

Paul referred to himself at 3:6 as a "servant (*diakonos*) of a new covenant," and at 6:4 as a "servant of God." And, as he is about to narrate in vv. 23-29, he has a mile-long record of performance beyond the call of duty to prove it. The fact that suffering is a principal feature of the servant-figure in Isaiah, especially chap. 53, offers Paul an easy transition to his recital of performance far beyond the call of duty. At the same time he is able to meet standard Greco-Roman perceptions of what constitutes exceptional personhood. As was pointed out in connection with 2 Cor. 6:3-10, an impressive topic in Greco-Roman recitals of distinguished performance was the "endangered benefactor" who comes through a perilous circumstance or "peristasis." The specific ordeal can therefore be called a peristatic recital. Moreover, such accounts appear in autobiographical as well as biographical documents. In his speech titled *On the Crown* (173), Demosthenes boasts about his loyalty to Athens in a time of dire peril:

> I want you to know that I alone of all who addressed you on matters of policy did not in peril's hour abandon my post of loyalty to the state. No, I was there, speaking and writing, in the very midst of terrors, what was to your best interests.

Later in the same speech (249) he describes some of the opposition he encountered from political opponents:

> My opponents joined forces with those who had made up their minds
> to do me damage. They drew up indictments, inquiries, impeach-
> ments—all of it, but not at first under their own signatures, for they
> sought anonymity behind intermediaries. . . . They left nothing un-
> tried against me. But in all these hazards I was saved, thanks first
> of all to the gods, but also to you and to the rest of the Athenians.

By making such a similar recital about himself Paul does not in
fact violate canons of good taste, for instead of praising himself,
he recites what he has endured from others. It is a capital rhetorical maneuver. For at the end Paul will, in the judgment of
the Corinthians, be standing firmly on his feet as a distinguished
benefactor who has endured so much for the sake of the gospel.

The payment of a costly personal price for involvement in the
gospel mission is expressed in a fourfold list that echoes 4:7-18
and compares Paul's hazard-ridden life with that of his opposition.
"In trials and troubles frequently, in custody frequently, under
countless blows, close to death many times." The first item is a
general term that describes the wear and tear and general perils
associated with his mission labors (cf. vv. 27-28). The second refers
to incarceration, of which Acts 16:23-40 cites one example. The
third refers to blows that he endured under various circumstances, including some of the times when he was under arrest
(cf. vv. 24-25; Acts 16:23). The reference to death is expressed
in the plural ("in deaths many times"), perhaps in allusion especially to hazards undergone in the course of numerous sea
journeys (cf. v. 25; 1 Cor. 4:9; Acts 27); the plural form in this
sense is well established in Hellenic usage.

24—Paul's reference to **Jews** is not a general indictment, for
he writes "by Jews," not "by the Jews." Some Jews whipped him
at five different times (Paul's use of the phrase "the Jews" in 1
Thess. 2:14 is more general). This reference to Jews comes as a
touching note after Paul's affirmation of his ethnic identity. Paul
is accustomed to attacks from within the family. By keeping under
the limit of **forty lashes,** an effort was made to avoid degrading

the offender (Deut. 25:1-3). Josephus (*Antiquities* 4.8.21) is aware of the problem and terms the lashing a "most disgraceful punishment."

In connection with Paul's mode of narration, Anton Fridrichsen calls attention to the *Res Gestae*, in which Caesar Augustus repeatedly made use of numerals in reference to his achievements (see *Benefactor*, pp. 259-60, 265).

25—Paul's reference to a beating with **rods** has in mind the Roman custom of punishment meted out at the hands of officials called "lictors," who carried wooden rods with which they inflicted the blows. Acts 16:22, which has the same term (*hrabdizein*) that Paul uses, is the only passage that provides details of such a punishment in Paul's career. See also 1 Cor. 4:11. According to Roman law, such a punishment was not to be inflicted on a Roman citizen, as Paul was, but some Roman magistrates were on occasion as lax in support of consitutional rights as their counterparts at a latter day in the United States. Heinrici cites Cicero (*Against Verres* 2.62 [162]) in reference to a Roman citizen from Messina who cried out, "I am a Roman citizen," and yet was beaten.

Stoning was a Jewish procedure that ordinarily was terminal for the victim. For details see Deut. 17:5-7; 22:22-25. Acts 7:58-59 records the formal stoning of Stephen in Saul's presence. Since judicial stoning would result in death, the stonings referred to by Paul were probably mob actions, like the ones recited in Acts 14:5, 19, and which Paul managed to survive.

Acts 27 carries the only report of a shipwreck that involved Paul, and this one occurred later than the writing of 2 Corinthians. As Windisch notes, Paul's account is similar in some respects to one recorded by Josephus in his autobiography (3.13-15). At the age of 26, the Jewish historian went on a voyage to Rome, in the course of which the ship on which he was traveling, with about 600 aboard, sank, but Josephus and about 80 others swam all the night and managed to reach another ship.

26-28—Paul continues his "autobiography of perils" with a list of miscellaneous hazards encountered in the course of his frequent journeys in connection with his mission work. The phrase **frequent journeys** is to be taken as a heading for the experiences that follow, which are set forth in the rhetorical figure known as anaphora, with the noun **danger** appearing eight times in v. 26, and two prepositions being used a total of 10 times in vv. 26-27. The effect is one of an avalanche of suffering that climaxes in rhetorical questions in v. 29.

Rivers could be swollen from rains and hazardous for other reasons. Paul's comment about **robbers** deserves consideration in the light of an evaluation by Epictetus (3.13.9): "In our judgment Caesar appears to be responsible for unusual security, for we are no longer bothered with wars, battles, nor uncontrolled brigandage nor piracy; on the contrary, one can travel at any hour of the day, or sail from sunup to sundown." From other sources one can conclude that the Roman presence ensured a more general sense of security than the world had ever experienced under other political conditions, but brigandage, as Epictetus's carefully phrased description acknowledges, remained a hazard in some localities.

Paul's reference to hazards from his **own people** is amplified repeatedly in Acts, which includes numerous accounts of Paul's expulsion from synagogues and threats to his person (see Acts 9:20-29; 13:44-45; 14:1-6, 19-20; 17:5-9; 18:6-17).

Acts suggests that hostility against Paul **from Gentiles** was infrequent, but Luke's otherwise sketchy treatment of Paul's experiences does not permit one to draw hard and fast conclusions. In any case, for the period under discussion, see Acts 16:19-24.

The reference to **false brethren** ("false brothers and sisters") again contributes a touching note. Dangers from robbers, towering waves, and swollen rivers Paul took in stride. But insincerity within the fellowship cut him deeply.

In the phrase **toil and hardship**—a combination or doublet known in rhetoric as *synonymia*—lurks an echo of 1 Thess. 2:9. The end-rhyme of the Greek expression adds to the pathos. Whether Paul refers to his labors as a tentmaker or merely generalizes about his intense absorption in the cause of the gospel cannot be determined. The words **through many a sleepless night** recall 6:5, but it is not possible to determine specifically what caused them. Yet some indication of Paul's restlessness can be gleaned from his remarks in 2 Cor. 7:5.

The expression **hunger and thirst** may refer to hardships

brought on by famine and drought in the areas where he traveled. Such times as well as others, including shipwreck, exposed him to hunger (**often without food,** cf. 6:5).

Traveling of the sort described by Paul would include bone-chilling exposure to the elements. Many ancient letters include requests for garments, and a later letter ascribed to Paul puts in such a plea (2 Tim. 4:13). Epictetus (3.22.45) asked: "And how can one who has nothing, one who is naked, without a home or hearth, in squalor, without a slave in attendance, and without a city, live without a care?" One of Paul's numerous answers is recorded in 2 Cor. 4:11.

Some conception of what Paul means by the **pressure** involved in care of God's assemblies may be gleaned from the numerous replies he makes to questions that have been addressed to him on various matters. Paul was much in demand for advice, and the correspondence that has survived under his name is only a small percentage of what he must have produced. Also, the numerous miles that Paul covered to serve his constituency at Corinth are some indication of the large investment of time he spent in follow-up ministry. Luke's book of Acts provides further commentary on this aspect of Paul's missionary responsibility.

29—In this verse Paul provides specific examples of the kinds of problems that took up his administrative time. Paul cares deeply for his converts. He was not one to say, "I can't get too personally involved." Out of such concern derives his uncompromising resistance to any dilution of the gospel. In short, he is their benefactor, and his recital has been the story of an endangered benefactor. As Windisch notes, Cicero wrote along similar lines (*In Behalf of Archia 6.14*):

> For unless I had been persuaded from my earliest youth by the precepts of many, and by many writings, that there was nothing in life of such importance as the glory of an honorable life, but that in the pursuit thereof, one must experience excruciating bodily pains and constant peril of death and exile, I would never have exposed myself in the interest of your safety to such tremendous risks as are involved in the daily attacks of these wicked men.

Similarly, Seneca (*Consolation of Polybius* 7:2) says of Caesar:

> Caesar can have anything he wishes, but for this very reason many things are denied to him. His wakefulness provides sound sleep for all others; his toil releases all others from their burdens; his labor brings enjoyment to all others; his industry spells time off for all others.

Paul's recital of hazards, as pointed out above on 6:3-10, is not an isolated phenomenon in the world of his time. Statecrafters were fond of reciting hazards endured in behalf of their constituencies, and ability to endure perils was expected of anyone who presumed to qualify for recognition as a person of exceptional merit. Since philosophers, following the line of Socrates, liked to think of themselves as the ultimate benefactors of humanity, the *peristasis* found a place in philosophical writing. Thus, Epictetus (3.24-29) explains that a budding philosopher must not expect a life of ease, for our very environment and people with whom we must associate are such that one can expect the following: "cold and heat, inadequate diet, travel by land and sea, winds and all manner of perils. One person they destroy, another they drive into exile; one they send out as an envoy, another they draft for the army." Dio Chrysostom (8.16) wrote in the same vein.

30-33—It is probable that Paul's opponents criticized Paul for what appeared to be a skin-saving exit from Damascus. With tongue in cheek Paul swears (see on v. 10) that he does not lie— an apparent thrust against charges that Paul covers up some of his more embarrassing activities and at the same time a jab at the "false apostles" (see vv. 13-15). He therefore turns his undignified departure from Damascus into another exhibit of his status as a benefactor to the people of God, but only after celebrating God as the Supreme Benefactor, **who is blessed forever.**

In connection with Paul's unusual method of escape, some of his addressees who knew the Bible would have recollected the story of the two spies who had been let down through an aperture in the wall of Jericho under the guidance of Rahab (Joshua 2). David's wife Michal used a similar tactic to rescue the future king of Israel from Saul's assassins (1 Sam. 19:11-12). Wettstein cites numerous examples of similar escapes. Athenaeus (5.52, p. 214a) says of an Athenian ruler that he had posted guards at the gates, for many of the Athenians had premonitions of what was going to happen and were escaping by letting themselves down from the walls. Plutarch (*Aemilius Paulus* 26. 269a) relates that Perseus of Macedonia was forced to let himself and his family down from the city walls through a narrow window; the biographer notes that it was an unaccustomed hardship for a family that had been brought up to enjoy the soft life.

Far from ending on a note that would suggest humiliation or disgrace, this story confirms that Paul, not the adversaries, is ultimately in the right. Paul did not run away from a responsibility. As many a great leader before him, he was prepared to endure incredible hazards on behalf of his constituency. Of Julius Caesar it was said that his ability to endure hardships beyond normal human endurance astonished his soldiers. Paul challenges his opponents to match his own record. Suetonius (*Julius Caesar* 64) records that Caesar was once engaged in attacking a bridge at Alexandria. A sudden assault by the enemy forced him to take refuge in a small boat, but when many others tried the same tactic, he plunged into the waters and swam about 200 paces, all the time holding up some papers with his left hand and with his teeth pulling his cloak, to keep it out of the hands of the enemy. In the face of insurmountable odds, Paul survives—not by his wits, but, as he will shortly say, by the Lord's beneficence and power (12:9).

By using this illustration as the climactic moment in his recital, Paul shows how absurd it is to engage in any bragging contest. There is no indication that Paul had Prov. 21:22 in mind.

Neither the identity of the governor ("ethnarch") nor his specific function in Damascus is known. Some ethnarchs headed ethnic groups within or outside a large city; some were in charge of an entire city. The king is Aretas IV, who reigned at Petra from 9 B.C.E. to about the year 40. His daughter was divorced by Herod Antipas in favor of Herodias, the wife of Aretas's half-brother, Herod Philip (cf. Mark 6:17-20). These data help fix the time for Paul's presence in Damascus (see Gal. 1:17), and his escape may have been made before the end of 40 C.E.

Ecstatic Experiences and a Thorn in the Flesh (12:1-10)

1—Paul says that he is compelled to brag, he **must boast.** The Greco-Roman world goes in for honorary decrees, and those who wish to be considered successful as leaders must be able to produce credentials that merit an award. There is no indication in the Corinthian correspondence that Paul's opposition boasted of visions any more than they boasted of the type of experiences cited in 11:24-27.

The RSV's rendering, **there is nothing to be gained by it,** obscures a subtle satirical thrust. The first part of v. 1 is better rendered: "I can't escape boasting. It won't be helpful to you, but I will go on to visions and revelations of the Lord." In this clause Paul uses the adjective *sympheron,* a term that appears frequently in honorary inscriptions in reference to benefactors whose actions or deeds "are helpful" to the people. By negating the value of such "achievements," Paul aims at directing the attention of his addressees to his really weighty apostolic contributions and benefactions.

Paul's precautionary statement, coming as it does after a statement that requires some hedging, is known in rhetoric as *epidiorthosis* (cf. 3:5; 7:8; 11:21, 30; 12:11, 16; 1 Cor. 7:10; 15:10; Gal. 1:6; 2:20). Demosthenes makes frequent use of this figure in his speech *On the Crown.* To cite but one, about the middle of his speech (126) he declaims to the jury:

> Inasmuch as the proper and just vote has been pointed out to all, probably I must, despite the fact that I am not fond of invective, speak about him (Aeschines) because of the reviling statements made by him. In the process all I have to do is just state the facts regarding him, without engaging in a great quantity of lies (as he does).

Demosthenes does not want to take the course he does, but he is driven to it by the nature of the case.

To claim receipt of a vision (*optasia*) or revelation (*apokalypsis*) suggests that one has an extraordinary means of contact with the deity. In Gal. 1:12-15 Paul writes about one such revelation, but not in a boastful way, for he refers to his abominable revolt against God exhibited in his persecution of Christians and contrasts that with the staggering grace of God in selecting him for the mission to the Gentiles. Luke records four special communications that Paul had concerning his mission responsibilities (Acts 16:9-10; 18:9-10; 22:17-20; 23:11), but these were scarcely of the type that Paul records in 2 Cor. 12:2-4.

In view of the reference in the very next verse to "Christ," it is probable that the term **Lord** refers to him (cf. vv. 8-9). The genitival construction is colloquially imprecise but suggests that in his receipt of the visions and revelations Paul enjoyed a privileged relationship with Christ.

2—The descriptive mode exhibited in vv. 2-4 is known in ancient rhetoric as *diatyposis*. The opening phrase, **I know a man,** is also used by Epictetus to introduce a story (1.10.2). Frequently such stories satirically illustrate the consequences of improper approach to the philosopher's task. Paul's very use of the introductory form to such an illustration would therefore suggest to the Corinthians that Paul is indeed boasting with tongue in cheek. The use of the third person in autobiographical narration was used with capital effect by Julius Caesar in the report of his exploits in Gaul. In Paul's account it is demanded by the aura of detachment that the apostle wishes to convey and by his interest in maintaining a contrast between such experiences and his preference for boasting in his weaknesses. At the same time, he achieves the effect that Demosthenes (*On the Crown* 321) sought to elicit when he adopted the third person of a "rather modest citizen" in an introductory paragraph to a catalog of personal service on behalf of the state: "For by adopting this mode of speaking (in the third person) I may speak in what will be accepted as the most inoffensive manner."

Out of all his extraordinary psychical experiences, Paul selects one that made an especially profound impression on him. He knows the exact year, and his mention of it rules out most of the visions recorded in Acts. Yet it is impossible to relate Paul's account with any precise data outside this epistle.

Paul's choice of verb, **caught up,** is a masterful piece of satire. His opponents in Corinth pride themselves on qualifying for the role of exceptional persons, and Paul must enter the competition. How about an apotheosis!

The ultimate experience of a person of extraordinary merit was to be made one of the immortals, that is, one who merited status among the gods who are imperishable. Included among the immortals were such heads of state as Romulus, Alexander the Great, Julius Caesar, Caesar Augustus, the philosopher Empedocles, and the physician Aesclepius. Various stories of their ascension into the heavens were in circulation. So common had the practice become that Nero's chaplain, the philosopher Seneca, wrote a spoof about the deceased Emperor Claudius's thwarted ascension under the title, *Apocolocyntosis* (Pumpkinification) *of Divine Claudius*. Upon his very undignified death at the age of 64, in Seneca's account, Claudius knocks at the gate of heaven to seek admittance among the deities. At the height of a vigorous debate on the question of his admittance, the deified Augustus, horrified at the thought of honoring Claudius in this manner, moves his deportation from heaven within 30 days, and from Olympus by the fourth day. Mercury then escorts him to the nether world, where he is sentenced by Aeacus, one of its three judges, to rattle dice forever in a box that has holes in the bottom, whence they forever do their vanishing act. Rescued from this fate by the ex-emperor Gaius (Caligula), who claims him as his slave, he is handed over to Aeacus, who in turn makes a present of him to his freed slave Menander, who makes Claudius his law-clerk.

Although written after Paul's correspondence with the Corinthians, this satirical work is a sample of the kind of sentiments that were in circulation with respect to overindulgence in honorific dedications. By writing in tones suggestive of an apotheosis, Paul in effect invites his addressees to rethink their attitudes and to keep in perspective any expectations they may have concerning the persons of their leaders. Ultimately, as Paul repeatedly reminds them, the apostle of true merit is the one who sets forth the supreme excellence of God as manifested in the gift of Jesus Christ.

Apart from the satirical effect, Paul's reference to an ecstatic journey would be a recognizable part of Hellenic cultural tradition. Wettstein called attention to the importance of Plato's Myth of Er (*Republic* 10.614c) in connection with Paul's recital. In the myth a messenger leaves the body so that his soul could go on a journey to the other world and return with a report.

The very uncertainty that Paul expresses as to details is satirical. The apostle refers to an experience that falls into the category of psychokinesis, a movement of the psyche that is independent of the body's locomotion. So unusual was the experience that Paul is not certain about the details. He does not know whether he was in the body or out of the body. In related manner the narrator of the *Apocolocyntosis* (2) says that he is not certain precisely at what hour the proceedings took place on 13 October 54, alleging that philosophers and clocks don't always agree on the time.

Conceptions of the number of "heavens" varied so much in Jewish circles that it is impossible to know why Paul selected the digit *three* but, in view of his description in v. 4, it appears that he considered **the third heaven** the ultimate in celestial experience.

By adding that only **God knows** the facts in the matter, Paul suggests that the experience was utterly fantastic. At the same time, he suggests that he is treading on dangerous ground. The matter is so sacred that he ought not to be talking about it. But, being the "fool" that he is, he proceeds.

Paul's suggestion of reticence would have been filled with further meaning for many of the Corinthians, who would associate Paul's recital with their own acquaintance with mystery religions (the term *religion* here being distinguished from *theology*). These secret cults prescribed certain initiation ceremonies. Among the most well-known ones were the "mysteries," or sacred rites, of Demeter, whose most celebrated locale was Eleusis. Because of them, there were Greco-Romans who could "live with joy and die with greater hope." Like Paul, even those who dared to talk about the rites moved on to other things just at the point of revelation, and details concerning the mystery rites remain, as noted below on v. 4, one of the best-kept secrets of the ancient world.

3—The repetition in this verse contributes to the satirical tone by adding a note of feigned suspense at the threshold of the ultimate disclosure.

4—Paul picks up the thread of v. 3. Will he now break the

190

code of silence that all antiquity imposed on initiates into mysteries?

The term **Paradise** suggests a king's park. To be invited into "paradise" meant that one enjoyed intimacy with the royal household. Hence the significance of the promise that Jesus made to the malefactor (Luke 23:43): Jesus as king counts the outlaw one of his intimates. The other occurrence of the term is in Rev. 2:7, which echoes Gen. 2:9.

In God's paradise the apostle hears **things that cannot be told** (*arrēta*). With the rest of antiquity, Paul seals his lips on the frontier of telling all about his own exposure to great mystery. For example, Herodotus (6.134) provided some account of the rites of Demeter, but when it came to revealing one of the principal actions in the sacred enclosure, he wrote a frustrating parenthesis, to the effect: "I cannot say what it was." An ancient commentator on Aristophanes' *Clouds* (302) noted about the Hellenic world: "The mystical story has to do with the unutterable (*arrēta*) mysteries. For they (the ancients) are very conscientious about publicizing nothing concerning these matters." Lucian satirized the tight-lipped attitude in his spoof on a descent into Hades (*Mennipos* 2). One of the characters asks a man named Menippos what novel enactments have been made against the rich. Menippos replies: "It is not permitted to expose them to the public, lest someone indict us for impiety before Rhadamanthus (judge of the underworld)."

In view of the numerous occurrences of *arrēta* noted by Wettstein and Windisch in connection with the mysteries in Greek literature, including Philo, it is probable that Paul was conscious of the quasi-technical nature of the term. And the Corinthians would be impressed with his piety, one of the fundamental characteristics of a person of merit in the Hellenic world.

5-7—If Paul were to boast about his visions, he could himself become the center of a personality cult. But the truth of the gospel would be up for grabs; for each claimant of special revelation could put in a pitch for the loyalties of God's people. Paul refuses to take that route and prefers to boast only about his weaknesses, for through Paul's weaknesses the divine strength is displayed. With this statement he indicates, of course, that he disavows the validity of all his boasting that was done in irony in the paragraphs that preceded. The Corinthians could not fail to grasp the implications for their own assessment of the apostle. Any charges of lack of theological sophistication do not hold up. Paul could sound very esoteric, if he wished, but it would not be to the Corinthians' best interests.

Most of the Corinthians would by now be applauding Paul's cascading oratorical brilliancies. By maintaining the charade of talking about a person other than himself, Paul facetiously suggests that he avoids the distaste attached to self-praise. In his essay *On Inoffensive Self-Praise* (542e), Plutarch states that "people who feel compelled to engage in self-praise will make it easier for themselves if they do not attribute everything to themselves but shift the burden of glory to fortune or to God."

Four centuries earlier, Demosthenes had modeled the thought. In the middle of one of his self-evaluations as defender of the interests of Athens, Demosthenes says that he could say much more, but is cautious about arousing resentment because of his apparent boasting (259). People who receive favors ought to be honorable enough to express appreciation, he says, "but one who has conferred them ought to forget them immediately." Hence, he goes on to say, "I will not be inveigled into saying any more about them. The respect I have already reaped because of them suffices" (269). It is a line of thought rooted in the Delphic maxim, "Know yourself."

Paul knows the rhetorical code and states that he is worried lest the very **abundance** of the revelations should lead to any one's overestimation of the apostle. The opening clause of v. 7 in the Greek text consists of the words, *kai tē hyperbolē tōn apokalypseōn* ("and because of the abundance of revelations"). This phrase has caused difficulty because of uncertainty about its grammatical connection. The RSV construes it with the words that follow, but stylistic and textual-critical considerations weigh against such interpretation. At the same time, those who construe the phrase with the preceding verse encounter difficulty in the conjunction *dio* (which is ignored, apparently for textual-critical reasons, by the RSV). The problem is best resolved along the following lines. (1) The phrase is to be taken with v. 6, and is to be rendered: "(than he sees and hears from me), especially (*kai*) because of the abundance of revelations." (2) The connection between this phrase and the succeeding clauses is expressed colloquially. The apostle's thought leaps ahead of his grammar. Abundance suggests hazard, and consideration of hazard requires a transition that involves use of a causal conjunction; hence the choice of *dio* ("therefore"). Verse 7 should, then, be rendered: "(than he sees or hears from me), especially because of the abundance of revelations. Therefore, to keep me from being too elated, a thorn was given me in the flesh. . . ."

With the keen sense of humor that prompts comedians to make themselves butts of their own jokes, Paul says that in the face of an array of revelations he received an antidote. The apostle maintains the strain of folly that runs through the entire autobiographical speech by characterizing the antidote as a benefaction (*edothē*, **was given**). The logical grammatical donor is Satan, for the donation of the **thorn** is defined as Satan's messenger. But it is generally understood by biblical writers that Satan performs his functions within the boundaries of divine permission. The humor in Paul's reference to Satan lies in the fact that Satan, who is known in Jewish tradition as God's arch-rival, with a colossal ego, would cross the rhetorical stage as a competitor who sends Paul an antidote to possible pride and arrogance. Since God is ultimately responsible, the humor is doubly sharp. In the sophisticated rhetorical context of the "Fool's Speech," an anecdote like this communicates with several circuits open.

Just as second-century Christian storytellers loved to fill in biographical holes left in the Gospels and Epistles, so commentators have filled the literature of interpretation with a long list of equations, ranging from epilepsy to competitive congregational leaders, for Paul's delightfully inscrutable "thorn." But its identity, like that of various ritual acts in antiquity, will be an eternal mystery. Certain it is that the "thorn" was a source of pain and humiliation for the apostle, and more probably a physical disability or deficiency than hostility from human opponents. In any case, the lesson for the church is obvious—evaluation of service, when otherwise well rendered, is not to be contaminated by consideration of physical disabilities.

193

8—This verse establishes that Jesus Christ was for Paul a healing Savior. The expression **I besought the Lord** follows the form used by a patient at the healing center of Epidauros. Grateful for his recovery through the beneficence of Asclepius, Apellas thanks the deity and observes that one of the instructions was for gargling with cold water to overcome inflammation of the uvula. Apellas observes that he had "besought the deity for this" (*peri toutou parekalesa ton theon, SIG*[3] 1170.30-31). Apellas received a positive answer, Paul a negative.

The numeral **three** is firmly entrenched in Jewish traditions, but is also significant in the Greco-Roman world. Euripides (*Hippolytus* 46) has Aphrodite say that it is "not in vain to pray to the deity three times in succession." Horace notes the magical value of the triple performance (*Odes* 3.22.3; *Satires* 2.1.7; *Epistles* 1.1.37).

In view of the context, v. 9, it is probable that Paul addressed these three petitions to Christ. If such is the case, it is a unique departure from Paul's custom, which is to address God as the one who is ultimately responsible for everything (cf. 5:18; Rom. 11:33-36). Paul's Jewish liturgical tradition is still firmly entrenched, but Christ is the natural object of his petition here, for it is in the proclamation of his service for all humanity that Paul is engaged. An answer coming from Christ will indeed be especially meaningful.

As Windisch notes, the Corinthians could not fail to have perceived the difference between Paul's chronic malady and the successful cures experienced by visitors to healing shrines. Therefore the Corinthians would find all the more meaningful the divine response recorded in v. 9.

9—Paul could, of course, count on people with a background in Jewish tradition to understand words about trouble/**power**. Had not psalmists and the author of Job celebrated the idea? But adept as Paul was at being a Hellene among Hellenes, he knew that the Corinthians would be at home with the sentiment. A related tradition of the value of suffering was well established in the Hellenic ethos from the time of Homer. Aeschylus put it in crisp form: "Learning through suffering" (*Agamemnon* 177, *pathei* *mathos*). And Epictetus (1.1.10-13) summed the Greco-Roman preachers' counsel:

> Now what does God say? "Epictetus, if there had been any other way, I would have made that little body of yours and your tiny holdings free and unencumbered. But things being as they are— let it not escape you—this body is not your own but merely some cleverly compounded clay. Yet, since I was not able to give you the other, we have provided you with some small part of ourselves, namely the faculty of choice and refusal, of desire and disinclination, or, to put it simply, a discriminating approach to impressions. If you make this your chief interest and your soul's ultimate concern. you will never feel frustrated, you will not groan, you will not complain, you will not flatter any person. Well, then? Does this offer strike you as being too stingy?" "No, certainly not!" "Then you're satisfied?" "It's my prayer."

But in Philo's *Life of Moses* (1.69) we encounter the closest parallel to Paul's formulation. The Jewish philosopher said of the bush which was not consumed that it was a voice proclaiming to sufferers: "Take courage, your weakness spells strength." Paul, of course, moves the thought to a far different plane. The word **power** means the ability to function. That ability is best exhibited in weakness, for it is in weakness that the full extent of Christ's capacity for overcoming obstacles can be observed. To one who has overcome death all else seems trivial.

The words **made perfect** render the verb form *teleitai*, which expresses completion: "is carried out." In the context of the sacral references made in vv. 1-8, this word would strike the Corinthians with special force. One spoke of "carrying out" sacred rites (cf. Plutarch, *Table Talk* 671e). The "mysteries of Christ" are experienced in the kinds of **weakness** that Paul experienced.

To emphasize the quality of the divine response, Paul calls the refusal of his petition a manifestation of grace, that is, beneficence. Paul is a benefactor in a special sense to the Corinthians, but Christ is the Great Benefactor, to whom all else in Paul's thinking is subservient. Now it is even more apparent why he put so little stock in visions and revelations. His denigration of their significance provides the framework for appreciating the climactic emphasis on weakness.

Remarkable is the fact that this quotation is the only saying of Jesus used by Paul in the entire epistle, and it has to do with the endorsement of weakness as opposed to what humanity ordinarily sets up as standards for excellence, such as ancestral advantage, ability to win debates, impressive presence, and spectacular performance.

The words **rest upon me** would bear more Jewish than Hellenistic freight, for the verb "rest" (*episkēnoō*) would suggest the kind of imagery that is found, for example, in Exod. 40:34, concerning the glory of the Lord that floods sacred space.

Paul's confession of strength in weakness suggests personal integrity. One can boast of weaknesses and attract attention to oneself for possessing a magnificent ability to endure. But unless one can show others how they can acquire and manifest such ability, the possessor of such experience and alleged virtue is nothing. Such is not the case with Paul. He leads others to the source of his strength in weakness: Christ. Thus he surpassed Epictetus in awareness of spiritual resources. For Epictetus (4.8.30-31) had spoken in a related vein, but lacked Paul's ultimate treatment. Adopting the Cynic's role, the Greek philosopher says:

> So that you may see for yourselves, O people, that you are searching for happiness and serenity, not where they are but where they are not, behold, I have been sent to you by God as an example—one who has neither goods, nor house, nor wife, nor children—no, not even a bed, or a shirt, or a pot. Yet you can see how healthy I am. Make trial of me, and if you see me maintaining my tranquillity, then listen to my remedies and the treatment that cured me.

10—This verse provides the concluding framework for the vignette that began at 11:21b, with special focus on 11:25-33. In v. 9 Paul referred to the functioning ability of Christ. Now he identifies with that power. His thought is of a piece with the affirmation made, for example, in 13:4; Gal. 2:20; Phil. 1:21.

Paul has written what is in reality a success story in the face of immense obstacles. The endangered benefactor of the Corinthians emerges as some miraculously victorious paraplegic. In his recital there is consolation for those who endure hostility in the face of faithful witness. But the indolent, those who make no waves and wait to see which way the wind will blow before they move, can take no comfort in a text that displays the kind of record piled up by the apostle Paul.

Transition (12:11-13)

11—Near the end of his oration *On the Crown* (256), Demosthenes turns to Aeschines and says that he is driven by the latter's defamatory allegations to enter into discussion of personal matters. Paul declares himself a fool for having to engage in the same type of tactics. Dependence on such rhetorical protective ointment is prompted by the awareness that comes up for discussion in Plutarch's essay *On Inoffensive Self-Praise* (539c). The raconteur from Chaironeia observes that one ought not to celebrate one's own achievements. "Even those who are crowned for victories in the games," he states, "are proclaimed victors by others, who thereby remove any stigma of self-adulation." Along similar lines, Paul tells the Corinthians that it would be more appropriate if they recited his praises. And through his words there sounds the plaintive note that attended the rebuke given by Themistocles in the face of Athenian mistreatment: "Why, dear people, are you so weary of being treated well?" (Plutarch, *Political Precepts* 15[812]).

Paul proceeds to discharge a devastating blast of wit that could not fail to win plaudits from Hellenes whose cultivated taste for the bon mot is prodigally documented in antiquity. But before entry into comment on the statement, it is necessary to catch the wordplay of the original: "In nothing (*ouden*) do I come short of your superlative apostles, even though I am nothing (*ouden*)." The joke is patent. After recounting his long tale of "weaknesses," he declares that he is a **nothing**; yet in his nothingness he is superior to those who have been ogled by Paul's constituency. The more sophisticated among his addressees might well have thought of Odysseus and the time when he cried out to the blind and befuddled Polyphemus, who had asked his identity: "Nobody!" (*Oudeis*). According to Epictetus (4.8.25), Socrates proclaimed that he was in effect "nothing," if he waited for someone else to aid him. Dio Chrysostom uses the ploy to advantage in his 32nd discourse (39). In reference to speakers who flatter their audiences, he makes this rejoinder: "They are clever people, mighty sophists, charmers all. As for us, our speech may sound ordinary and pedestrian, but our subject is by no means second-rate. Our words may lack grandiloquence, but their subject matter is of the utmost importance." For further discussion see Betz (*Der Apostel*, pp. 121-132).

The apostle's description of his opponents as "superstar apostles" is to be entered under the rhetorical classification of syncrisis (see on 11:12-15). We know, of course, from 11:19-20, that they are exceptionally expert in being the opposite of what an apostle ought to be. Hence the impact of irony in the present passage.

12—It was also understood in antiquity that in the absence of defense from others it was essential to praise oneself. Plutarch (541d) expresses a consensus: "It is expected that a public servant who has been wronged is granted the right to say something about himself to his harsh critics." In support he appeals to the Hellenic bible, Homer's poems, and cites Achilles, who in the face of numerous indignities boasted that he had sacked 12 cities with his ships (*Iliad* 9.321-32).

In line with such hallowed tradition, Demosthenes, after having endured the calumnies of Aeschines, cites his own record of beneficence (257):

> When I was a child I possessed the necessary means to avoid doing anything that might have been degrading because of poverty. And when I reached maturity I acted in similar fashion. I met expenses for choruses and triremes, I paid the war tax, and showed no slackness in private or public service, but put myself at the disposal of both the city and my friends.

In keeping, then, with recognized custom, Paul catalogs notable activities in which he had been engaged on behalf of the Corinthians, for no one shall rob him of his conviction that he has been their benefactor. Since the Corinthians have been in default in their recognition, it is no more a fool's part that Paul plays here than in Rom. 15:18-19.

Awareness of Paul's use of the benefactor motif helps one see that this verse is intimately linked with the argument that precedes it. In vv. 1-10 the emphasis was placed on Paul's weakness. Here he makes the transition from weakness to display of extraordinary deeds. This is a powerful answer to the charge that he is all talk, no action (see 10:10-11). As indicated above, on 6:3-10, **patience** (*hypomonē*) is the mark of an endangered benefactor. Paul's beneficence to the congregation is all the more evident in view of the hazards that he has undergone on their behalf and also in view of the insults that he has had to take from some of their number.

Paul's reference to his miracles is akin to the emphasis placed on them in Rom. 15:18-21, where he sets them alongside his proclamation of the gospel as manifestation of his role as a benefactor who demonstrates his identity in "word and deed" (v. 18). Reference to proclamation of the gospel is lacking in 2 Cor. 12:12 for the simple reason that the argument requires a focus on the apostle's ability to demonstrate his apostolic credentials in deed. His past performance, of which the Corinthians have knowledge, should be a sufficient disclaimer of the validity of the opposition's charges that Paul is all words without performance.

The threefold terminology for miracles—**signs and wonders and mighty works**—is also found in Acts 2:22; Heb. 2:4. The OT makes repeated reference to "signs and wonders." Acts records numerous healings through Paul (Acts 13:6-12; 14:8-18; 15:12; 16:16-18; 19:11-12; 28:3-6, 7-10), but none in connection with his stay at Corinth.

Since this is a "fool's speech," which incorporates the principal topics and themes that found expression in praise of superstars, divine or human, Paul's reference to extraordinary performance would not be lost on Greco-Roman addressees. Numerous miracles were attributed to the hero Asclepius, who is mentioned in Homer's "Ships' Catalog" (*Iliad* 2.729). For example, to a certain Lucius who was "afflicted with pleurisy, and given up by everyone," Asclepius revealed that he should "come and take ashes from an altar to the Three Gods, and mix them up well with wine and apply the mixture to the afflicted area. And he was healed and gave thanks publicly to God, and the people rejoiced with him" (*Benefactor*, p. 194). The Elder Pliny (*Natural History* 7.13) reports that Crates of Pergamon states that "in the Hellespont around Parium there was a race of people, whom he calls Ophiogenes, who could relieve the bites of serpents by personal contact and draw out the poisons from the body simply by placing their hand on the afflicted part." The miracles reported in apocryphal legends about the apostles and those attributed to Apollonius of Tyana are well-known.

13—The reference to **the rest of the churches** appears to echo the statement in 11:28 concerning his care for "all the churches." Apparently Paul was criticized for taking too much on himself and in the process neglecting the Corinthians. Some of his opponents may well have been among those who offered to step into the breach.

Paul's defense is that his interest in others has not been purchased at the expense of the Corinthians' claim on his time. Indeed, he emphasizes at v. 14, he is about to see them for the "third" time.

Once again the apostle refers to his refusal to take subsidy from Corinth (cf. 10:7-10). The words are tinged with the sarcastic wit for which Demosthenes was famous. "My only mistake, evidently, was my refusal to take advantage of you. Forgive me such injustice!" Paul can perpetrate this type of rhetorical ploy because of the cultural background against which its bite would be less mordant than it sounds to modern ears. The Corinthians would consider themselves properly chastised, for they had violated the Hellenic sense of reciprocity. Paul was their benefactor, and they permitted him to be treated in a manner disgraceful to the national ethos. Evidently they like nonbenefactors!

Final Protestation of Affection (12:14—13:10)

Paul No Free-loader (12:14-18)

14—This verse is the antidote to what had to be said in v. 13, and the Corinthians would readily see how big the heart of Apostle Paul really was.

The first of the three visits mentioned by Paul was made when Paul founded the congregation. The second was his "painful" visit (2 Cor. 2:1). The third is the one he plans to make after the dispatch of 2 Corinthians (see 13:1). For further details see the introduction.

With the words **I seek not what is yours but you** Paul sounds a warm note of the type cited by Wettstein from Cicero, *On the Ends* (2.26.85): "If we are to be true friends, you must love me for myself and not for my possessions."

Paul's use of proverbial wisdom is a strong rhetorical tactic. Firmly entrenched is the understanding that parents are responsible for their offspring. Isis declared about herself: "I set the penalty for parents who lack affection" (*Benefactor*, p. 29). In his *Life of Moses* (2.245), Philo notes that "it is a law of nature that children are the heirs of their parents, not parents of their children." Paul could have cited other proverbial wisdom to the effect that parents ought to be provided for by their children, but he chooses to opt for the parental responsibility. Again, the Corinthians could not have failed to note the striking tack taken by the apostle. For other use of the parental figure by Paul, see 1 Cor. 4:15; 2 Cor. 6:13.

15—In illustration of Paul's thought, Windisch cites Seneca (*On Providence* 5.4), who says of benefactors: "they are industrious, they spend, they are spent, and that quite readily."

To give oneself for others was the recognized mark of a benefactor. Of Menas, outstanding citizen in Sestos, it was proclaimed that he "dedicated himself unstintingly" for the welfare of his city (*Benefactor*, p. 322).

As if the pain were one too deep for tears, Paul asks, "Because I have so much affection for you, do I come short of yours for me?" Or, "Is your love inversely proportionate to mine?" The point is that Paul's affection is so great that the challenge to reciprocity is apparently too much for the Corinthians. Evidently they would like to have him show less. The question is, of course, ironical. It was taken for granted in Hellenic society that affection is a two-way avenue. In an essay, *Marriage Precepts* (143c), Plutarch observes that affection elicits affection, and it was normal to expect a benefactor to continue dispensing generosity. For example, the people of Iasos passed a decree of appreciation for services rendered by the city of Priene, which included the resolution that the decree was to be delivered, "with encouragement that they (the people of Priene) continue their past policy toward our people" (*Benefactor,* p. 90). Similarly, the people of Lycia brought the generosity of Opramoas to the attention of Emperor Antoninus Pius with these words (*Benefactor,* p. 136):

> The Province of Lycia considered it appropriate and right once again to render testimony to Opramoas and to report to the Lord Imperator . . . that through his (previous) approval of Opramoas he has made him all the more eager to be of service to our cities.

16—It is necessary to grasp the colloquial character of the two sentences in this verse: "Very well, 'You didn't freeload,' you will say to me. But in the same breath, 'Ah, but you were clever and took advantage of us in our naiveté.' " Paul imagines to himself a dialog with the Corinthians and expresses it succinctly in the first person.

At 11:20 Paul chided the Corinthians for their readiness to be taken in (*lambanō*) by theological swindlers. The formulation is grammatically similar but not semantically equivalent to one in Sophocles' *Philoctetes* (101), where Odysseus says to Neoptolemos, "I say, by stealth take Philoctetes." Paul uses the verb in the transferred sense that is found in such an expression as, "Take someone to the cleaners." He is a con man, master of theological shell games.

17-18—The apostle's satire demands that his refusal to accept maintenance had to do with offsetting charges that he was exploiting the Corinthians in some way through his fund-raising efforts, and probably through third parties to cover his tracks. Evidently he wished to nip any suspicions in the bud by refusing to accept any maintenance from the Corinthians, and they had to grant that he was no financial burden to them. "But," some among them apparently charge, "he slipped one over on us and involved us in a heavy assessment for the benefit of Jerusalem." In rebuttal, Paul proceeds to write about his envoys.

The structure of assumed charges and defense follows the pattern used by Demosthenes in an address to Aeschines in the speech titled *On the Crown* (117):

> Did I make a contribution? Yes, and I receive praise for that, without being subject to audit for what I donated. Did I hold offices? Yes,

and I rendered an accounting for my discharge of the same, but not for donations. Indeed, but was I a corrupt official? Well, if that were the case, why did you not accuse me when the auditors called me in?

Like Demosthenes, Paul plays the role of a barrister in his own defense.

"Did I use some of my envoys as a screen for my personal interests?" Answer: "Look at the credentials of those whom I dispatched—Titus and the brother (whom you all know). Titus hasn't ever used you to feather his own nest, has he? Well, haven't we conducted ourselves with the same kind of spirit? Didn't we walk in his footsteps?"

Evidently Paul could count on the Corinthians viewing Titus as a Christian above reproach. The diction is reminiscent of either 8:6 or 8:16-22. If 8:6 is in mind, the reference is to the first of two visits by Titus, namely, when he broached the matter of a collection to the Corinthians. But it is odd that Paul makes no mention in 8:6 of any "brother." If in 12:17-18 Paul has 8:22 in mind, the reference is to Titus's second visit when he was to help the Corinthians go through the final phase of their collection. But it is odd that in such a case Paul makes reference only to "the brother," whereas 8:22 includes "the brother" mentioned in 8:18. In any event, the view that 12:17-18 refers to 8:16-22 assumes that the aorist tense *synepempsamen* (8:22) is to be understood as an epistolary aorist, "as of this writing we are sending." A major question remains. What point in time is referred to in 12:18? The argumentative structure, with its answering of charges, suggests that the dispatch has taken place and that Paul compares his own track record to the one already set by Titus and "the brother." In that case, chaps. 10–13 are best viewed as having been written after Titus had arrived in Corinth to aid the Corinthians in the final phase of the collection process. This view assumes that Paul dropped his pen for a time after the writing of chaps. 1–9, and in the light of new information completed 2 Corinthians.

Fears about the State of the Community's Health (12:19-21)

19—The opening clause is a further instance of *praemunitio* or rhetorical protective ointment. "Here goes Paul again, defending himself," the opposition is thinking. "Yes," says Paul, "and we do it in the presence of God, under the control of Christ. And it's all in your interest."

With this approach Paul moves in a familiar pattern of rhetorical expectations. Refutations of charges of guile and other allegations, with protestations of concern for the public interest, were part of the orator's rhetorical art and Demosthenes was an expert in their use. Aeschines alleged that Demosthenes obfuscated issues through rhetoric. "Yet I perceive," argues the self-styled bene-factor of Athens, "that it is the audience that for the most part moderates the persuasiveness of public speakers, who gain a rep-utation for acumen only in proportion to your acceptance of them and your demonstration of goodwill." And if you examine the record, he goes on to say, "you will all discover that my skill has been exercised openly on your behalf, and not against you, not even in private" (*On the Crown* 276-77).

Plutarch documented the procedure in his essay *On Inoffensive Self-Praise:* "One who is censured for the very things that con-tribute to the public welfare will invite no blame for praising his own policies" (541e). A few paragraphs earlier, after having taken account of the offence that gratuitous self-praise evokes, he ac-knowledges that under certain circumstances a politician might well indulge in what is termed self-adulation, not for personal prestige or self-gratification, but because the welfare of others may be connected with the truth about himself: in such cases orators should not be reluctant to relate their helpful political achievements and thereby render a further service. As is the case with seeds, writes Plutarch, such praise produces a fine crop, for many more and nobler praises are generated by it (539e-f).

20—The warning in the opening phrase of this verse is in keep-ing with epistolary form of the type described in a work falsely attributed to Demetrius of Phaleron (8). The rhetorician defines the type as follows: "When we use vehement expression to arouse fear for what has either been done or will be done." He then suggests a script for the "threatening" mode: "If you think that you can escape indictment for what you have done, try it. But you will quickly discover that it will be useless to try to gain time by slinking off and going into hiding. There is no way that you can possibly escape paying the consequences."

Hellenes were fond of lists. Greco-Roman audiences were conditioned to recitals of many types, which were recited with or without conjunctions. Aeschylus (*Seven* 610) has Eteocles say of Apollo's seer, that he is a "prudent, upright, good, pious" person. Aristophanes spoofed the habit by composing one of the longest words in any language. In it he cites an exhaustiing list of exotic ingredients for an outrageous salmagundi (*Ekklesiazousai* 1169-75). Philosophers and itinerant preachers composed lists of vice and virtue. Philo ran Aristophanes competition with a series of about 150 vice terms in *Sacrifices of Abel and Cain* (32). The moral philosopher Cebes (19) catalogs the problems of one of the characters in his script who comes to be instructed in virtue. An elderly man explains that the prospect has come to be cured of a variety of maladies. "Of what sort?" asks the participant in dialog. The man tabulates: "His ignorance and error . . . and haughtiness and desire, and incontinence and dissipation and greed and all the rest with which he was infected." In a description of the philosopher Zeno's views, Diogenes Laertius (7.110-116) shows how the Stoics map the structure of the soul through classifications of vice and virtue. The following statement typifies Zeno's approach: "Inordinate desire is an irrational longing, under which fall the following: dissatisfaction, hatred, rivalry, anger, love, wrath, ill temper" (113). Related is the list in Wis. 14:25-26: "All is in confusion (among worshipers of idols): blood and murder, theft and fraud, corruption, disloyalty, violence, perjury, assault on fine citizens, defilement of minds, sexual perversion, broken marriage vows, adultery, and debauchery." Other lists in Paul's writings include Rom. 1:29-31; 13:13; 1 Cor. 5:10-11; 6:9-10; Gal. 5:19-21; Eph. 4:31; 5:3-5; Col. 3:5, 8; 1 Tim. 1:9-10; 6:4; 2 Tim. 3:2-4; Titus 3:3; see also 4 Macc. 1:26; 2:15; Mark 7:21-22; 1 Pet. 4:3; Rev. 9:21; 21:8; 22:15). The list of combative characteristics in 2 Cor. 12:20 is strikingly paralleled in the "Catalog of Greek Astrological Texts" (*polemous, phonous, machas, schismata*, wars, murders, fights, divisions; see BAGD, s.v. *schisma*). In J. H. Kent's collection of inscriptions found at Corinth (*Corinth VIII.3 The Inscriptions* [Athens, 1966], 22-26, nos. 119-121) one can determine the importance that party politics had for the Corinthians.

Partisan politics is suggested by all the terms in Paul's lists, but the first two focus attention on the partisanship as such, with the rest of the terms describing the heat generated by such narrow perspectives. Paul's choice of terms is particularly appropriate in the situation to which he addresses himself. The entire list, which echoes 1 Cor. 3:3, deals with divisive attitudes and conduct (cf. Rom. 1:29-30; Gal. 5:20). The term *eris* (**quarreling**) refers to the discord generated by partisan interest. Partisan politics is suggested by the word *zēlos* (**jealousy**): one party is jealous of another party's success in drawing adherents. Party strife leads to ill will and resentments (**anger**), which involve all participants in its corollary, contentious bickering (**selfishness**). The inevitable result is name-calling (**slander**), which is paired with malicious whispering campaigns (**gossip**) emanating from puffed-up people (**conceit**) who leave a constituency in total disarray (**disorder**). As Dio Chrysostom (31.18-19) instructed the people of Rhodes, such sins as "jealousy, folly, and contentiousness prevailed over virtue" and led to the descent of Hellas from its pinnacle of greatness. Paul fears that the Corinthians will similarly fall from the prestigious position that he defined at 3:2-3.

It is important to note that the word **perhaps** (*pōs*) is Paul's way of indicating to the addressees that he is not suggesting that the majority of the Corinthians are actually guilty of all the vices that he is about to catalogue. Rather, he is conveying his anxiety. As he stated in v. 15, he is extremely fond of them and cannot stand the thought that they might revert to some of their past ways. In short, this is preventive maintenance and encouragement to hold fast in the face of clever maneuvers by manipulative competitors of Paul.

21—The contemplated visit will be the first since his "sorrowful visit" (2 Cor. 2:1). Paul's reference to a possible humiliation may be a designed echo of 11:7, in which he made reference to his self-humiliation in working among them without cost to the Corinthians. It is also probable that Paul had in mind the "sorrowful visit." In any event, the humiliation, if indeed it takes place, will be an experience that he accepts from God as the price to be paid for trying to keep the Corinthians on the correct track. On the other hand, as Plummer notes, they will have to accept the responsibility for whatever shame the apostle experiences in such an encounter.

That Paul does not actually indict the Corinthians appears to be clear from his choice of the verb **sinned before.** That is, many of them were guilty of sins. But Paul fears that their repentance might not have been genuine. Again he is expressing his great concern for their spiritual welfare. There is no real conflict with his joyful response to the news of the Corinthians' repentance in the case described in 2 Corinthians 7. His concern for their morality goes on. The ball is now in the Corinthians' court. They can say, "We better clean up the rest of our act so we don't embarrass our apostle." Or, "Won't our brother Paul be pleasantly surprised when he comes to visit us? How good of him to be so concerned about us."

It has seemed strange to some interpreters that Paul should recite the catalogs of vice recorded in vv. 20-21, after having apparently settled affairs with his addressees. Why open old wounds? But the moral feature must be viewed from the Greco-Roman perspective. In vv. 19-20 we have an indirect attack on certain elements at Corinth who have in Paul's judgment exploited his converts and have passed themselves off as "superlative apostles" (2 Cor. 11:5; 12:11). If they are permitted to continue their activities, the results will be as described in vv. 19-20, and perhaps worse. For praise of such people, as Plutarch wrote in another context (*On Inoffensive Self-Praise* 545d-e), can lead to emulation that results in shameful conduct. In other words, Paul is saying that through the type of theology presented by him the vices which he catalogs can be overcome (cf. 1 Cor. 6:9-11). But if his opposition wins the upper hand, Paul fears that the consequences will be of the sort described. As Plutarch continues in the passage cited above, one renders a service by denouncing vice. This Paul does in vv. 20-21, and thereby qualifies for Plutarch's further judgment expressed in *Precepts for Governing a State* (*Moralia* 810c): "When blame is mingled with praise, and is expressed with complete frankness, yet devoid of disdain, and induces repentance rather than ire, it appears well-disposed and remedial."

Paul's Wish for a Pleasant Visit (13:1-10)

Chapter 13 climaxes the line of thought developed in 12:19-21. The apostle is conscious that he has not spared the feelings of the Corinthians. He has completely leveled with them. And they know where he stands. At the same time, he wants them to know that he has written so bluntly because he cares so much for them.

1—Paul's first visit was the time when he introduced the Corinthians to the good news; his second, when he found the Corinthians at odds with the aims and purposes of the gospel. Now he contemplates a third visit, which he hopes will be pleasant. Just as chaps. 8–9 were designed to help the Corinthians prepare for the final stages of their pledged collection, so chaps. 10–13 are designed to prepare the congregation for this third visit.

The biblical reference is from Deut. 19:15 (cf. Matt. 18:16). Its use here signals a strong judicial tone without necessarily referring to procedural matters. Some of the Corinthians might well have noted the numerical correlation of number of witnesses and visits. If so, the first visit would serve as testimony for the constitutional base, the gospel, that some of the Corinthians have violated since that first visit. The second visit provided evidence of such violation. And the third will determine whether there are parties guilty of the type of activity against which the apostle warns in 2 Cor. 10-13.

2-3—Paul is concerned about Corinthians who may be sliding back into old patterns of sexual aberrations and partisan politics, but his warning is inclusive. He proposes to stamp out any last pockets of rebellion and at the same time is on guard against any outbreak of new fires. Just what form Paul's disciplinary measures might take is not spelled out, but 1 Cor. 5:5 suggests one recourse, namely, "handing" someone "over to Satan." Such a process would be put in the context of magic by people in the Mediterranean world. A magician is one who can bring into play forces or powers that lie outside normal experience. In Acts 8:9-24, Luke relates the attempt of a magician named Simon to acquire Christian magical powers. Another magician, Elymas by name, opposed Paul and Barnabas at Paphos (Acts 13:6-12). Both learned that Christian magic was not at the disposal of anyone for purposes of exploitation. At Ephesus, seven sons of Sceva discovered that it could backfire in the hands of those who wanted to use the name of Jesus for personal ends; and the incident had such a ripple effect that eventually thousands of dollars worth of magical recipes went up in smoke (19:13-20). After warning the Galatian Christians about the use of potions (Gal. 5:20; RSV, "sorcery"), which would involve invocation of numerous deities and frequently be used to control or exploit another person, Paul himself makes a playful allusion to magical practice at the close of his letter to the Galatians. "Let no one make trouble for me," he writes, "for I carry the marks of Jesus in my body" (Gal. 6:17). In short, the ultimate magic is the power of Jesus. And the Corinthians, like the Galatians, better not tamper with it.

Earlier Paul had said that he had penned a letter in order to "test" the Corinthians' credentials as obedient Christians (2:9; cf. 9:13). Now it is the Corinthians who are putting Paul to a test of his apostolic credentials as spokesperson of Christ. Is he a genuine apostle or not? The sentence beginning **He is not weak . . .** is introduced with a relative pronoun in the Greek text: "Christ, who. . . ." Such a relative serves since the time of Homer to focus attention on the one who is described. Paul argues from a position that is held on all sides. The Corinthians will certainly affirm that Christ is **not weak,** and they will most certainly not deny that he is **powerful** in or among them. Paul is, of course, setting the hook to affirm the source of his own ability to function as an apostle of the first rank.

4—Paul now reviews with the Corinthians the meaning of power. The significance of Christ is based on his acceptance of a degrading role, that of a crucified criminal. By emphasizing that Christ lives through God's **power,** Paul focuses the Corinthians' attention on God as the one with whom they must ultimately

deal. At the same time he prepares the groundwork for the conclusion which he expresses about himself. His apostolic claims
derive their force from the fact that he shares the weakness of
Christ as the degraded one, but lives with him out of God's power,
and in connection with that power relates to the Corinthians.
Weakness is never left out of sight. And recollection of Christ's
weakness, of which the cross is the principal symbol, can keep
the Corinthians from being embarrassed by manifestations of
weakness in Paul, such as lack of personal "presence" and oratorical sophistication (cf. 10:10). God's power, the ability to bring
life out of death and to restore recalcitrant Christians to obedience, is exhibited in the gospel. There is a message of hope for
the Corinthians in Paul's emphasis on God's power in connection
with Christ. Paul's entire approach is in terms of his experience
of the love of God, who suffers the humiliation of the crucifixion
of the Son and yet reaches out with longing love for the return
of sinful human beings.

5—After creating the bridgework in v. 4, Paul invites the Corinthians to form their own judgment in the matter. "Examine
(*peirazete*) yourselves to see whether you are controlled by faith;
subject yourselves to review (*dokimazete*)." **Holding to your faith**
(*peirazete*) does not mean maintaining a firm creedal stance in
the face of calamities and the associated doubts to which they
give rise. Rather, the first of the two verbal synonyms refers to
self-examination in an effort to determine one's real identity. If
we call ourselves believers, then we must ask whether we actually
live in terms of the faith we profess. The second term, **test yourselves** (*dokimazete*), suggests an examination for genuineness.
The words are an echo of 2 Cor. 8:8. It is the term one would
use in connection with the process for determining the genuineness of rare metal (1 Pet. 1:7). We are to scrutinize ourselves to
determine whether our attitudes and decisions can really be
called Christian. The apostle goes on to state the latter explicitly.
By putting it in the form of a question, he gives the Corinthians
an opportunity to answer it in the affirmative. His concluding
conditional sentence is a bit of rhetorical needling. The RSV's
rendering **meet the test** is one word in Greek (*adokimoi*), which

Paul uses to play on the verb *dokimazō*. They are to administer the test to themselves. Will they fail to pass their own test?

6—This verse actually affirms that they will most certainly pass the test, for the apostle has done his apostolic work so responsibly that they will produce the proper fruits of the gospel. Paul has a pride in the job. The Corinthians' new way of life will be the best proof of Paul's apostolic credentials. He is willing to stake his reputation on their performance.

7—Paul affirms in v. 6 that he will pass the test as an authentic apostle if the Corinthians respond positively to the gospel. But in v. 7 the apostle protects himself against misunderstanding by a rhetorical ploy known as *epidiorthōsis:* "I do not mean to say that we want you to avoid what is vulgar, so that we may come off with flying colors. On the contrary, we want you to do what is first class, even if in the process we appear to lack the proper credentials (that some people think might be better demonstrated by severe action on my part in your midst)."

A number of points require consideration in support of the interpretation offered here. (1) The RSV's term **wrong** renders the Greek word *kakon,* which means something that is second-rate and lacking in "class." The antonym **right** means behavior that is first class and merits the highest approbation. (2) Paul's motivation is not to find mere ratification for the truth of the statement that he made in v. 6. (3) If they do what is noble or first class, there will be no need to demonstrate his ability to be severe in person. (4) There will be those who, in the absence of a demonstration of extraordinary administrative intervention—because of the Corinthians' fine response that is anticipated—will assume that Paul is still all verbal hot air with no capability of action (2 Cor. 10:10). But Paul has no anxiety about that. The word **though** renders the particle *hōs,* which suggests that the term governed by it is not a statement of fact but is so viewed from the perspective of one or another observer.

8-9—Paul declares that all his energies are invested in support of (*hyper*) the **truth** that is the gospel, not against (*kata*) it. In support of this affirmation, he says that he rejoices when the Corinthians function as Christ's people, even though he is charged with having a number of inadeqaucies. The apostle seeks only their **improvement** (*katartisis*). The proof he says lies in the product. To rephrase a commercial, "With a reputation like Paul's, the product has to be good." Paul has now set the hook. The Corinthians cannot wiggle off. Their own reputation as his living epistle (3:3) is at stake. Will their own audit of themselves (13:5) come up with a negative verdict? And if they affirm themselves as a fine product of the gospel, despite all of the liabilities charged up against Paul by his opposition, his own apostolate is vindicated.

Along similar lines Demosthenes (*On the Crown* 277) defended himself against charges of Aeschines that he manipulated the assembly with cheap rhetorical tricks: "All of you will discover," he says, "that whatever skill I possess has been exercised, both in public and in private, on your behalf (*hyper*)—never against (*kata*) you."

10—In a final attempt to answer the charge expressed in 10:10, that he writes threatening letters but when present in person loses all his bluster, Paul states that he does so in the present case so that on arrival he might not have to use apostolic clout upon arrival. He is not interested in merely throwing administrative weight around in Corinth. He is a builder, not a demolition expert. This last clause echoes 10:8 and indicates that the line of thought expressed in chaps. 10–13 has come full circle. To build (*oikodomē*) is the function of a benefactor, and it is this positive reputation that Paul wishes to enjoy at Corinth. Should some "tearing down" (*karthairesis*) be necessary, so be it, but that is not the mark of a benefactor and certainly not the primary badge of an apostle.

Closing Words (13:11-14)

Plea for Mutual Affection (13:11-13)

The RSV's noninclusive term **brethren** does not accurately reflect the Greek term *adelphoi* in the social context of this letter. Paul is addressing the entire Corinthian membership, male and female. The phrase **mend your ways** paraphrases the verb form *katartizete*, which echoes the noun *katartisis* in v. 9. The central meaning is restoration. Paul urges them to be receptive to his invitation to restoration as a first-class assembly of God's people.

The expression **agree with one another** (*to auto phroneite*) does not mean to sweep things under the rug or maintain a diplomatic truce, but to accept and provide counsel and encouragement. The point is that the membership ought to be clear about its purpose as a Christian community. To **live in peace** means that they marshal all their resources to realize their purpose for existing as a Christian community instead of engaging in competitive bickering.

The **holy kiss** is the sacred sign of affection. Paul says that it should be "holy," that is, it should be genuine and not disguise insincerity or hostility, as did the kiss of Judas (cf. Luke 22:48). This appeal for expression of concern and feeling is followed in the modern practice of "passing the peace." Paul would have found incomprehensible the objection that this is an intrusion on privacy in public devotion.

In v. 13 Paul reminds the Corinthians of the reputation that they enjoy in many of God's assemblies. It is a final plea to look beyond themselves and grasp the larger picture of God's reality in Christ.

Benediction (13:14)

This benediction is not a mere formality. For the last time, it focuses the Corinthians' attention on the beneficence (*charis*) of Jesus Christ. This term, often rendered **grace,** carries with it the implication of a call to thanksgiving. The title **Lord** reminds everyone that Jesus Christ is in charge of all Christians everywhere. The mention of **Jesus Christ** in turn suggests the ultimate expression of divine affection. The **Holy Spirit** makes possible a relationship between believers and God and at the same time opens up a myriad of possibilities for shared enterprise among those who share the one Spirit.

This benediction is the climax of Paul's closing prayerful approach that had begun at v. 7. In similar fashion, taking account of both his opposition and the welfare of his beloved Athens, Demosthenes ended his speech titled *On the Crown* (324) with a prayer. After summarizing a tale of treason, he raises his voice in a final patriotic plea:

> May none of all you Deities in Heaven show them a single nod of favor, but may you try to instill even in them some better mind and

sense. Yet should they be past healing, take them by themselves and expose them to swift and utter perdition on land and sea. And grant to all the rest of us a sure salvation in swift release from threatening fears.

The difference in tone between Demosthenes' conclusion and that of Paul is striking. Demosthenes asks the jury to inflict penalties on his opponents. Paul never loses sight of his own opponents, but his closing words concentrate the attention of his addressees totally on divine magnanimity.

BIBLIOGRAPHY

This bibliography lists books and studies that are either referred to in the commentary or will be especially useful to those who wish to pursue further study of 2 Corinthians. General readers who are limited to English will find much that is helpful in the items marked with an asterisk (*). Fuller bibliographies are available in the works by Furnish, Martin, and Betz (Hermeneia volume).

Commentaries

*Barrett, C. K. *A Commentary on the Second Epistle to the Corinthians*. Harper Commentaries. New York: Harper, 1973.
*Betz, Hans Dieter. *2 Corinthians 8 and 9: A Commentary on Two Administrative Letters of the Apostle Paul*. Hermeneia. Philadelphia: Fortress, 1985.
Bultmann, Rudolf. *The Second Letter to the Corinthians*. Translated by Roy A. Harrisville. Minneapolis, Augsburg, 1985.
*Furnish, Victor Paul. *II Corinthians: A New Translation with Introduction and Commentary*. Anchor Bible 32A. Garden City, N.Y.: Doubleday, 1984.
Heinrici, C. F. Georg. *Der zweite Brief an die Korinther*. Revised edition. Göttingen: Vandenhoeck & Ruprecht, 1900.
Lietzmann, Hans. *An die Korinther I/II*. Handbuch zum Neuen Testament 9. Tübingen: J. C. B. Mohr (Paul Siebeck), 1949.
*Martin, Ralph. *2 Corinthians*. Word Biblical Commentary 40. Waco, Texas: Word, 1986.

*Plummer, Alfred. *A Critical and Exegetical Commentary on the Second Epistle of St Paul to the Corinthians*. International Critical Commentary. Edinburgh: T. & T. Clark, 1915.

Windisch, Hans. *Der zweite Korintherbrief*. MeyerK 6/9. Göttingen: Vandenhoeck & Ruprecht, 1924.

Special Studies

Betz, Hans Dieter. *Lukian von Samosata und das Neue Testament*. Texte und Untersuchunzen 76. Berlin: Akademie-Verlag, 1961.

_____ . *Der Apostel Paulus und die sokratische Tradition: Eine exegetische Untersuchung zu seiner "Apologie" 2 Kor 10–13*. Beiträge zur historischen Theologie 45. Tübingen: J. C. B. Mohr, 1972.

Bultmann, Rudolf. *Der Stil der paulinischen Predigt und die kynisch-stoische Diatribe*. Göttingen: Vandenhoeck & Ruprecht, 1984 (1910).

*Charles, R. H. *The Apocrypha and Pseudepigrapha of the Old Testament in English (APOT)*. 2 volumes. Oxford: Oxford University Press, 1913.

*Danker, Frederick W. *Benefactor: Epigraphic Study of a Graeco-Roman and New Testament Semantic Field*. St. Louis: Clayton Publishing House, 1982.

_____ . "A Form-Critical Study of Linguistic Adaptation in Romans," in *Festschrift to Honor F. Wilbur Gingrich*, pp. 91-114. Edited by E. H. Barth and R. E. Cocroft. Leiden: Brill, 1972.

*Kennedy, George A. *Classical Rhetoric and Its Christian and Secular Tradition from Ancient to Modern Times*. Chapel Hill: University of North Carolina, 1980.

Marshall, Peter. *Enmity in Corinth: Social Conventions in Paul's Relations with the Corinthians*. Wissenschaftliche Untersuchungen zum Neuen Testament, 2 Reihe 23. Tübingen: J. C. B. Mohr (Paul Siebeck), 1987.

Schmithals, Walter. *Gnosticism in Corinth*. Translated by John E. Steely. Nashville: Abingdon, 1971.

_____ . *Paul and the Gnostics*. Translated by John F. Steely. Nashville: Abingdon, 1972.

Selected Bibliography

Wettstein, Jakob. *HĒ KAINĒ DIATHĒKĒ. Novum Testamentum Graecum.* 2 vols. Amsterdam: Dommerian, 1751–1752.

Wilckens, Ulrich. *Weisheit und Torheit: Eine exegetisch-religionsgeschichtliche Untersuchung zu 1 Kor. 1 und 2.* Beiträge zur historischen Theologie 26. Tübingen: J.C.B. Mohr (Paul Siebeck), 1959.

Zmijewski, Josef. *Der Stil der paulinischen "Narrenrede": Analyse der Sprachgestaltung in 2 Kor 11.1—12.10 als Beitrag zur Methodik von Stiluntersuschungen neutestamentlicher Texte.* Bonner Biblische Beiträge 52. Cologne: Hanstein, 1978.

Lexicons

Bauer, Walter. = BAGD. *A Greek-English Lexicon of the New Testament and Other Early Christian Literature.* A translation and adaptation of Walter Bauer's fourth revised and augmented edition by William F. Arndt and F. Wilbur Gingrich (1957) (BAG). Second edition revised and augmented by F. Wilbur Gingrich and Frederick W. Danker from Bauer's 5th edition. Chicago: University of Chicago Press, 1979.

Moulton, James Hope, and George Milligan. *Vocabulary of the Greek Testament Illustrated from the Papyri and Other Non-Literary Sources.* London: Hodder and Stoughton, 1952 (1930).

Papyri and Inscriptions

*Benefactor, see Danker, above.

Corpus Inscriptionum Graecarum. Edited by August Boeckh and others. Berlin, 1825–1877.

Dittenberger, Wilhelm, editor. *Orientis Graeci Inscriptiones Selectae* (= *OGI*). 2 volumes. Leipzig, 1903–1905.

―――― . editor. *Sylloge Inscriptionum Graecarum (SIG³).* Third edition. 4 volumes. Leipzig, 1915–1921.

Gärtringen, F. Freiherr Hiller von, editor. *Inschriften von Priene.* Berlin: Georg Reimer, 1906.

Inscriptiones Graecae (IG). Edited by A. Kirchhoff and others, in process since 1873.

Inscriptiones Graecae ad res Romanas pertinentes (IGR). 4 vols. Paris: Leroux, 1906–1927.

Schroeter, F. *De regum hellenisticorum epistulis in lapidibus servatis quaestiones stilisticae*. Leipzig: Teubner, 1931.

Welles, C. B. *Royal Correspondence in the Hellenistic Period: A Study in Greek Epigraphy*. London, 1934.

INDEX OF ANCIENT AUTHORS AND WRITINGS

Jewish, Jewish-Christian, and Patristic

Acts of Paul and Thecla, 155
Apocalypse of Moses, 174
Augustine, 165
1 Enoch, 162-163
2 Enoch, 92
Josephus, 46, 181, 182 2x
Life of Adam and Eve, 174
4 Maccabees, 70, 111, 163
Philo, 55, 77, 80, 94, 104, 110, 128 2x, 152, 174, 191, 195, 201, 205
Testament of Gad, 111
Testament of Issachar, 118
Testament of Simeon, 63

Greco-Roman

Inscriptions

Benefactor (see Bibliography), 15, 20, 21-22, 23, 36, 42, 66, 75, 79, 83 2x, 86, 88, 89-90, 91, 95, 116, 117 2x, 120 3x, 122, 123, 124, 125-126, 127 2x, 130 2x, 132 2x, 133 2x, 135, 138-139, 140 2x, 142, 143, 144, 149, 156, 166, 168, 169, 182, 199, 201-202
CIG, 33 2x
IG, 76, 91
IGR, 137
OGI, 35, 36, 90, 106, 112, 117-18, 120, 122 2x, 131, 132, 133, 145, 169
Priene, 75, 132
Schroeter (see Bibliography), 123
*SIG*³, 92, 93, 94, 100, 101, 105, 106, 113, 114, 119, 120, 122, 122, 126, 129, 130, 136 2x, 137, 139, 150, 179, 194
Welles (see Bibliography), 123, 133

Papyri

Papyri Oxyrhynchus, 157
Sammelbuch der griechrischen Urkunden, 73

General

Aeschines, 155, 160
Aeschylus, 33, 73, 194, 205
Antiochos I of Commagene, 89, 117, 143
Antiphon, 157
Appian, 97
Apuleius, 99, 117, 147
Aristides, 142
Aristophanes 150, 191, 205
Aristotle, 24, 120, 127, 128 2x, 139
Artemidoros, 65
Athenaeus, 186
Augustus, 50, 82, 83, 91, 132, 142, 149, 182
Cebes, 110, 205
Cicero, 132, 138, 142, 182, 184
Demetrios of Phaleron, 204
Demosthenes, 24, 41, 86, 99, 103, 126, 127, 134, 135, 137, 149-150, 160, 161, 163-164, 165-166, 170 3x, 171 4x, 172, 175, 178 2x, 179, 187, 188, 192, 197, 198, 200, 202-203, 204, 212, 213-214
Dio Cassius, 79, 155
Dio Chrysostom, 137, 162, 165 2x, 176, 178, 185, 197-198, 206
Diodorus of Sicily, 133
Diogenes Laertius, 157, 205
Dionysius of Halicarnassus, 45
Empedocles, 60
Epictetus, 36, 49, 51, 60, 65, 66, 79, 86, 87, 89, 94, 95, 96 2x, 100 2x, 152, 155, 156 2x, 157, 183, 184, 185, 188, 195, 196, 197
Euripides, 98, 103-104, 194
Hermogenes, 179

Herodotus, 46, 98, 191
Hesiod, 139
Hierocles, 111
Homer, 20, 46, 55-56, 88, 97 2x, 119, 156, 165, 198, 199
Horace, 50, 65, 67, 91, 104, 194
Iliad, see Homer
Isaeus, 137
Julius Caesar, 188
Juvenal, 38
Libanius, 107
Livy, 50, 59, 119
Lucian, 49, 104, 191
Marcus Aurelius, 84, 86, 88, 94, 159
Menander, 60, 128
Odyssey, see Homer
Persius, 157
Pindar, 20, 50, 70, 76, 87, 175, 179
Plato, 20, 49, 54, 66, 69, 73, 77, 80, 86, 93, 100, 127, 157, 176, 189
Pliny (Elder), 199-200
Plutarch, 24, 38, 45, 51, 84, 87, 88, 90, 97, 110, 149 2x, 155, 159, 160, 165, 170, 175 2x, 186, 192, 195, 197 2x, 201, 204, 207, 208
Polybius, 86, 88, 128, 156
Seneca, 49, 66, 69, 70, 85, 139 2x, 185, 189, 190, 201
Simonides, 34
Sophocles, 33, 54, 63, 72, 98, 202
Suetonius, 107, 186
Tacitus, 51
Teles, 89
Theognis, 72, 142
Theophrastus, 137
Thucydides, 46, 51, 70, 88 2x, 106, 179
Velleius Paterculus, 42
Vergil, 79, 84, 152
Xenophon, 138, 140, 141, 166
Zeno, 205

GLOSSARY

Most technical terms are defined in their context, but the following loanwords from Greek are to be noted:

arete *(aretē)* = exeptional excellence, superior merit

gymnasiarch *(gymnasiarchos)* = head of gymnastic training

peristasis; plural, peristaseis *(peristasis, peristaseis)* = experience of crisis, recital of perils

ABOUT THE AUTHOR

Frederick W. Danker, Professor Emeritus of the Lutheran School of Theology at Chicago, is an ordained minister of the Evangelical Lutheran Church in America. He received his Ph.D. from the University of Chicago. Besides holding pastorates in various parishes, he served as instructor of New Testament for 34 years until his retirement in 1988. At that time, he and his wife, Lois, an administrator at the University of Chicago Medical Center, returned to St. Louis, where Dr. Danker had served Concordia Seminary and, later, Christ Seminary.

His numerous writings range from lexicons, books, and articles in learned journals to publications in newspapers and popular magazines. Through his pioneering work *Benefactor* (1982), Danker has encouraged the study of epigraphic materials (especially documents written on stone) for sharper understanding of the New Testament. His commentary on St. Luke's Gospel, *Jesus and the New Age*, revised in 1988, is valued by specialists as well as nonspecialists. Because of his ability to bridge academic and general interests, Danker is in frequent demand as a public lecturer on such varied topics as the politics of the Scriptures, proclamation based on the three series of the church year, and Jewish-Christian relations.